Introducing Urban A

MW01096819

This book provides an up-to-date introduction to the important and growing field of urban anthropology. This is an increasingly critical area of study, as more than half of the world's population now lives in cities and anthropological research is increasingly done in an urban context. Exploring contemporary anthropological approaches to the urban, the authors consider:

- How can we define urban anthropology?
- What are the main themes of twenty-first-century urban anthropological research?
- What are the possible future directions in the field?

The chapters cover topics such as urban mobilities, place-making and public space, production and consumption, politics and governance. These are illustrated by lively case studies drawn from a diverse range of urban settings in the global North and South. Accessible yet theoretically incisive, *Introducing Urban Anthropology* will be a valuable resource for anthropology students as well as of interest to those working in urban studies and related disciplines such as sociology and geography.

Rivke Jaffe is Associate Professor in the Centre for Urban Studies and the Department of Human Geography, Planning and International Development Studies at the University of Amsterdam, the Netherlands.

Anouk de Koning is Assistant Professor in the Department of Cultural Anthropology and Development Studies at Radboud University Nijmegen, the Netherlands.

Introducing Urban Anthropology

Rivke Jaffe and Anouk de Koning

Routledge
Taylor & Francis Group

LONDON AND NEW YORK

First published 2016
by Routledge
2 Park Square, Milton Park, Abingdon, Oxon OX14 4RN

and by Routledge
711 Third Avenue, New York, NY 10017

Routledge is an imprint of the Taylor & Francis Group, an informa business

British Library Cataloguing-in-Publication Data
A catalogue record for this book is available from the British Library

Library of Congress Cataloging-in-Publication Data
Jaffe, Rivke.
Introducing urban anthropology / Rivke Jaffe and Anouk De Koning.
     pages cm
  Includes bibliographical references and index.
  1. Urban anthropology. I. Koning, Anouk de. II. Title.
  GN395.J34 2016
  307.76–dc23   2015018436

ISBN: 978-0-415-74480-5 (hbk)
ISBN: 978-0-415-74481-2 (pbk)
ISBN: 978-1-315-66939-7 (ebk)

Typeset in Bembo
by HWA Text and Data Management, London

Printed and bound in the United States of America by Publishers Graphics,
LLC on sustainably sourced paper.

Contents

Figures and boxes

Figures

Boxes

Preface

We hope that *Introducing Urban Anthropology* will be able to fill a significant gap in the range of existing introductory textbooks that cover anthropology and its subfields. We are both city enthusiasts, interested in getting to know different cities, and excited to experience the diversity, creativity and unexpected encounters they offer. We are also committed to analyzing the various social problems found in cities, such as inequality, insecurity and pollution. We hope our passion for city life and our critical engagement with urban questions is evident throughout this book.

As is true of any text, and certainly of anthropological texts, our own personal and academic trajectories inform the content of this book. While this book seeks to cover the most important themes in current urban anthropology and includes a wide geographical range of cities, our emphases will betray the influence of our own trajectories. Our location in the Netherlands may provide the reader with a slightly different perspective on urban anthropology and on cities across the world than if we were located in, for instance, the United States. Our academic trajectories also influence the examples we give, our selection of case studies to illustrate specific themes, and the particular insights we bring to bear on the wider field of urban anthropology.

Rivke has worked mostly in the Caribbean, particularly in Kingston, Jamaica. Her earlier research concentrated on urban pollution and environmental justice in Curaçao and Jamaica, followed by a research project on the governance role of criminal 'dons' in Jamaica. Her current research examines the political implications of the pluralization and privatization of security provision in Kingston, Jerusalem, Miami, Nairobi and Recife. In addition, her research has focused on the role of popular culture (music, video clips, street dances, murals and graffiti) in how people experience and communicate urban exclusion and solidarity.

Anouk's academic career started with a study of middle-class professionals in neoliberalizing Cairo, and she maintains strong ties to the city. Following this, she studied Surinamese social history, including a focus on the bauxite mining town of Moengo. She then turned to study her own city, Amsterdam, analyzing how new nationalist, racialized public discourses shaped policy and everyday life in this multi-ethnic city. Her current research uses migrant parenting as a vantage point from which to explore how citizenship is negotiated in a Europe where migrants have increasingly been framed as a burden or a threat.

Writing *Introducing Urban Anthropology* has been a stimulating journey. It has expanded our understanding of current research in the field, and helped us discover the work of colleagues around the world. Many of them have been kind enough to provide us with photos to illustrate our discussion of their work. We have also benefited from informal crowdsourcing, asking our colleagues for advice and tips.

We are grateful to the many people who have helped along the way. In addition to the anonymous reviewers who provided constructive comments, we want to thank our friends and colleagues who read parts of this manuscript closely and provided us with invaluable feedback: Freek Colombijn, Henk Driessen, Martijn Koster, Eileen Moyer and Martijn Oosterbaan. Rivke would also like to thank Peter Nas for encouraging her interest in urban anthropology from early on in her career.

This book would not have come about if it were not for our editor at Routledge, Katherine Ong, who launched the idea and helped us along the way, assisted by Lola Harre. We also thank our partners, Wayne Modest and Ivo Bol, for their encouraging words and patience throughout the process of writing. We are grateful to Anouk's parents, Marijke and Tom de Koning, for their baby sitting, which allowed us to go on writing retreats together. We hope that this book will find its way into the classrooms and onto the bookshelves of readers who are curious to learn more about the distinct approach to city life that urban anthropology can provide.

Amsterdam, May 2015

Rivke Jaffe and Anouk de Koning

Chapter 1

Introduction

For the first time in history, more than half of the world's population now lives in cities. This demographic change, resulting from rapid urbanization, has coincided with a shift within anthropology towards doing research in cities. Anthropology that takes place in cities, therefore, has become increasingly common. Part of this research has explicitly taken the urban as its object of study, understanding the city more as a set of processes than as a setting, and taking its material and spatial form into explicit account (Low 2014: 16–17). Urban anthropologists seek to understand the changing nature of urban social life, the influence of urban space and place, and more broadly what constitutes a city in the context of global flows and connections.

This textbook provides an introduction to urban anthropology, an increasingly important field within anthropology. While anthropology's traditional focus was on small-scale communities in non-urban settings, cities have become a prominent context for anthropological research. However, the fact that many anthropological studies are conducted in cities does not necessarily make them urban anthropology in our view. In this respect, we differ from some other authors, who consider any anthropological research conducted in the city to be urban anthropology (e.g., Sanjek 1990; Pardo and Prato 2012). This book takes as its starting point that, while urban anthropologists study a broad range of social phenomena, what makes their work *urban* anthropology is their explicit reflection on the implications of the urban context in which these phenomena occur.

This introductory chapter gives a brief overview of the development of urban anthropology. It starts with a section that discusses the background factors that influenced the growth of urban anthropology in the twentieth century, and the distinctions between urban anthropology, general anthropology and other disciplinary approaches to urban life. In the next section, we sketch the historical development of the field, starting from nineteenth-century predecessors and describing a number of 'schools' and trends or 'turns' that characterized urban anthropology in the twentieth century. This section also briefly explores the themes and approaches that are specific to anthropological research on the twenty-first century city. The third section discusses the specificities of doing anthropological research in and on urban settings, elaborating how the concerns and methodologies of ethnographic research are adapted to urban contexts. We address a number of approaches and methods, including 'studying up' and 'studying through', mobile methods, cognitive and participatory mapping, and the study of popular culture. The chapter ends with an overview of the structure of the book.

Why urban anthropology?

The emergence and growth of urban anthropology can be related to a number of background factors. Two main factors have been global processes of rapid urbanization and shifts within broader anthropology. The first straightforward factor feeding into the growth of urban anthropology, then, has been the growth of cities. For most of human history, the majority of people did not live in cities. This is not to say that cities are a new phenomenon. Around 5000 BCE, concentrated 'proto-urban' settlements emerged in the fertile floodplains of the Nile and Mesopotamia, with temple complexes or royal compounds housing populations who did not work in agriculture. Other early urban areas developed as trade cities. The number, size and political reach of such dense ceremonial, administrative and commercial settlements grew gradually over the millennia, until the concept of a 'city' had become commonplace in most parts of the world (see Box 1.1 on city typologies).

In the nineteenth century, Europe saw rapid, large-scale urbanization as the Industrial Revolution concentrated masses of factory laborers in overcrowded shanty towns. Twentieth-century industrialization and urbanization swelled the cities of countries across the world. Notwithstanding these long histories of urbanization, agriculture long remained the most important source of livelihood for the majority of the world's population, and most people continued to live in rural areas. It is only in the twenty-first century that more than half of humanity lives in urban areas. The social, cultural, political and economic changes that accompanied this massive demographic shift drew the attention of anthropologists.

Whereas the growth of industrial cities in Europe and North America in the nineteenth century was key in the development of sociology as a discipline, urban anthropology has

Box 1.1 City typologies

In his classic work on urban anthropology, Ulf Hannerz (1980) used the typology of Courttown, Commercetown and Coketown to distinguish between cities that develop and function as administrative centers, versus those that depend on their trade function or on the concentration of industry. The first type, Courttown, refers to ceremonial cities. These urban areas were grounded in the concentration of political and ceremonial power, centered on the court and monumental political buildings. The second type, Commercetown, emerged as the consequence of the growth of trade networks, within which cities developed as crucial nodes. In such trade cities, the marketplace played a crucial role and represented an important urban site (and continues to do so, as we discuss in Chapter 5). Coketown, finally, refers to a new city type that came into being in the nineteenth century. These massive industrial cities were marked by their economic basis in, for instance, textile manufacturing.

While useful in thinking through different trajectories of urban development, such functional typologies obscure some of the diversity and dynamic nature of cities. Many cities, of course, combine various functions. In addition, shifts in political function or economic activities can drastically transform urban landscapes, leading to the eventual decline or even abandonment of urban sites. This is illustrated by the decline of some of the earliest Mesopotamian cities, or in recent years by the deserted stretches of urban space in former 'Motor Town' Detroit.

developed along multiple trajectories. While a number of important early studies were based on fieldwork in North American and European cities, urban anthropology also developed in the global South, where researchers studied processes of urbanization in the colonial and postcolonial world, often in relationship to research on development, modernity and decolonization. Notwithstanding, the growth and diversification of cities in North America and Europe, and the social problems associated with these changes (such as overcrowding, pollution, criminal violence and ethnic conflict), similarly garnered anthropological attention.

In the late twentieth century, processes of urbanization were increasingly associated with major social, cultural and economic transformations often grouped under the rubric of globalization. The central role of cities in globalization (see Chapter 7) has meant that the attention of anthropology and other social sciences to global processes has often involved an increased interest in urban processes and urban social life.

In addition to these broader demographic and societal changes, shifts within the discipline of anthropology itself have been a second important factor informing the growth of urban anthropology. Anthropology's earliest roots are entangled with the history of colonialism. While not a straightforward 'handmaiden of colonialism', the discipline did develop as a colonial science, stimulated by a demand for enhanced knowledge of 'native populations' (Asad 1973). Early European anthropologists conducted research on these subjugated populations within the parameters of colonial imperatives, which included facilitating control of colonial subjects and justifying European domination. In the United States, in a tradition that became known as 'salvage anthropology', early research concentrated on documenting Native American cultural practices, which were thought to be in danger of becoming extinct.

In the 1970s and 1980s, the move to decolonize anthropology involved a critique of the disciplinary focus on 'the Other' (Hymes 1972; Clifford and Marcus 1986). Critical anthropologists questioned the discipline's preoccupation with 'exotic' difference and its tendency to privilege fieldwork in sites far away from the researcher's home (Gupta and Ferguson 1997). They sought to expand the long-standing interest in people living in 'traditional' hunter-gatherer or peasant economies, by giving more attention to social life in 'modern' urban economies.

This decolonizing movement within anthropology emphasized the need to 'bring anthropology home' and to study those sites where researchers themselves lived and worked – often cities in Western Europe and the United States. The move to study countries 'at home' in many cases also meant a turn to urban anthropology. In 1970s France these two shifts – towards an anthropology of the modern, and an anthropology at home – were even indistinguishable; the move from the traditional subjects and sites of anthropology to an 'anthropology of the present' inaugurated a flurry of work on French cities (Rogers 2001).

Situating urban anthropology

Urban anthropology has developed into a sprawling field that uses a highly interdisciplinary approach to study an extremely varied range of topics. How can we distinguish urban anthropology from general anthropology, and from adjacent fields such as urban studies, urban sociology and urban geography? In this book, we define 'urban anthropology' as anthropology that engages explicitly with the question of how social life is structured by and experienced within urban contexts. Such urban contexts are characterized by specific features such as size, density, heterogeneity, anonymity and inequality (see Box 1.2 on definitions of the city).

In urban settings, people tend to engage in a broad variety of social relations, ranging from intimate and personal relations amongst household members, close friends and kin, to more segmented relations structured by clearly delimited roles (such as economic relations), to very fleeting, anonymous encounters, for example in traffic. The heterogeneity of urban populations and the prevalence of public spaces such as sidewalks and plazas mean that cities are often the site of unexpected encounters between people with diverse socio-economic and cultural backgrounds.

Box 1.2 **What is a city?**

One of the enduring debates in urban anthropology and urban studies more broadly has been on how to define the field's core concept: *the city*. Early definitions tended to emphasize the functions of cities in relation to their surrounding 'hinterland'. From this perspective, cities are local centers of power, places where political, economic, cultural and religious activities converge and are concentrated. Other definitions emphasized physical form and demographic characteristics, focusing on the crowded built environment and dense population of cities. An influential definition by Chicago School sociologist Louis Wirth (1938: 8) included size, density and population heterogeneity as the three main characteristics of a city: 'for sociological purposes a city may be defined as a relatively large, dense, and permanent settlement of socially heterogeneous individuals'.

Wirth also focused on different types of social relationships and attitudes to define *urbanism as a way of life*. In contrast to rural areas, which he saw as characterized by face-to-face, intimate social relations between family, friends and community members, Wirth argued that what defined the city were the impersonal, formal and business-oriented relationships between its residents, and their blasé attitudes. The association of cities with anonymity and heterogeneity has been very influential, shaping our understanding of urban space as a public realm, which Richard Sennett defines as 'a place where strangers meet' (2010: 261).

Definitions drawing from constructivism understand the city as a *social construct*: a city is a city, rather than a village or a town, if people believe that it is one. In essence, a city might just be a line on a map that enough people have agreed should be there. This attention to the social constructedness of cities also means studying who has the power to define a city as such. Political and administrative definitions that allow a place to label itself as a city have fiscal, economic and legal implications. Municipal authorities can tax residents and businesses independently of national governments, while real-estate prices and zoning regulations might vary drastically based on whether a site is inside or outside the city limits.

More recently, scholars have begun to approach city not so much as a place but as a *social-material-technological process*, or an *assemblage* (Brenner et al. 2011). From this perspective, cities are the intersection of multiple dynamic and unstable networks and flows of people, animals, money, things, ideas and technology. Emphasizing the interwovenness of cities and nature, urban political ecologists frame the city as the process of the urbanization of nature (Swyngedouw 1996).

Moreover, the size and diversity of cities facilitate the emergence of particular scenes or subcultures, for example based on lifestyle choices or popular culture preferences, leading to an association of the urban context with cultural creativity and aesthetic innovation. Demographic density enables the very urban phenomenon of the crowd, which has strong social and political implications – crowds can shape sensations of anonymity, loneliness or freedom, but they can also be the start of riots and other forms of collective violence and political action. More broadly, cities are often places where political power manifests itself in spectacular ways. Official buildings are monuments to state power and particular visions of society; symbolically important public spaces provide the grounds for both state spectacle and political contestation.

These various characteristics of the urban context inform the type of questions that urban anthropologists ask. Crucial concerns include the following broad questions: how do cities shape forms of identification and social relations? What cultural repertoires and imaginaries emerge in urban contexts of anonymity, diversity and inequality? How do urban spaces shape power relations between groups or institutions, and, conversely, how do power relations shape urban spaces?

Anthropology has turned to the city relatively late in comparison to related fields such as urban sociology and urban geography. While it has often been inspired by and in dialogue with studies in sociology and human geography, urban anthropology has distinguished itself from these adjacent fields in a number of important ways. From early on, urban anthropologists studied cities in Africa, Asia and Latin America as well as those in Europe and North America. This has given urban anthropological research a more global character than more 'mainstream' urban studies, which tended to focus exclusively on European and North American cities.

Urban anthropologists have also distinguished themselves from urban sociologists and urban geographers through their methods. While they often draw on a range of methodological tools including surveys, interviews and media research, urban anthropologists tend to rely primarily on ethnography and its main component, participant observation. Participant observation provides access to hidden aspects or segments of urban life, to intimate, informal and illegal processes. It allows researchers to map tacit knowledge that cannot easily be verbalized, and can shed light on the many less obvious routines that structure social life in the city.

The use of ethnographic methods also connects to the distinctive anthropological focus on everyday life in the city, and on the less quantifiable imaginaries and symbols through which people make sense of their urban surroundings. Perhaps the most significant contribution of urban anthropology has to do with the hallmark of anthropology as a discipline: its insistence on understanding people and social situations in their full complexity, rather than seeing them as abstracted from their contexts or as easily generalizable. Urban anthropology tries to capture the complex social and cultural lives that people develop in cities, and documents how they negotiate heterogeneous, unequal and constantly changing urban landscapes.

Historical developments

Urban anthropology only really emerged as a distinct subfield in the mid-twentieth century. However, tracing its historical development draws our attention to a number of important predecessors in the nineteenth and early twentieth centuries. In this section, we start with a discussion of these early antecedents to urban anthropology, followed by an overview of twentieth- and twenty-first-century developments in the field. This overview is somewhat skewed towards anthropological literature published in or translated into English, and hence does not fully cover those urban anthropological traditions that developed in other languages, such as French, German, Spanish or Dutch.

Urban anthropology's predecessors

A number of urban anthropology's ethnographic and analytical predecessors can be found in the nineteenth and early twentieth centuries. We can distinguish three broad groups of influential writers describing and analyzing urbanization and industrialization in European and North American cities: literary journalists, academically minded reformers and empirically oriented sociologists studying Chicago. The first group consisted of non-academic writers, including investigative journalists and novelists. Middle-class, educated authors such as English writer and social critic Charles Dickens (1812–1870), English novelist Elizabeth Gaskell (1810–1865) and French writer and journalist Émile Zola (1840–1902) sought to research the lives of the urban poor in the context of industrial urbanism.

What was it like to work in a factory or to live in a slum? In order to find answers to such questions, journalists attempted to immerse themselves in the lived realities of the urban poor. Their semi-ethnographic forays resulted in sometimes sensationalist accounts of poverty, overcrowding, squalor and disease. Many of these journalistic and literary writings did have a political purpose: the authors wanted to highlight the exploitation of the urban poor and used their 'research' to make a case for governmental and charitable interventions.

As photography became increasingly accessible, illustrated accounts provided similar arguments in visual form. In his famous book of photojournalism, *How the Other Half Lives: Studies among the Tenements of New York* (1890), social reformer and journalist Jacob Riis (1849–1914) documented the squalor of New York City slums in order to mobilize the public to address the deplorable living conditions of the urban poor (Figure 1.1).

A second prominent group of nineteenth-century predecessors to urban anthropology consisted of more academically oriented authors. In addition to semi-ethnographic methods, some of them began to draw on statistics and cartography, novel methods at the time. Like their more journalistic contemporaries, many of these researchers were associated with the Victorian-era political project of sanitary reform (see Chapter 8), while others were more radical.

An important author was German social scientist and philosopher Friedrich Engels (1820–1895), who wrote *The Communist Manifesto* with Karl Marx. In 1844, Engels published a harrowing account of the conditions of the working class in England's industrial cities. This book followed two years of observations in Manchester and Salford, where his working-class partner Mary Burns introduced him to the slums. The cholera epidemics that ravaged many cities in the nineteenth century also fed into urban research, including early forms of social epidemiology and detailed medical mapping. In London, philanthropist and social researcher Charles Booth (1840–1916) compiled a seventeen-volume publication on the lives of the city's poor, *Lives and Labour of the People in London* (1889, 1891), based on years of statistical data collection and analysis. These works highlighted the high rates of death and disease that the urban poor suffered, and demonstrated the relation to low wages and overcrowded, unsanitary living conditions.

Figure 1.1 Bandit's Roost, Mulberry Bend, New York City 1888 (photograph by Jacob Riis)

Moving into the twentieth century, an important body of urban research emerged from the University of Chicago, at the first sociology department in the United States (see Hannerz 1980: 19–58). From the 1910s to the 1930s, an influential group of professional sociologists researching the city developed what came to be known as the *Chicago School*. The Chicago School was founded by two unconventional scholars: William I. Thomas (1863–1947) and former journalist and activist Robert Park (1864–1944). Thomas is perhaps best known for the Thomas theorem ('If men define situations as real, they are real in their consequences'), while Park laid the foundation of the human ecology model that guided much early Chicago School research. This model understood human behavior in cities to be shaped by the urban environment and its competitive character.

Like these founders, the next generation of Chicago sociologists, including Louis Wirth, Nels Anderson, Florian Znaniecki and St. Clair Drake, emphasized the importance of empirical data and especially fieldwork. They instructed their students to view the city as their laboratory, urging them to leave their desks and libraries in order to study urban people and places from up close. In addition to direct observation, they experimented with various methods, exploring the use of cognitive mapping and oral history as tools for urban research.

The Chicago School produced numerous classic urban studies. Much of the research these scholars conducted in the early decades of the twentieth century consisted of case studies of marginalized groups and neighborhoods, including new immigrant groups and ethnic enclaves. Louis Wirth, the author of an influential text on 'urbanism as a way of life' (see Box 1.2), also became known for his book *The Ghetto* (1928), a classic study of the organizing logic of Chicago's Jewish ghetto, and examined the interaction between elective ethnic concentration and majority discrimination. William Thomas and Florian Znaniecki explored Chicago's immigrant neighborhoods in *The Polish Peasant in Europe and America* (1918–1920), their landmark study of Polish immigrant families. This five-volume study, based on personal documents, is considered a prescient forerunner of transnational migration studies. In 1923, Nels Anderson, a Chicago sociologist who had once been homeless himself, published *The Hobo*, a pioneering ethnographic study of homeless persons that championed participant observation. *Black Metropolis* (1945), by African-American scholars St. Clair Drake and Horace Cayton, remains a classic study of Chicago's Black neighborhoods. While most studies of the Chicago School concentrate on the work of these male academics, women were also involved in similar types of urban ethnography. One example is Jane Addams, a Chicago-based reformer who ran a center called Hull House. Addams worked closely with the university-based sociologists and also published her observations of urban life in what was essentially an ethnographic style.

The boundaries of the three groups of journalists, activists and academics distinguished here are blurred. For example, while nineteenth-century sociologist Max Weber is identified less with the empirical tradition of the radicals and reformers listed as the second group, his book *The City* was an influential publication that approached cities as a form of social organization. Friedrich Engels was a journalist, activist, social scientist and political ideologue all in one. Chicago School leader Robert Park is known as an academic, but he worked extensively as a journalist before joining the university as an urban sociologist. He also studied with the German sociologist and philosopher Georg Simmel, an example of the various connections between US and European traditions.

Early urban anthropology

Following these early urbanists, in the mid-twentieth century more explicitly anthropological researchers began to train their lens on the city as well. In the 1920s and 1930s, Chicago-trained anthropologist Robert Redfield (who also happened to be Robert Park's son-in-law) worked to define 'folk society' in contradistinction to the 'modern city', understanding the former as a culturally uniform, face-to-face community with limited division of labor. Redfield later elaborated his notion as a folk-urban continuum, with progressive degrees of cultural disorganization, secularization and individualization (e.g., Redfield 1941; Hannerz 1980: 59–61).

Against the background of massive rural-to-urban migration in the global South, anthropologists began to follow their 'peasant' interlocutors as they moved to the cities, studying how these migrants coped in new urban environments. This early urban anthropology was often primarily interested in processes of urbanization, rather than the urban quality of the social life they studied (Foster and Kemper 2002). Anthropologists working at the Rhodes-Livingstone Institute in British Central Africa and at the University of Manchester studied life in mining towns in the African Copperbelt, situated in present-day Zambia and the Democratic Republic of Congo. The Rhodes-Livingstone Institute was set up by the governor of Northern Rhodesia in 1937. Its first director, Godfrey Wilson, together with his wife Monica Wilson, decided to focus on the study of the emerging mining towns, where life was regulated strictly in accordance with the needs of the industry, providing temporary housing for its male workers, and offering little space for family life (see Chapter 5 on mining towns).

These so-called Copperbelt studies, conducted from a 'colonial liberal' perspective, traced the social transformations associated with rural-to-urban migration and industrialization in the 1940s and 1950s. British anthropologists such as Max Gluckman, Albert Epstein and Clyde Mitchell, as well as American anthropologist Hortense Powdermaker, sought to analyze the 'African Industrial Revolution' and develop a concept of 'African modernity'. This work also developed innovative methods to capture urban life. Coming out of a tradition of British anthropology that focused on social structures, these studies argued for analyses that focused on particular cases or situations to capture the dynamic nature and complexity of urban social life. A famous example of such a study is Mitchell's *The Kalela Dance* (1956), which analyzed the performances of a dance troupe in the Copperbelt town of Luanshya. The dancers had developed a repertoire, featuring doctors and nurses dressed in white, that clearly spoke to their urban experiences, as did their emphasis on stylish urban fashions. While these studies tried to disrupt ideas of Africans as tied to unchangeable rural life and tribal cultural tradition, their ideas of urban modernity tended to be defined in Western terms of progress (see Ferguson 1999).

Not much later, anthropologists such as Oscar Lewis and Ulf Hannerz began working in African, Latin American, Caribbean and North American cities, demonstrating a similar concern with urbanization and new migrants' adaptation to urban life. This early urban anthropological work, extending from the 1950s into the 1970s, drew on the ethnographic 'community studies' done by sociologists, most prominently William Foote Whyte's classic *Street Corner Society: The Social Structure of an Italian Slum* (1943). In the late 1930s Whyte spent over a year living in Boston's North End, at the time a notorious slum inhabited primarily by Italian-Americans. He wrote evocatively about the social world of street gangs and 'corner boys', explaining how local life was organized. In doing so, he showed that common assumptions about social disorganization in poor communities were false. Whyte was familiar with anthropological work and adopted ethnographic methods, relying primarily on participant observation.

The anthropological work inspired by such community studies more explicitly sought to bring anthropological methods that had been developed in rural, village environments to bear on urban neighborhoods. Ethnically homogeneous neighborhoods and 'ghettos' were understood as close-knit 'urban villages' characterized by strong local ties. This approach served to counter earlier accounts (such as those by sociologists Louis Wirth and Georg Simmel) of urban relationships as anonymous and business-like. However, this view of neighborhoods as more or less bounded, contained social units represented 'communities' as static entities and ignored the embedding of neighborhoods within the larger city.

Both Hannerz and Lewis did research in non-Western cities and in US cities. Lewis developed his 'culture of poverty' thesis through urban anthropological research in Mexico City and New York City, while Hannerz studied a 'ghetto' street in Washington DC in the 1960s and urban life in Kafanchan, Nigeria, in the 1970s (see Figures 1.2 and 1.3). In 1980 Hannerz published his now classic *Exploring the City*, in which he develops a more theoretical anthropological approach to city life.

In their North American studies, Lewis (1966) and Hannerz (1969) discussed the socio-cultural life that developed in marginalized, impoverished neighborhoods. A major point of contention concerned the relation between culture and poverty, a debate centering on Oscar Lewis' notion of a *culture of poverty*, which held that a culture developed in response

Figure 1.2 Fieldwork in Kafanchan, Nigeria, 1975; Ulf Hannerz with Chief Ladipo, leader of the Yoruba ethnic community in Kafanchan (photograph courtesy of Ulf Hannerz)

Figure 1.3 Fieldwork in Kafanchan, Nigeria, 1975; Silver 40, a commercial artist and major informant, in front of his workshop (photograph courtesy of Ulf Hannerz.)

to conditions of urban poverty helped reproduce the marginalization of people in poor neighborhoods (see Box 2.2).

Late twentieth-century 'turns'

In the 1970s and 1980s, anthropologists working on cities increasingly drew on a *political economy* perspective. In tandem with urban geographers and sociologists such as David Harvey and Manuel Castells, anthropologists such as Ida Susser (1982) and Leith Mullings (1987) drew on Marxist theories to understand how everyday urban lives and neighborhoods were shaped by the structures of capitalism and the associated relations of production. The City University of New York (CUNY) provided an important meeting point for an interdisciplinary group of scholars, who studied urban life drawing on intersecting perspectives from political economy and anthropology.

In Africa, Latin America and the Caribbean, this interest in political economy was also evident in a focus on the urban *informal economy*, which developed in part through an anthropological engagement with development studies. Anthropologists studying sectors unregulated by the state, such as street vending and small-scale manufacturing, attempted to understand this type of labor and productivity in relation to cities' formal economic sectors (see Chapter 5). In this period, anthropologists working in Latin America mainly studied informal, marginalized urban places, such as Brazilian *favelas* or Peruvian *barrios jovenes*. In Africa, in line with the British tradition of urban anthropology, anthropologists primarily focused on urban social relations, such as exchanges in the marketplace or political alliances (Low 1996: 386–387).

Building on these political economic approaches, but also extending them in new, poststructuralist directions, in the 1990s the interests of urban anthropologists reflected the influence of what has been called the *spatial turn*. Across disciplines, people began to focus on the power inherent in configurations of space. This turn inaugurated a revitalization of urban anthropology, with an increasing number of anthropological studies that explicitly focused on the relation between urban space and social and cultural life in cities. This spatial turn drew strong inspiration from French thinkers such as Michel Foucault, Henri Lefebvre and Michel de Certeau. In urban anthropology, Foucault's conceptualization of power, as regimes of truth that shape the world around us and our understanding of it, has perhaps been the most influential (see Box 8.1). Two key studies published in 1989 signal this new direction in urban anthropology. Paul Rabinow's *French Modern: Norms and Forms of the Social Environment* drew on Foucault's insights on the productive nature of power to explore the planning of North African cities as a technology of colonial rule. James Holston's *The Modernist City: An Anthropological Critique of Brasília* similarly studied the design of the new Brazilian capital of Brasília as a technology of state power (see Chapter 8).

Lefebvre (1991) argued that space is a social product, and that it often works to reproduce the interests of the powerful. His work calls attention to the social production of space and the way in which this produced space, in turn, influences how people can think and act. The struggle over how urban space is shaped is thus one over the right to reinvent one's own life. Lefebvre famously captured this in the idea of *the right to the city* (see Box 9.1).

Where Foucault and Lefebvre emphasize the importance of urban planners and professionals, de Certeau paid more explicit attention to the everyday ways in which people negotiate urban landscapes. He argued that while the powerful can use *spatial strategies* to dominate spaces and define them according to their needs, the powerless rely on more

Figure 1.4 Setha Low interviewing in Parque Central, San Jose, Costa Rica, 2014 (photograph by Joel Lefkowitz)

ephemeral *spatial tactics*, which materialize only temporarily, in what he calls pedestrian speech acts (1984: 37). Such tactics include the informal economic activities in spaces where the police regularly crack down on street vendors. The police enforce the strategies of the powerful, who define what is allowed or prohibited in particular spaces; the vendors resort to flexible tactics to occupy urban spaces that they can vacate at a moment's notice to avoid having their goods confiscated.

In the course of the 1990s, anthropologists also increasingly began to see *consumption* rather than production as the main characteristic of the late modern city. Authors such as James Ferguson, Setha Low, Chua Beng-Huat and Arlene Dávila began to study new urban lifestyles and leisure landscapes, as well as the commodification of urban culture (see Chapter 6). Setha Low has been instrumental in the consolidation of urban anthropology in the 1990s, not only through her own work on public space in Costa Rica (2000) (see Figure 1.4), but also through her many overview articles and readers (see e.g., Low 1996, 1999).

The study of consumption in urban anthropology intersected with the cultural turn in geography, in which influential LA School urban geographers such as Edward Soja and Mike Davis sought to characterize postmodern urbanism based on the fragmented or 'kaleidoscopic' consumer-oriented landscape of Los Angeles, as distinct from the modern city that promised a more unified, inclusive project, in which production governed urban form.

Anthropologists and the twenty-first-century city

This book focuses on recent themes and trends in urban anthropology. Below, we briefly introduce urban anthropology in the twenty-first century, highlighting some of the themes that we examine at length in the chapters that follow. The earlier schools, themes and 'turns' discussed above continue to influence urban anthropology in the twenty-first century. Important themes within the field include *urban space, place and the built environment*. Anthropologists are interested in the cultural meanings that people construct around political, economic and religious places and buildings (Chapter 2), how and why they move through the city in specific ways (Chapter 3) and how social interaction is structured in open public spaces such as streets, parks and squares (Chapter 4). In addition, urban *social difference, inequality and solidarity* remain central political and economic concerns. More broadly, the majority of urban anthropologists pay close attention to the workings of *urban power, politics and governance*. While the interest in place, space, economy and politics is shared with other urban researchers, what distinguishes anthropologists is their close attention to everyday urban life and to forms of urban *imagination* and *cultural representation*.

However, ongoing social transformations have influenced researchers' interests and priorities. In particular, changes associated with *globalization*, including large-scale *migration* and the reach of *mass electronic media*, have shifted the ways anthropologists understand cities. We now see cities as inseparable from *global networks and flows* of people, material goods, ideas and money (see Chapter 7). In addition, the past few decades have seen the rise of what has come to be known as *neoliberalism*: a set of theories and policies that promote market-based solutions to a broad range of problems, reconfiguring the relations between the state, citizens and the private sector. Anthropologists have studied how neoliberal reforms take shape in and through the urban landscape, and have analyzed the new *urban entrepreneurialism* that encourages cities to compete for global flows of people and investments (see Chapter 8).

Anthropological engagement with the two interrelated developments of globalization and neoliberalization has produced new perspectives on 'traditional' urban anthropological concerns such as poverty, crime and social diversity. For instance, many anthropologists now study urban problems such as *violence and security* in relation to the changing role of the state in protecting its citizens (see Chapter 10). Similarly, anthropologists who study urban places now emphasize the role of international migration or globally circulating popular culture in shaping how people feel at home in the city (see Chapter 2), or focus on neoliberal policies that encourage the privatization of urban services (see Chapter 8).

In addition, the attention on *consumption* that started in the 1990s has continued to grow, in tandem with a new interest in studying urban middle classes (see Chapters 5 and 6). This meant a move away from urban anthropology's traditional attention on more marginalized urban groups and areas. In many postcolonial settings, these *new middle classes* of cosmopolitan, globally savvy professionals are seen as a group that can successful mediate between global and local scales (see Chapter 7). While some studies focus on the work lives of these professionals, and their position in the urban economy, much anthropological work has focused on how they position themselves through their consumption choices.

Research on *social movements* has also been on the rise in the twenty-first century (see Chapter 9). An important focus in these studies has been the alter-globalization movements, which tried to counter the globalization of capital through global social movements. This type of research was boosted with the worldwide urban protests and revolts that rocked the world in 2011. Urban anthropologists were quick to engage ethnographically with the largely urban-based uprisings in North Africa, the large-scale protests against austerity measures in Southern Europe and the Occupy movements in the United States, which quickly spread to cities across the world.

A final trend in urban anthropology is the attention paid to *mobility, infrastructure and technology*. Anthropologists increasingly study various forms of mobility, and what they tell us about urban inequalities. Studies of traffic, for example, provide an excellent vantage point for the everyday negotiation of inequality (see Chapter 3). Related to traffic is the study of urban infrastructure, which examines how the very material organization of the city structures social life (see Chapter 8). Urban anthropologists also pay attention to the way new communication technologies impact urban social life, not only in the spectacular cases of the mass mobilizations of 2011, in which all kind of social media played an important role, but also in everyday life, where there is a constant interaction between offline and online lives.

Doing urban anthropology

We have briefly discussed the historical developments underlying the formation of urban anthropology, and the themes and topics that urban anthropologists have studied. But what about their actual research practices – how do researchers go about 'doing' urban anthropology?

Ethnographic fieldwork remains anthropology's central methodology, and this holds largely true for urban anthropology as well. However, urban anthropology generally faces rather different conditions from those in which the broader discipline and its methods were developed. In cities, people may spend much of their time in relatively inaccessible places of work, leisure and home. At the same time, their lives are generally tied into social networks that spread out over the urban landscape. Moreover, this urban landscape clearly extends beyond people's specific experiences and horizons, and is shaped by economic and political processes at the scale of the nation and the region. These features complicate the archetypical forms of anthropological fieldwork, based on long-term immersion in the socio-cultural life of a local community.

Below we discuss a number of methodological dilemmas and considerations one may encounter while doing urban anthropological research. A first set of issues has to do with the demarcation of, and access to, the field. A further set of issues relates to the networked nature of urban social life, and specifically to the size of urban areas and the high degree of mobility in people's life in the city. Do such features require specific urban methodologies? A related point concerns the intricate connections between local-level urban activities and processes, and those at other scales. While these various issues – the difficulties of defining the field, and the highly networked, mobile and multi-scalar nature of social life – are not fully unique to cities, they have shaped urban anthropological methods in clear ways, as we outline below.

Not your usual field?

One of the most obvious issues that urban anthropologists face is how to define and delineate *the field*. In general, urban anthropology cannot fall back on the clearly circumscribed field sites with their dense, bounded social life that used to be the staple of anthropological research. The idea that communities that can be studied as clearly demarcated entities has been criticized for ignoring the significance of wider networks and ties, and portraying rural sites in a simplified, static manner. The notion of a bounded community seems even more problematic in urban settings.

In urban contexts, it is often impossible to reproduce the 'traditional' anthropological conditions of intensive participant observation in the social life of a spatially circumscribed community. Social relations branch out in space, connecting people to various parts of the city in idiosyncratic ways that reflect their class position and individual circumstances and preferences. While certain working-class neighborhoods may harbor some of the concentrated, localized social life that anthropologists traditionally studied, people's lives often spread out across and beyond the urban landscape. Their urban trajectories include spaces of residence, work and leisure to which anthropologists may not have easy access.

There is no single answer to the question of where and what exactly the field is. A simple answer would be: it depends. What shapes a researcher's field will depend on the theme or phenomenon that she wants to study, which also determines what methods are most appropriate. To study middle-class lives in Cairo, for example, Anouk found it useful to move with middle-class professionals in their daily trajectories across the urban landscape. It allowed her to explore their cognitive maps of the urban landscape, which included safe and dangerous spots, places where they wanted to be seen, and those they would rather avoid. It also allowed her to assess the tacit logics that guided urban mobilities (de Koning 2009).

Doing research in Kingston, Jamaica, on the governance role of criminal leaders known as 'dons', Rivke found it important to engage in 'deep hanging out' in one inner-city neighborhood. In addition, this research also led her to examine popular cultural expressions related to dons, such as murals, popular music and street dances (Jaffe 2012). To understand how the Jamaican state was entangled with the informal rule of the dons, she also needed to move out of downtown Kingston in order to speak to politicians, bureaucrats and other government officials (Jaffe 2013).

In other cases, for example in research on urban policymaking, there might not be an easily recognizable social life to study, or if there is one, it might not be accessible. In policymaking, much of 'the action' happens along networks that connect various actors who may rarely meet face to face (see, e.g., de Koning 2015). This again requires other research strategies and creates a very different sense of the field from, for example, research primarily located in an urban working-class neighborhood.

Urban methods

Urban anthropological fieldwork may clearly have a different character from fieldwork in rural sites. In urban anthropological fieldwork, researchers are more likely to have to deal with a wide range of people who occupy diverse social roles: from local politicians, wealthy merchants and directors of charity organizations to neighborhood strongmen, informal vendors and security guards. Moreover, many contacts during such fieldwork may be more fleeting, making it harder to establish long-term connections and rapport. Finally, urban anthropologists are more likely to study people who are highly educated and plugged into the same social media as themselves. This means that their informants are more likely to engage with and speak back to the anthropologists' findings and analyses. Relationships with such interlocutors may also extend beyond the fieldwork period more easily, since contacts can be maintained through the Internet and social media. While these characteristics all enrich anthropological research, they require a high level of flexibility and sensitivity. Drawing on the broader shifts in the discipline, described above, urban anthropologists may use *auto-ethnography* to reflect in detail on how their own urban positioning, experiences and interactions influence their analyses (e.g., Ulysse 2008).

Most urban anthropology requires a combination of research techniques and a triangulation of various kinds of data. This may entail using existing statistical data, generating new data through surveys, or engaging in analysis of a broad range of cultural 'texts', which may include political debates and policy documents as well as online media and a wide range of popular culture expressions. Even more than rural research, urban anthropological fieldwork is characterized by flexibility, inventiveness and a reliance on serendipity. It involves what can be described as eclecticism or even a kind of 'pragmatic amateurism' (Gusterson 1997: 116), qualities that seem well suited to urban settings.

Doing urban anthropology often stimulates inventive use of methods and research strategies. Heather Horst and Daniel Miller (2005), for example, used mobile phone contact lists to map people's social networks in urban Jamaica. Devising similarly creative methods may be necessary to chart the interaction between online and offline activism, as Jeffrey Juris (2012) did in his research on the #Occupy movement (see Chapter 9), or to understand how social media networks interact with urban landscapes to create offline/online realities and feedback loops.

While there are no methods that are specific or exclusive to urban anthropology, some methodological approaches have often been especially pertinent to researchers working in cities. One example is research on urban scenes or social movements, where the analysis of popular culture expressions such as music, dance or street art may an important method in understanding how urban identities are experienced and communicated (Jaffe 2014). For instance, anthropologists working in cities from Los Angeles to São Paulo have drawn on the analysis of hip hop lyrics, performances and styles to understand how residents negotiate class, gender and racial identities and respond to urban change (e.g., Pardue 2008; Peterson 2012). Similarly, they combine ethnographic research with visual analysis of community murals to understand how such images construct and represent place identities, local heritage and alternative histories (e.g., Sieber et al. 2012).

This type of research often involves developing sensory methods that concentrate on urban sounds, images, tastes, smells and movements – a range of embodied sensations sometimes called the *urban sensorium* (Goonewardena 2005). Sensory methodologies can help researchers to understand how such sensations may be central to the formation of communities or to urban politics. For instance, dancing together, eating together, or joining a dense crowd of protestors can produce powerful, embodied feelings of belonging. In particular, participatory visual methods have often proven useful for researchers interested in developing new, sensorially distinct ways of understanding, representing and taking part in urban place-making (e.g., Pink 2008).

In the next two subsections, we discuss two other sets of methods that have been associated with urban anthropological research: the 'studying up' and 'studying through' approaches, and spatial methods including mobile methods and mental mapping.

Studying up and studying through

As anthropological research moved into the city, it also increasingly focused on groups that hitherto had hardly been studied: middle classes and elites. Laura Nader's (1972) call to *study up* is still the classic statement on research on relatively powerful actors. Nader argued that in order to understand processes of domination, anthropologists should study powerful actors and institutions in the United States, rather than focus only on the underdogs or marginalized groups. Increasingly, anthropologists study such privileged groups, both those 'at home' in the United States or Europe, and the postcolonial elites in those countries where anthropologists have traditionally done fieldwork. Sherry Ortner (2010) has recently pointed out that much 'studying up' research actually entails studying sideways. The interlocutors in anthropological research on relatively powerful actors often include lawyers, politicians, stockbrokers, policymakers or scientists – people in class positions that are often not so different from the academic researcher's own position.

Studying up presents anthropologists with a number of methodological issues. Anthropologists wanting to study up often have trouble gaining access to fieldwork sites and possible informants. Powerful people have the ability and perhaps also more of an inclination to keep prying strangers out of their lives (Gusterson 1997). They may be protective not only of their privacy, but also of their time, making it difficult to organize interviews. For instance, Mitchel Y. Abolafia (2002) was able to negotiate his initial access to Wall Street only through his old college friends and later relied on the intercession of former students at the business school where he taught.

However, it may not be possible to arrange invitations to the halls of power for participant observation, or to secure ample interview time. Many anthropologists may have no choice but to rely heavily on what Ortner calls interface ethnography. This involves 'doing participant observation in the border areas where the closed community or organization or institution interfaces with the public' (Ortner 2010: 213). Such events may be film festivals, in the case of the Hollywood movie industry studied by Ortner, or public political debates in the case of a study of local politics. Such interface events present anthropologists with a way to observe some of the actual workings, implicit logics and cultural rules of an inaccessible community or industry.

The newly developing field of the anthropology of policy is also highly relevant for urban anthropological research. In urban settings, the impact of policymakers and politicians is often felt very clearly, and anthropologists often want to understand how urban social spaces or phenomena are shaped by policy. The anthropology of policy has pointed to the importance of studying the way policies connect various urban sites and networks, such as the bureaucratic offices where policies are designed and operationalized and the streets, squares, clinics, community centers and private homes they target.

Janine Wedel, Cris Shore, Gregory Feldman and Stacy Lathrop (2005) have called such tracing of a specific policy theme through the various layers of a policy chain *studying through*. They define studying through as 'following the source of a policy – its discourses, prescriptions, and programs – through to those affected by the policies' (Wedel et al. 2005: 39–40). This studying through approach is reminiscent of the analysis of social networks and extended case studies that were a hallmark of earlier urban anthropological research (see Hannerz 1980). It may also be relevant to the study of other types of networks and relations than those initiated by policymaking, and may thereby lend itself well to studying complex, multi-scalar urban phenomena.

Mobile methods and mental mapping

Mobility is constitutive of social life and expresses and contributes to social hierarchies (see Chapter 3). As noted above, the everyday activities of many urban dwellers are rarely contained in one locale, but are often dispersed across the urban landscape. In order to study urban lives, it is therefore useful to employ *mobile methods* that allow one to tag along with informants and to make sense of their mobility patterns and urban trajectories.

Mobile methods help to track the movement of people, goods and ideas, but they can also enable us to understand the larger structures that organize this movement (Büscher et al. 2011). The most obvious mobile method is following and observing people's movements through the city. A more participant 'walking with' or 'riding with' makes it possible to grasp experiences and logics of movement, as well as the tacit knowledge of the urban landscape that such movement presupposes (Kusenbach 2003; Jirón 2011). Like participant observation more generally, such practices of 'moving with' can also provide insight into the embodied, sensory aspects of urban life: the smells, sounds and affects that are central to experiences of the city (see Chapter 2). Another mobile method involves asking informants to keep diaries of their movements throughout the day, which the ethnographer can then discuss with them (Haldrup 2011). Such discussions can reveal much about daily lives and movement that informants would not be able to articulate unaided, allowing us 'to uncover how ... mobilities are choreographed, sensed and made sense of' (Haldrup 2011: 69).

To understand how people relate to the urban landscape, researchers can also use a variety of methods that involve mapmaking. One is *mental mapping* (or cognitive mapping), which involves asking people to draw maps of particular areas (such as a neighborhood or a city). Often, researchers also ask their interlocutors to highlight particular characteristics, for example the presence of facilities, particular groups or, more generally, landmarks or features that are important to them (e.g., Ben-Ze'ev 2012).

As Bjørn Sletto (2009: 445) argues, 'maps are representational objects intimately implicated in projects of place-making, and therefore they are tools of power'. Mapmaking exercises can be a method to elicit various experiences and visions of urban landscapes, but they may also be tools that empower less heard or even suppressed representations of space in so-called counter-mapping exercises. However, such mapmaking may also become part of contestations between different local actors, with particular maps validating certain claims over others. For example, a mapping workshop Sletto (2009) organized in Trinidad provided a group of local fishermen with the opportunity to represent their knowledge as the most accurate knowledge. This claim positioned them as *the* experts with respect to contested swamplands. Such processes of mapping may thus also provide rich insights into competing claims and visions of landscapes.

Structure of the book

Following this introduction, the chapters of this book are organized into three main parts that focus on important domains of contemporary urban anthropological research into the twenty-first century. These three parts each consist of three chapters that focus on specific subthemes, which are illustrated through case studies drawn from a diverse range of urban settings. Each chapter ends with a number of questions for further reflection and a list of suggested reading and suggested viewing.

The first part, 'At home in the city?', focuses on place-making and belonging. It includes three chapters that introduce anthropological ways of understanding urban places, mobilities and public spaces. The second part, 'Crafting urban lives and lifestyles', examines production and consumption and includes three chapters on urban economies;

consumption, leisure and lifestyles; and cities and globalization. The third part, 'Politics in and of the city', discusses politics and governance. The chapters that make up this part focus on urban planning; cities, citizenship and politics; and violence, security and social control. A concluding chapter explores emergent themes and future directions in urban anthropology.

Rather than producing generalizing theories of urban life, anthropology draws on in-depth case studies to understand the social complexity of cities in particular contexts. The theoretical insights that emerge from such case studies are used more to inspire understanding of other urban cases than to provide clear-cut general models. Working from this approach, this book draws extensively on ethnographic case studies conducted by anthropologists working on cities across the world.

Discussion questions

1 How would you define a city? What are the most important features of a city, in your opinion?
2 What main background factors explain the emergence of urban anthropology as a subfield of anthropology?
3 What do you consider the most important differences between urban anthropology and related fields such as urban sociology and urban geography?
4 Comparing urban anthropology in the mid-twentieth century and urban anthropology in the twenty-first century, what different interests and emphases can be distinguished?
5 What are the methodological dilemmas you might encounter when doing urban anthropological research?
6 What methods do you think are particularly productive for urban anthropological research?

Further reading

Bridge, Gary and Sophie Watson, eds. (2010) *The Blackwell City Reader*, second edition. Oxford: Blackwell.

Büscher, Monika, John Urry and Katian Witchger, eds. (2011) *Mobile Methods*. London and New York: Routledge.

Gmelch, George and Walter P. Zenner, eds. (2009) *Urban Life: Readings in Urban Anthropology*, fifth edition. Long Grover, IL: Waveland Press.

Hannerz, Ulf (1980) *Exploring the City: Inquiries toward an Urban Anthropology*. New York: Columbia University Press.

Low, Setha M., ed. (1999) *Theorizing the City: The New Urban Anthropology Reader*. New Brunswick, NJ: Rutgers University Press.

Nonini, Donald M., ed. (2014) *The Blackwell Companion to Urban Anthropology*. Oxford: Wiley-Blackwell.

Part I

At home in the city?

Chapter 2

Urban places

This chapter examines urban places, and discusses different ways of thinking about their role in structuring urban belonging and everyday experiences of the city. Specifically, we focus on the relationship between processes of physical construction and meaning-making, to understand how people make a home in the city. The process of transforming abstract space into concrete, meaningful place is often referred to as *place-making* (see Box 2.1 on the relationship between *space* and *place*).

In the first section of this chapter, we introduce the theoretical discussion of place-making, home and belonging. We focus on discursive and sensory forms of place-making and discuss sacred place-making as an important example. The second section examines the role of buildings as urban places, with specific attention to architecture and domestic space. Built structures gain specific meanings through the combination of material forms with ceremonial and everyday uses. We examine different types of architecture, including religious and colonial structures, and discuss how studying the design and furnishing of domestic space can help us to understand changing family relations and ideologies. The third section focuses on neighborhoods. Neighborhood spaces have long been a popular site for urban anthropological research. Much of this work has concentrated on marginalized and informal settlements, from North American ghettos to Brazilian *favelas* and Turkish *geçekondus*. More recently, there has been an increase in studies of wealthier city dwellers and the ways they inhabit urban space, including work on elite gated communities and other fortified enclaves. Increasingly, anthropologists have studied these different types of urban places and place-making relationally, understanding them as central to processes of segregation and discrimination. Finally, the fourth section discusses new ways of thinking about urban places in the context of globalization, addressing relational place-making in the context of transnational migration and trade.

Place-making, place attachment and the politics of belonging

What does it mean to turn space into place? Urban place-making involves individual and collective acts of territorial meaning-making. This process often starts with marking spatial boundaries, either physically or discursively. This boundary-making could be as simple as talking about a room in an office building as 'Anouk's office', building a wall around what we see as 'our' residential community or marking the borders of a neighborhood on a

Box 2.1 **Space and place**

Starting in the late twentieth century, urban anthropology has been inspired and transformed by concepts of space and place, tying into a broader 'spatial turn' within the social sciences and the humanities. Anthropology – along with other fields such as sociology, political science history, visual culture studies and literary criticism – began to draw on theories and concepts from geography. One main discussion in this regard has concentrated on the distinction between space and place.

Space is generally seen as a more abstract phenomenon. *Place*, in contrast, is commonly understood as a bounded form of space that has concrete physical features, is shaped by human experience and imbued with meaning. Places are bounded in the sense that they can usually be located in space, either on a map or by using geographical coordinates. Places tend to have concrete material characteristics, for instance in the form of architecture or natural features. In addition, space becomes place when it is lived in. It is made meaningful in different ways: first, through our everyday embodied experiences and the attachments and connections we form to places, and second, through the often politicized discourses that also define the meaning of a place (Cresswell 2004).

Place has often been associated with rootedness, authenticity and the 'local'. As late twentieth-century scholarship began to focus on globalization, this understanding of place shifted. In his influential work *The Information Age*, the urban sociologist Manuel Castells (1996) argued that new information and communication technology had resulted in a distinction between the 'space of flows' and the 'space of places'. The space of flows refers to 'the technological and organizational possibility of practicing simultaneity without contiguity' (Castells 2013: 34). This is a more abstract, partly digital space, where infrastructural and social networks and nodes facilitate the global movement of money, goods and information. In contrast, the space of places is based on meaningful locality and experience.

Castells' concept of the space of flows connects to what French anthropologist Marc Augé (1995) has termed 'non-places': places that are characterized by transience and uniformity rather than by rootedness and unique features. He focuses on spaces of circulation, consumption and communication, such as airports, hotels, shopping malls. However, Augé's characterization of such spaces as bland, standardized non-places can be critiqued. For people whose passports do not allow for easy travel, airports can be very anxious places. In addition, airports, hotels and shopping malls increasingly incorporate design features intended to make them stand out rather than be anonymous and identical.

Another recent perspective on urban places has come from assemblage theory and actor-network theory (Farías and Bender 2012). Anthropologists, sociologists and geographers drawing on this perspective see urban places as inherently dynamic and heterogeneous. They understand places as made up of networked human and non-human elements (such as buildings, water, trees, garbage).

government map. These bounded spaces are recognizable to us through physical features: the number on the door, the painting on the wall, the tree in the yard or the street signs at each intersection.

As we give names to these bounded places and use them – for living, working, studying or consuming – they become imbued with positive or negative emotional associations, memories or aspirations. Through our everyday uses and narratives, and through more spectacular experiences or interventions, spaces gain meaning and become places. By using and talking about places, people form attachments to them. The geographer Yi-Fu Tuan (1974) coined the term topophilia (literally: place-love) to refer to this type of positive affective bond. Related to this emotional type of bond between people and places is place identity, a concept that describes how people's sense of who they are, and to what larger communities they belong, is rooted in place. Place-based identities – developed in relation to a neighborhood, or a street or a school – can complement or overlap with other forms of belonging, such as those based on age, gender or religion. People also have functional relations to places, where they rely on a specific place for social, economic or political support.

Discursive and sensory forms of place-making

The process of place-making always entails the construction of meaning in relationship to the physical environment, a process that can take both discursive and sensory forms. Naming – of cities, neighborhoods or streets – is an important discursive part of place-making and negotiating power. A well-known example is the Greek city of Byzantium, renamed Constantinople under the Romans and Istanbul under the Ottoman Empire. European colonial claims were often also made through such naming practices, for instance in the case of Batavia (the present-day Jakarta, the Indonesian mega-city), or Léopoldville (currently known as Kinshasa, the third largest urban area in Africa). The urban origins of what is now known as Jakarta go back to the fourth century AD. Dutch conquerors, having destroyed the city in the seventeenth century, built a new fort and city called Batavia, named after the mythical ancestors of the Dutch, a Germanic tribe called the Batavi. After independence the city was renamed Djakarta and later Jakarta, a new formulation of Jayakarta, the city's name prior to colonial conquest. Léopoldville was established as a trading post at the site of a number of fishing villages by the Welsh explorer Henry Morton Stanley at the behest of the Belgian King Léopold II, who considered the Congo his personal possession. Under the postcolonial ruler Mobutu's Africanization program, the capital of newly independent Zaïre was renamed Kinshasa after one of the original fishing villages. Each of these names connected to larger narratives of belonging and authority, intended to frame these different places culturally and politically.

People also make places through a range of practices other than naming and narratives. Experiences of place are multi-sensory: in addition to sight, these experiences also involve smell, sound, touch and taste (Feld and Basso 1996). Place-making practices often entail a visual marking of space to indicate the presence of an individual or a group, as in the case of graffiti artists (or, conversely, state's efforts to control such visual expressions in public space). Visual signs may also help mark a place as appropriate for specific types of behavior but not others, or they may serve as a declaration of identity. For example, the sense of place changes when a tailor in Cairo puts up a poster of the Virgin Mary, an embellished Holy Quran, or a poster of Egyptian pop star Amr Diab in

Figure 2.1 Pentecostal church *Deus é Amor* (God is Love) in Rio de Janeiro (photograph by Martijn Oosterbaan)

his shop. Such signs can also serve as clues as to which people are welcome in that space, and which are unwanted.

While the visual has often been privileged in studies of the city, anthropologists increasingly also pay attention to other senses in order to get a fuller picture of the urban sensorium: the embodied, sensorial dimension of urban experience. For instance, music, and more generally sound, presents another powerful form of place-making. In his study of the soundscape of a *favela* neighborhood in Rio de Janeiro, Brazil, Martijn Oosterbaan (2009) demonstrates how music can communicate group identity and reproduce social boundaries in a dense social space like the *favela*. The Rio *favela* where Oosterbaan worked was marked by a competition over who could dominate the local soundscape: those who enjoyed funk music and attended *bailes* (public dance parties), or adherents of Pentecostalism, who saw going to a *baile* as immoral, 'leading one straight into the arms of the devil' (Oosterbaan 2009: 88–89). The local Pentecostal church (Figure 2.1) was strategically located along a main road, directly across from the samba school where funk parties were held. Those who attended samba practice would thus also be drawn into the Pentecostal service, by '[t]he loud, amplified voice of the pastor, alternated with shouts of the audience, followed by the music and the singing that mark the particular style of Pentecostalism' (Oosterbaan 2009: 90).

This example indicates the contestation that place-making often involves. Structural forces and powerful actors often shape processes of place-making, limiting the range of meanings one can attach to a particular place. Think of a shopping mall that is designed and policed to ensure that it remains defined as a space for consumption. When belonging to places is only accorded to a specific group, place-making can take on an exclusionary form, for instance in neighborhoods segregated by class, ethnicity or religion. The meanings and uses of specific places are often contested, not only between 'insiders' and 'outsiders', but also amongst 'insiders'. These disputes mean that urban places can be important sites for studying urban politics. Focusing on urban places, then, not only sheds light on feelings of home and belonging, it also directs our attention to socio-spatial structures of inequality and exclusion, and to contestations over definitions of urban space.

Sacred place-making

While cities are often associated with modernity and are therefore often implicitly pictured as secular, the example of the *favela* soundscape already hints at the important role of religion in place-making. Anthropologists increasingly study urban forms of religious innovation and community, as well as the ways that religion shapes city spaces and urban life (Hancock and Srinivas 2008; Becci et al. 2013). Religious place-making has discursive and experiential dimensions, and often relies on important markers (such as monuments or places of worship) in the built environment. A number of cities, including pilgrimage sites, are known primarily as religious places. While the origins of certain cities lie in sacred sites, which acted as catalysts for urbanization, other cities have, over time, been engulfed by the significance of their religious shrines. This is the case, for instance, in Mecca, the birthplace of the prophet Mohammed and home to the Kaaba, the holiest Islamic site for many Muslims. Life in Mecca is governed by the religious calendar and the influx of millions of pilgrims, who come each year to perform the hajj. Cities that contain such important pilgrimage sites are often strongly connected to similar places, through the movement of people who travel between them, by the exchange of ideas and goods, and sometimes even by institutional arrangements.

Many cities, however, are not defined as strongly by their religious sites, but still contain many places that are sacred in less spectacular ways (Kong 2010). Religious architecture is one of the most obvious forms of sacred place-making. Mosques, churches or synagogues mark particular neighborhoods or smaller spaces as sacred ground, delineating religious communities and enabling spiritual experiences. More ephemeral shrines may similarly insert a religious sensibility into the urban landscape: 'market shrines, road-side temples or habitations for new and old deities ... serve to anchor the sensibilities of the faithful in place or mark the infringement of space by routinized or unexpected expressions of devotional sentiment' (Hancock and Srinivas 2008: 624) (Figure 2.2). The presence of religion in public space may become the subject of intense contestation, as is the case in many European cities, where the presence of Islamic buildings, sounds or attire gives rise to profound controversies (Oosterbaan 2014). Meanwhile, smaller, less spectacular places of worship such as the numerous Pentecostal churches that have popped up in cities across the world (see for example Figure 2.1) may be less subject to scrutiny. However, these churches are also important ethno-religious places for diasporic groups, and play a role in the re-enchantment of the urban landscape (Garbin 2013).

Figure 2.2 Roadside shrine in Mexico City, 2010 (photograph by Eileen Moyer)

Buildings

Buildings have been an important focus within the anthropological study of urban places. Government buildings, offices, shops and homes are all sites of experience and meaning-making. Buildings' design often reflects dominant ideas about appropriate social relations. In many cases, commissioning authorities, architects and designers have explicit ideas about the meanings they want a building to convey. However, as soon as a construction is completed, these meanings may begin to shift. Buildings only really become places when people begin to use them, discuss them and develop emotional attachments to them. In studying urban buildings, two fields that have received increasing anthropological attention are architecture and domestic space.

Architecture

One way of looking at how buildings play a role in shaping urban places is through the lens of the anthropology of architecture. Buildings have an obvious functional dimension: they shield their occupants from the elements, protecting them from the heat, the cold or the rain. The exterior and interior design of buildings structures the activities that take place inside, shaping the behavior of occupants or users. In addition, buildings have important symbolic qualities. Intentionally or accidentally, their specific form and design trigger associations and emotions. Different types of political, religious or social authorities often use these symbolic features to assert their power. However, built structures also acquire meaning in ways that have nothing to do with official government strategies. In fact, everyday place-making may run counter to official goals.

Spectacular skylines, buildings or monuments have come to play an increasingly important role in projecting a city's identity, in deliberate processes of city-branding (see Chapter 8). Think of New York City's famous skyline including the Statue of Liberty and the Empire State Building, the Eiffel Tower in Paris, Kuala Lumpur's Petronas Towers or Sydney's famous Opera House. Built structures designed by famous architects (or 'starchitects'), such as Frank Gehry, Zaha Hadid or Daniel Libeskind, can imbue cities with the type of cachet that attracts tourists and investors. In addition to such economic considerations, governments often use built structures to represent the past and to inscribe social memory in the urban landscape. Examples are the 9/11 monument in New York City, the Museum of the Revolution in Havana or the tsunami monument in the Indonesian city of Banda Aceh.

The meaning of formal state monuments is not always stable. What Pierre Nora has called 'sites of memory' (in the original French, *lieux de memoire*) may be appropriated or re-signified by less powerful groups. Their uses of, or stories about, monuments may disrupt state narratives. One example is the twelve-foot high statue of the Spanish conquistador Juan de Oñate in Alcalde, New Mexico. As a colonial governor in the sixteenth and seventeenth centuries, Oñate was known for his brutal treatment of Native Americans, including ordering the amputation of a foot of each Acoma Pueblo man. When the 400th anniversary of his arrival was commemorated in 1998, anonymous protestors cut off the statue's right foot (Dürr 2003). Notwithstanding, in 2007 the Texan city of El Paso unveiled a huge bronze equestrian statue of Oñate, and, again, the celebration of a historical figure associated so closely with colonial cruelty elicited much protest.

Like monuments, religious architecture is a good example of how power can be expressed through buildings. Mosques, temples, synagogues and cathedrals are usually not just neutral 'containers' for religious services and ceremonies. As noted above, they are also designed to mark the urban landscape in specific ways. However, these buildings do more than just express religious identity or power to the outside world; they play a central role in the experiences and identifications of religious adherents. The materiality of these buildings, combined with the different ways that people use them (for instance in rituals and ceremonies), contributes to the formation of religious subjects. Specific architectural forms and styles, from minarets to stained glass, have an affective power – like other buildings, religious architecture can be understood as affective places that *move* people. Oscar Verkaaik (2014: 12) argues that

> … religious spaces have a kind of agency. They are manmade products that have an impact on human experience. Concretely, buildings limit or direct movement, impress visitors, affect the senses, evoke connotations. Neither an empty cipher with no intrinsic meaning whatsoever nor an authoritative text, a building provides opportunities for processes of identification within a particular social context. We are being trained to interpret and experience buildings in a certain way, but that does not exclude the possibility that they may, positively or negatively, overwhelm us and make us look at ourselves and our communities in a new or renewed way.

Colonial architecture constitutes another category of 'powerful buildings'. In colonial cities, monumental structures served to communicate the cultural superiority of their inhabitants and the political and religious order they could impose on colonized populations. These buildings represented a material manifestation of (colonial) modernity and progress. They were often designed not just to impress and inspire awe; they were also meant to induce and facilitate new, modern ways of living that were different from the surrounding, 'native' city. At its most optimistic, some of such buildings were thought to bring about the birth of a new, modern type of subject.

In addition to erecting imposing government buildings and grand elite residences, colonial authorities often introduced regulations to change 'native' construction practices and styles. In colonial Kingston, Jamaica, houses and huts were not allowed to have more than one entrance – a law intended to facilitate searches by the authorities. In colonial Accra and Bombay, the British colonizers tore down 'unsanitary' housing and introduced building codes aimed at preventing epidemics (Pellow and Lawrence-Zúñiga 2014). These policies reflected a concern for public health, but also the colonizers' need to maintain a healthy urban labor force.

Colonial architecture did more than enable control. In his work on colonial and postcolonial Indonesia, Abidin Kusno (2010) discusses the connections between the built environment and political consciousness. He sees architecture as a mode of communication and transformation: buildings serve to stimulate, define and express urban change; they are created to herald and hasten the arrival of new times. Focusing on modernist colonial architecture in early twentieth-century Javanese towns, Kusno argues that the new built environment involved more than techniques of colonial domination. It also enabled the formation of new social and political identities. In royal towns such as Surakarta and Yogyakarta, the Dutch colonizers developed a modernist urbanism that countered the traditional Javanese courtly architecture (see Figure 2.3). As new monumental buildings symbolically challenged the power of the traditional ruling class, a new type of urban subject began to emerge. A generation of educated young men began to see themselves as 'urban' and 'modern', and this new self-awareness translated into a movement of popular radicalism and the birth of anti-colonial nationalism.

Domestic space

A number of urban anthropologists have focused on domestic space to understand how people 'make place' in the organization, decoration and use of their homes. We often associate domestic space with personal taste. From an anthropological perspective, the way we use and adorn our residences is not only a matter of individual likes and dislikes. We are also interested in how such decisions and preferences are shaped socially and culturally, in different time periods and in different places. Interior design tells us something about people's identities, how they see themselves and how they want to be seen by visitors. In addition, domestic space is also shaped by larger state and corporate processes, such as municipal housing policy, commercial real-estate development, or the global rise of big-box furniture stores such as Ikea. While the home is a very local type of place, it is also a place where transnational ties and the influence of global forces are visible.

Anthropologists have pointed out that the interior design and layout of houses is often highly symbolic, and expresses dominant ideologies and social relations. As Pierre Bourdieu (1973) demonstrated in his classic discussion of the Berber house, the layout of houses reflects important aspects of social organization. Bourdieu argued that the design of the house according to a series of paired opposites (male/female, night/day, culture/

Figure 2.3 An example of Dutch colonial modernism in Indonesia (photograph by Freek Colombijn)

nature and so on) functioned as a tacit reminder of society's structure and ideology. Moving through the house, people learn to master fundamental cultural schemes. The spatial divisions of the home and the objects within it (from furniture and wall decorations to toys and technological gadgets) can tell us something about the social relations between people within and beyond the household.

Inge Daniels (2010) shows how in the twentieth century, as part of a state modernization project, Japanese dwellings began to be constructed that introduced the distinction between private rooms, including bedrooms, and family rooms such as a living-dining-kitchen. The state's promotion of Western models of domesticity also included a shift away from tatami mats towards sofas and chair-based living. However, family relations did not necessarily adapt completely and Western and Japanese styles of furnishing were often blended. Sleeping arrangements did not necessarily conform to the 'master bedroom' model: couples often slept separately, while parent–child co-sleeping remained common. Tatami rooms and Buddhist home altars have continued to be important features in Japanese urban homes, although their use and maintenance have undergone continuous renegotiations as intergenerational and gender relations change.

Daniels' work shows how the design, decoration and uses of domestic space incorporate important socio-cultural ideas about family life, privacy and leisure. In Japan, housing design has reflected larger national projects that were intended to 'modernize' structures' social interactions, but this design was also prone to change 'from below'. Design is also shaped by individual forms of expression and communication: it is part of social distinction strategies where people position themselves through their house.

Like other places, domestic space is gendered. The home is often seen as a 'female' domain, a space of care, child-rearing and intimacy. However, this domestic ideology that associates women with private, domestic space is by no means universal. Gendered distinctions between male public space and female private space are closely linked to European and North American bourgeois ideals that emerged in the nineteenth century. This involved the imposition of middle-class norms of a 'good home' on working-class households, a process that was often resisted by the urban poor (Löfgren 1984).

The negotiation of gender relations in and through the home continues to be contested. In Amsterdam, a minor scandal erupted in 2012 when a social housing corporation that was renovating an apartment complex sought to adapt the domestic plans of apartments to the perceived preferences of Muslim tenants. These adaptations involved extra storage space in the hallway for residents and guests to remove their shoes on entering, and extra faucets in the bathroom for them to perform the ablutions before Muslim prayer. In addition, the apartments offered the possibility to close off open kitchen plans, so that women could socialize and cook separately from men. The media, tapping into xenophobic sentiments, branded these apartments as '*halal* houses', and opponents complained that the building plans would encourage 'un-Dutch' gendered relations. These narratives saw the promise to introduce some 'Islamic' features as a wrong-headed multiculturalist compromise that entailed compliance with unwanted, even 'backward' gender norms. This case illustrates common assumptions about the role of domestic space in changing or perpetuating social norms such as those relating to gender.

Neighborhoods

We use the word 'neighborhood' all the time in urban anthropology and in our everyday conversations about cities. Neighborhoods are prime sites for the normative and emotional responses we develop to urban places, and for thinking about place-making more broadly. But what does this taken-for-granted term mean? It can be argued that (like the term 'communities') neighborhoods do not exist in any straightforward way. In his work on 'the production of locality', Arjun Appadurai (1996: 183) argues that we can never understand neighborhoods as existing separate from other places: 'neighborhoods are inherently what they are because they are opposed to something else and derive from other, already produced neighborhoods'. We recognize a 'good' neighborhood because it is not a 'bad' one, a Hindu neighborhood because it is not a Muslim one.

In many ways, neighborhoods operate as micro-versions of 'imagined communities' that take shape through both mundane and highly political practices and narratives. From one perspective, neighborhoods are constructed socially by people living in a certain urban area who feel some kind of commonality with their neighbors. By socializing and working together to solve collective problems, residents may develop a shared place-based identity, involving common norms and aspirations. Another way of defining neighborhoods involves understanding them as administrative units, with names and boundaries determined by municipal governments in order to facilitate urban governance. Governments give shape to neighborhoods by mapping them, collecting information and developing statistical analyzes in order to develop place-specific interventions – from 'hotspot policing' to customized service provision. In addition to residents and administrators, the media and other 'outsiders' also play a role in defining neighborhoods. Different types of media, from newspapers and television to soap operas and rap songs, contribute to how we 'know' different types of neighborhoods. Researchers, including anthropologists, also contribute to government and everyday knowledge of neighborhoods. Language (including the different terms we use to describe places) as well as visual representations are important aspects of these various processes of mediation.

Low-income and marginalized settlements

Urban anthropologists doing neighborhood-based research have often concentrated on low-income and socially marginalized areas. In both the global North and South, this research has studied areas known as ghettos, slums, *banlieues, bidonvilles, favelas, barrios bravos* and so on. An important development in these studies, which have strong roots in the ethnographic 'community studies' of the 1960s, has been a shift in focus from poverty to inequality. This shift also reflected a move away from the internal cultural dynamics of these areas to take into account larger political and economic structures that shape neighborhood life.

One of the most well-known scholars in studying low-income neighborhoods is urban anthropology pioneer Oscar Lewis, who saw these places as central in the development of specific cultural traits. In the 1960s, Oscar Lewis conducted research in New York City's Puerto Rican *barrio*. His classic urban ethnography, *La Vida: A Puerto Rican Family in the Culture of Poverty* (1966), relies on individual life story accounts of an extended Puerto Rican family in which several generations of women had engaged in sex work. Based on this work, and his previous work in Tepito, a *barrio bravo* in Mexico City, Lewis developed the 'culture of poverty' thesis, which argued that people living under structural conditions of long-term poverty may develop a particular set of cultural attitudes, beliefs and practices that work to perpetuate their marginal position, even when their structural conditions change. He claimed that this culture of poverty was transmitted across generations, keeping families locked into poverty. *La Vida* appeared around the same time as the infamous report on 'the Negro family' by US Assistant Secretary of Labor Patrick Moynihan, published in 1965, which diagnosed African-American family lives as plagued by 'pathologies' produced by histories of slavery and structural poverty.

The culture of poverty thesis and the Moynihan report were met with much criticism, particularly for their emphasis of cultural factors at the expense of an understanding of structural factors of unemployment and discrimination. The thesis that cultural habits kept people locked into poverty meshed well with popular understandings of poverty as the result of bad habits, and thus could easily feed into blaming-the-victim discourses (Bourgois 2001). Ulf Hannerz's early urban ethnography, *Soulside* (1969), tried to offer a more subtle reading of ghetto subculture, stressing internal variation within such neighborhoods, and understanding much of the more ghetto-specific (rather than mainstream) modes of behavior he encountered in Winston Street, Washington DC, to be directly related to poverty. These 'ghetto' ethnographies also informed later debates on the politics of representing poor urban neighborhoods (see Box 2.2).

Another influential author in the study of marginalized areas has been Janice Perlman, who started doing research in informal '*favela*' neighborhoods in Rio de Janeiro in the late 1960s (see Figure 2.4 for a recent image of a Rio *favela*). Initially, her work argued against the 'marginality model', a model that paralleled Lewis's 'culture of poverty' theory in its depiction of *favela* residents as culturally deviant and peripheral to the city and society. While Rio's poor suffered social exclusion, Perlman showed that they were very

Box 2.2 **Representing poor neighborhoods**

Issues of representation became subject to heated debate during the 1970s and 1980s, when anthropologists critically questioned how anthropology had constructed its object. Urban anthropologists working in US inner cities were confronted with such issues early on. The 1960s debate concerning Oscar Lewis's 'culture of poverty' thesis remains a landmark in discussions of the politics and ethics of representing poor neighborhoods. Specific representations, such as Lewis's work in New York and Mexico City, can inform or legitimize specific types of policy, including blame-the-poor policies.

Philippe Bourgois is critical of Lewis 'for presenting his subjects in a decontextualized pornography of violence, sexuality, and emotional brutality'. However, he argues that the politically motivated reactions to Lewis's ethnographic portrayals tended to deny the reality of the misery that Lewis described (Bourgois 2001: 11905). Bourgois discusses his own dilemmas in describing the lives of crack dealers in East Harlem, the same part of New York City where Oscar Lewis conducted his research (see Chapter 5). Such work in impoverished, crime-ridden areas raises tough questions about how to represent the misery one encounters. How to represent people who engage in self-destructive behavior without blaming the victim or, conversely, stressing structural forces of oppression at the danger of obliterating any sense of agency? Bourgois stresses the dangers of what he calls 'pornography of violence that reinforces racist stereotypes', but argues that censoring the social misery he had witnessed 'out of a righteous, or a "politically sensitive", fear of giving the poor a bad image' would make him complicit with oppression (2003: 15, 12).

Authors such as Bourgois have focused on *how* to represent urban poverty and deviance. In addition, some authors have questioned *why* urban research has paid overwhelming attention to the most marginal sections of society and the most spectacular manifestations of poverty. According to Steven Gregory (1998: 8), much of this research focused on a distinctive Black ghetto culture that was presented as a 'creative and adaptive response to an oppressive society and not merely a pathological deviation from its norms'. However, by focusing on what seems most distinct and distant from mainstream culture, such studies are at risk of reproducing assumptions and stereotypes of an isolated Black ghetto culture common to conservative mainstream representations. Instead, Gregory's own study in an African-American neighborhood in New York City (1998) focuses on political culture and activism.

The debate on the representation of poor lives in US inner cities is relevant beyond these specific sites. It shows us what dilemmas attend ethnographic portrayals of stigmatized or marginalized groups. Does documenting the gory or abusive aspects of life in poor neighborhoods play into existing stereotypes and blame-the-victim discourses? Conversely, does the censoring of such aspects of life not lead to a denial of actual suffering? Or, perhaps most damningly, is the portrayal of spectacular misery a ploy to boost book sales and academic fame? These questions involve both ethical (with respect to the obligations of anthropologists to the people they study) and political considerations (to what kinds of politics their research contributes).

Figure 2.4 Public square in the *favela* of Pavão-Pavãozinho, Rio de Janeiro (photograph by Martijn Oosterbaan)

much integrated in the urban economy, albeit asymmetrically, and that they displayed immense creativity and perseverance in trying to improve their socio-economic position (Perlman 1976). Continuing her research over the next four decades, Perlman (2010) found significant material improvements in her original research areas in terms of health, educational achievement, housing, infrastructure, and access to consumer goods. Nonetheless, Perlman's longitudinal study found that while absolute deprivation had decreased, relative deprivation – in other words, inequality – had increased and become even more entrenched, exacerbated by drug-related violent crime and enduring social prejudice. What it means to live in a *favela*, then, is not so much about access to material goods and services, but about residents' position in an urban hierarchy of people and places.

The words we use to describe deprived neighborhoods, such as those that Perlman studied, are often part and parcel of their marginalization. Terms such as 'ghetto', 'slum' or *'favela'* are not neutral descriptive labels. They play an active role in producing and reproducing area stigmatization. Noting a resurgence of the use of the term 'slum', Alan Gilbert (2007) warns of its sensationalist and stigmatizing effects. He argues that once dramatically different types of neighborhoods across the world are all labelled as 'slums', the word results in a homogenizing oversimplification. The term is used to map a social category (poor people) onto spatial terrain, and confuses the physical problem of substandard housing with the characteristics of the people who live there. This place–people confusion has important policy implications, for instance when slum demolition (a place-based intervention) is presented as a solution to urban poverty (a complex social problem).

'Ghetto' is a similarly controversial term. It is often used to describe the residential segregation of an ethnic group to one specific area within a city. Jewish ghettos in medieval Italian towns or in Warsaw during the Second World War are well-known examples; African-American ghettos in the twentieth-century United States are another. The French sociologist Loïc Wacquant has argued for defining 'the ghetto' more narrowly, as an analytic concept with strict parameters. To Wacquant (2002: 50), the ghetto is 'a relation of ethno-racial control and closure' that combines four criteria: stigma, coercion, territorial confinement and institutional parallelism. However, beyond this strict analytical definition, many urban residents see their own neighborhoods as ghettos, even if they might not meet all four of these criteria. In this sense the 'ghetto' can also be understood as an imaginative space. Disseminated globally through popular culture such as funk, hip hop and dancehall music and movies, this 'folk concept' of the ghetto connects marginalized neighborhoods from New York to Kingston and Dakar (Jaffe 2012).

Perhaps surprisingly, wealthier people are often attracted to marginalized urban areas and their cultural life, as the popularity of hip hop amongst middle-class youth demonstrates. Even while their residents suffer from area stigmatization, low-income neighborhoods often have a certain cultural cachet. Part of a larger process of the 'commodification of place' (see Chapter 6 on leisure and consumption), such areas become the source for 'ghetto fabulous' or 'favela chic' fashion. Similarly, slum tourism – visiting low-income neighborhoods in cities such as Rio, Mumbai or Johannesburg – has become a significant trend in global travel. Here, place-making can turn into place-marketing.

Segregation and displacement

As part of a shift in focus from poverty to inequality, urban anthropologists increasingly turned to study high-income urban areas. This also reflected a larger trend in anthropology towards 'studying up', the study of more powerful actors or institutions than those that anthropologists traditionally researched (see Chapter 1). Elite 'exclusivity' often literally relies on exclusion, and many of these neighborhoods incorporate physical features aimed at keeping out less wealthy urban dwellers. Anthropologists such as Teresa Caldeira (2000) and Setha Low (2003) have done ethnographic research in gated communities and condominiums. They show how high-income urban residents are fearful of crime, which they often associate with low-income ethnic others, and seek to construct defensible spaces that provide both safety and status (see Chapter 10).

This retreat by elites from the larger city is a stark example of class segregation, but even without walls and gates, different urban groups often live in separate neighborhoods. In most cities, the urban population is distributed unevenly across different neighborhoods along lines of class, ethnicity or occupation. Not everyone sees this clustering in communities as problematic. For instance, the development of the Castro district into San Francisco's main gay neighborhood meant that the lesbian, gay, bisexual, transgender (LGBT) movement had a safe 'home' area in the city (Duyvendak 2011). 'Ethnic enclaves' may provide recent migrants with access to networks and resources they need to get ahead in their new homes.

Residential segregation is often driven by exclusion and discrimination, as was most evident in colonial cities, or in South African cities under apartheid. In such cases, governments actively prevented socially mixed residential areas. In other cases, segregation is produced through market actors. In many US cities, for instance, African-Americans were unable to buy homes in White neighborhoods, because they were denied access to mortgages or restricted from viewing certain homes by banks, real-estate agents and homeowners. Segregation along lines of class, race and ethnicity often reinforces urban deprivation in terms of environmental degradation, exposure to health risks and restricted access to urban amenities. Anthropologists from Max Gluckman in 1930s South Africa to Setha Low in twenty-first-century United States have studied and critiqued segregation and its underlying structures of exclusion (Gluckman 1940; Low 2011).

In addition to studying segregation, anthropological research has studied many different kinds of displacement. The most evident type of urban displacement is when residents are removed from their homes through physical force, for instance in the context of political violence or through the demolition of informal settlements. In addition, displacement may occur through the real-estate market, in a less physically violent fashion. In the late twentieth century, scholars working in cities across the world began to recognize such processes under the rubric of gentrification.

Gentrification, a term coined by the British sociologist Ruth Glass in the 1960s, is used to describe the movement of wealthier residents into low-income urban areas. Tim Cresswell (2004: 93) defines gentrification as 'the purchase of run-down housing at cheap prices by middle-class incomers and the subsequent upgrading of the property and massive rise in property values'. This process usually involves the displacement of low-income residents, who can no longer afford the rental prices, or who sell their property to real-estate developers. In many cases, gentrification is promoted by municipal governments as part of urban regeneration or revitalization (see Chapter 8 on urban planning).

In her study of the socio-economically and ethnically diverse Washington DC neighborhood of Mount Pleasant, Gabriella Modan (2007) describes how residents responded to rapidly rising real-estate values that gradually displaced low-income inhabitants. Residents drew strongly on discursive strategies – both verbally and in written narratives such as grant applications – to assert their visions of, and claims to, the neighborhood and the people they felt belonged in that place. Some discourses constructed symbolic boundaries between 'inauthentic suburban' gentrifiers (often White and middle class) on the one hand, and 'authentic city people' (often low-income immigrants and people of color) on the other. Other moral discourses drew on these oppositions to debate the appropriate use of neighborhood space, contrasting 'clean' and 'orderly' individualized spatial practices with more public uses, which they presented as dirtier and signs of disorder. Modan's work shows how the political-economic processes of gentrification and displacement are always accompanied by symbolic, discursive forms of meaning-making and contestation.

Urban places in a global era

Where mid-twentieth-century community studies often approached urban places as if they had clear boundaries, in recent decades urban anthropologists have begun to study homes, streets, neighborhoods and cities in relation to other places and scales. In part, this shift built on the work of authors such Arjun Appadurai (1996), who emphasized that place-making is always relational: it is only possible to know 'here' because of its relation to 'there'. In addition, global migration and media flows challenged traditional anthropological approaches that saw people and culture as rooted in specific places (Gupta and Ferguson 1992). In a global era, people are connected to a diverse range of places, while places are marked by social and cultural diversity.

Drawing on a relational approach, anthropologists started to explore how urban places are produced through global flows and their relations to other places, both near and far (see Chapter 7 on global cities). Of course, these trans-local connections and mobilities are by no means new; they intensified and accelerated in the late twentieth century rather than emerging out of thin air. Colonial cities, for instance, have always been characterized by global connections, and in many cases were shaped by 'proto-globalization' since the seventeenth century. A relational approach to cities has pointed our attention to these processes, challenging traditional ideas of urban places as local, cohesive and rooted.

Researchers attempting to study urban places through a relational, global lens have often focused on urban residents' transnational ties, for instance by concentrating on migrant neighborhoods. In addition to such ethnic neighborhoods, 'transnational places' can also be bars, shops, restaurants or public plazas where migrants meet each other and recreate a sense of home. Many such studies have concentrated on migration from poorer countries to cities in Europe and North America, looking for instance at Puerto Rican neighborhoods in US cities or Turkish areas in Western Europe. However, South–South migration is equally significant, and many cities in Africa, Asia, Latin America and the Middle East have sizable immigrant districts. Cities across the world also have sizable communities of more privileged expat workers.

Beyond economic motives, migrants may also move because of political or ideological reasons. Following the Cuban Revolution in 1959, many wealthier Cubans in particular migrated to the United States and specifically to Miami. Over the past half century, these exiles have reshaped the city's public spaces as well as their private homes to evoke a nostalgic sense of Cuba as they would like to remember it. As Jenna Andrew-Swann (2011: 12) notes, 'The historical relationship between Miami and Cuba, especially Havana, is evident in place names, businesses, social clubs, arts, events and the individual and collective memories that continue to span the Straits of Florida'. Similarly, the Nairobi area of Eastleigh and the London neighborhood of Tower Hamlets have become hubs of transnational cultural, economic and political activity for Somalis who fled their country's political violence (Lindley 2010). In such places, people live in transnational fields, in which neighborhoods and villages are connected across physical distances and national boundaries (Levitt and Glick Schiller 2004), see Chapter 7.

Another relational and transnational approach to urban place involves tracing economic networks. A famous example is Theodor Bestor's (2004) work on Tokyo's Tsukiji market. Tsukiji is the world's largest market for seafood, and connects fishing fleets and rural fishing communities to sushi chefs, wholesalers and tourists. Combining urban and economic anthropology, this study analyzes the internal and external relationships that structure the market, its local rootedness and its global connections. Bestor (2004: xvi) shows how

> Tsukiji is closely attuned to the subtleties of Japanese food culture and to the representations of national cultural identity that cloak cuisine, but this is also the market that drives the global fishing industry, from Japanese long-liners in the Indian Ocean to Croatian tuna ranchers in the Adriatic.

The marketplace is a central institution in the urban life of Tokyo, both an important infrastructural hub and a repository of cultural heritage. As Bestor notes, 'if the emotional landscape of old Tokyo has a heartland, Tsukiji's partisans lay claim to a substantial chunk of it' (2004: 24). At the same time, this market plays a central role both in the national and international fishing and seafood industry, shaping global prices and driving the over-exploitation of marine resources.

These examples of markets and migrant neighborhoods show that while urban place-making always draws on local histories and a concrete built environment, these places are often equally shaped by global flows of people, representations, commodities and money (Appadurai 1996). In a global era, local places are produced through transnational connections. Global place-making involves flows of tangible goods – building materials, home decorations – as well as less tangible cultural flows consisting of images and ideas. For example, the case of popular culture representations of the ghetto, discussed earlier, demonstrates how globally circulating music and movies influence how residents see their own neighborhoods.

Conclusion

Cities include a broad array of urban places. This chapter has discussed how different types of urban places are made, and how they serve as forms of identification, communication and control. The home, often seen as the most private and intimate space in the city, reflects socio-cultural understandings of domestic life and family relations. The home can also be an important site for social distinction, through which people express ethnic and religious belonging, or communicate their ambitions to belong to a higher social class. Signature buildings also transmit messages about the city and its ambitions, for instance in place-marketing. While we no longer see neighborhoods as bounded communities, they remain prominent arenas for social organization and government interventions. For many people, they are still important contexts for socializing and sources of identity. A relational perspective on place emphasizes that these processes of place-making and belonging are informed by global flows and connections. Transnational place-making connects people, buildings, food, fashions, music and money beyond the city and across national borders.

Discussion questions

1   How are power relations expressed and reinforced through the interior and exterior of buildings? Can you recognize this in buildings you use regularly?
2   In what forms of place-making do you yourself engage? And how do you affect the spaces around you through these practices?
3   What forms of religious place-making can you identify in your urban environment?
4   What does it mean to take a relational approach to the study of neighborhoods?
5   In addition to transnational migration and trade, what are other examples of place-making in a global era?

Further reading

Becci, Irene, Marian Burchardt and José Casanova, eds. (2013) *Topographies of Faith: Religion in Urban Spaces*. Leiden and Boston, MA: Brill.
Briganti, Chiara and Kathy Mezei, eds. (2012) *The Domestic Space Reader*. Toronto: University of Toronto Press.

Cresswell, Tim (2004) *Place: A Short Introduction*. Malden, MA: Blackwell.

Low, Setha M. and Denise Lawrence-Zúñiga, eds. (2003) *The Anthropology of Space and Place: Locating Culture*. Malden, MA: Blackwell.

Rotenberg, Robert L. and Gary V. McDonogh (1993) *The Cultural Meaning of Urban Place*. Westport, CT: Greenwood.

Further viewing

Do the Right Thing (1989), directed by Spike Lee. Feature film on neighborhood relations in the Brooklyn area of Bedford Stuyvesant.

Unfinished Spaces (2011), directed by Benjamin Murray and Alysa Nahmias. Documentary on architecture and social change in Havana.

Chapter 3

Urban mobilities

People's lives in cities are not stationary. Much of what we do in cities involves movement: taking the bus to work, driving to the shop, walking to a friend's house. Some of these movements are experienced as frustrating, for instance daily commutes that involve spending hours stuck in traffic jams or squeezed in overcrowded subway cars. Other movements – leisurely walks along a boulevard, skateboarding with friends in a park – are part of what makes city life enjoyable to many people. This chapter focuses on people's movements in and through cities. It discusses both physical mobility (how we get from point A to point B) and the ways that these movements are represented and made meaningful. The chapter also explores why individuals and groups of urban residents move in different ways. People are not always able to choose their mobilities freely: different types of physical movement are shaped by physical ability, financial resources and existing transport infrastructures. In addition, anthropological studies demonstrate that our movements through the city are influenced by our social networks, the mental maps we construct, and culturally informed beliefs about who should be moving where, how and with whom. By limiting access to urban spaces of work, education and leisure, restrictions to mobility can reinforce socio-economic inequalities.

Anthropologists have long been interested in understanding how different social and cultural groups navigate their environments, but they originally tended to focus on the mobilities of hunter-gatherers, pastoralists, fisherfolk and other non-urban groups (Istomin and Dwyer 2009). Serious study of how city dwellers move around urban environments only really took off in the second half of the twentieth century, following the publication of Kevin Lynch's *The Image of the City* (see Box 3.1). James Holston (1989), for instance, studied the way in which residents of the planned city of Brasília find their way around town, while Andrew Maxwell (1998) explored how urban motorcyclists form communities in post-industrial US cities.

In the mid-2000s, a number of social scientists both within and beyond anthropology contributed to what became known as the 'mobilities turn', or even a *new mobilities paradigm* (see Box 3.2). This chapter explores the implications of this increasing attention on mobility of people, goods and ideas for urban anthropology. We start with a section on mobility and identities. What are the different ways in which people move through cities and how are social categories and identifications formed around these various mobilities? The next section looks at how differential mobilities are connected to urban inequalities, focusing on disability and on traffic and public transport. A final section looks at the cultural politics of mobility, focusing on the meaning given to different forms of movement and

Box 3.1   **Kevin Lynch's *The Image of the City***

A classic work in understanding how people move through cities is Kevin Lynch's *The Image of the City* (1960). Lynch was an urban planner interested in studying how people's perceptions of the city shaped the ways they navigated their urban environment. Based on studies in three US cities, *The Image of the City* sought to understand how people interpret and utilize urban form in their everyday 'way-finding'. Lynch (1960: 4) argued that in the process of way-finding, people draw on an 'environmental image, the generalized mental picture of the exterior physical world that is held by an individual'. This image of the city, which Lynch also called a 'mental map', is produced in an interaction between individuals and their environment. It is shaped both by the people's immediate sensory experience of their surroundings and by memories of earlier experiences, and is important for both practical and emotional reasons.

Lynch distinguished five elements in these mental maps: paths, edges, districts, nodes and landmarks. Paths are the different more or less linear routes that people follow as they move through the city, such as roads, sidewalks or rivers. Edges are the boundaries or breaks in continuity that people perceive as they move along these paths, such as walls or buildings. Districts are sections of the cities that share common characteristics, such as neighborhoods. Nodes are focal points or intersections such as plazas or crossroads. Landmarks, finally, are conspicuous, easily identifiable reference points such as striking buildings, monuments or artworks. Within the image of the city, Lynch made a distinction between studying how these different elements related to each other and to the observer, and what their practical and emotional meaning was. While these images or mental maps are individual, common images and systems of orientation emerge amongst members of specific social or cultural groups.

The Image of the City was influential in part because of its normative dimension. Lynch urged urban planners to pursue both 'legibility' (easily recognizable urban elements and patterns) and 'imageability' (elements that evoke a strong image). Lynch felt that planners should create cities that produce sharp, distinctive images and thereby allow residents to find their way more easily. He argued that less legible, disorderly surroundings produce fear, while more legible cities offer emotional satisfaction. This argument, which encouraged planners to take both urban aesthetics and residents' perceptions seriously, made a major impact in the discipline of planning.

Lynch's work has been important for urban anthropologists as a key text that focused on people's lived experience of the built environment. His research also had an impact on the methods researchers use to study urban life. Various urban anthropologists have taken up mental mapping (also referred to as cognitive maps) to understand how residents relate to, and move through, their surroundings (see Chapter 1). Lynch's work has also been subject to anthropological critique. Anthropologists studying urban symbolism have argued that Lynch pays insufficient attention to the meaning of urban elements (e.g., Nas and Sluis 2002). Lynch's emphasis on legible planning has been criticized by anthropologists whose studies show that residents may also resent an overly determined urban form, such as that of the planned city of Brasília (e.g., Holston 1989; see Chapter 8). In addition, authors have pointed out that Lynch's emphasis on visual elements in urban way-finding obscures the extent to which people rely on other senses – sound, smell or touch – when they navigate city environments.

Box 3.2 **The new mobilities paradigm**

A number of influential authors, including sociologists Mimi Sheller and John Urry, have argued that the social sciences have come to be characterized by a new paradigm (a set of practices that define the questions and methods of a field of research): the *new mobilities paradigm* (Sheller and Urry 2006; Hannam et al. 2006). Most twentieth-century social-scientists took a 'static' or 'sedentarist' approach, which assumed that being tied to specific places was the norm. From the 1990s sociologists, geographers and anthropologists increasingly began to focus on different aspects of mobilities to understand social life. A mobilities approach means that we cannot understand people, things and ideas only as rooted in specific places; we must also pay attention to the movements, flows and networks that connect humans to each other and to non-humans. However, a 'nomadist' view of the world in which everyone and everything is constantly on the move ignores the continued importance of fixity and rootedness. The mobilities paradigm emphasizes the importance of mobility and flows, but always in relation to immobility and fixity.

Another author whose work has been prominent in shaping the new mobilities paradigm is the geographer Tim Cresswell. He distinguishes three aspects that together make up mobilities (Cresswell 2010: 19). The first is *physical movement*, traveling from place A to place B. These physical movements constitute the 'raw material' from which mobilities are produced. The second aspect consists of *representations of movement*. Such representations can include official representations that distinguish 'good' and 'bad' ways of moving, for instance policy reports on bicycle-friendly cities or on homelessness. Less official representations of movements – such as depictions in news media, films or popular music – can also influence how we view different mobilities. The third aspect of mobilities that Cresswell recognizes is the *embodied and experienced nature of mobilities*. Being mobile, whether by walking through a city or flying across the world, is an embodied practice that involves sensorial experiences, from seeing and hearing to smelling and touching.

the aesthetics and materiality associated with these mobilities. This section discusses how certain mobilities come to be seen as transgressive or emancipatory, from low-rider car culture amongst Mexican Americans in US cities such as Austin, to cycling in Bogotá.

Mobility and identities

Social groups move through the city in different ways: individually or collectively, effortlessly or with difficulty, on foot, by car and by public transport. Mobilities shape and are shaped by identities. On the one hand, how we move shapes our identities. Different forms of mobility play a role in how urban residents are categorized by others. How we move around influences how others see us – most people would probably classify someone riding a donkey cart differently from someone driving a BMW. These same mobilities are also central to our own identifications: to which groups we understand ourselves as belonging. Skateboarders, joggers, commuters, biker gangs and soccer moms are just a few examples of urban types associated with specific forms of mobility and the lifestyles we connect to those mobilities. On the other hand, our identities also influence how we move. Pre-existing categorizations and identifications – such as gender, class, ethnicity and age – also shape our mobility preferences and opportunities. Elderly, low-income women tend to move differently through urban space than wealthy young men. Below, we discuss this relationship between mobility and identities, focusing on two types of mobility that have been studied specifically for the city: walking and driving.

Walking the city

Walking has always been an important way in which people get to know a city. In addition, the French philosopher Michel de Certeau (1984) argues, the everyday practice of walking also allows people to contribute to the production of the city, often in the face of more powerful political and commercial forces that structure urban space. He compares 'walking the city' to speaking a language: it is a routine, everyday practice that is often unconscious but is also productive, bounded by certain rules but able to transgress them. We can understand walking, de Certeau suggests, as an expressive form, as a way for pedestrians to tell stories about the city. Walking – taking detours, creating new paths, connecting different places – can be a creative way of subverting the urban system and its intended uses, and in so doing may 'remap' the urban order over time.

A central mobile figure in urban studies has been the *flâneur*: a figure who walks through the city, wandering through its streets, observing its population and enjoying its sights, sounds and smells. The flâneur is an urban stroller who is both detached from, and interested in, the sensations of everyday urban life. Historically, the flâneur has been associated with Paris, surfacing for instance in depictions of the city by the nineteenth-century French poet Charles Baudelaire and the twentieth-century German philosopher Walter Benjamin. Baudelaire described the flâneur as an anonymous spectator who strolled casually through the streets and arcades of Paris. His flâneur, a stranger who draws energy from the varied spectacle offered by the modern city, enjoys moving about aimlessly and losing himself in the crowd.

Benjamin analyzed Baudelaire's poetry to understand the development of nineteenth-century Paris as a space of modernity, changing dramatically as its architecture was transformed and consumer capitalism began to emerge. In particular, Benjamin drew on Baudelaire's work to try and understand how the development of the city's shopping arcades was connected to a new type of leisurely consumer. He saw the flâneur as a literary figure that could shed light on how the spectacle of modern city life impacted on the human psyche. The idea of the flâneur helped him theorize the accommodation of modern individuals to the shock of countless urban sensations. Where the urban sociologist Georg Simmel argued in the early twentieth century that this overstimulation would result in numbing or alienation, Benjamin suggested that the flâneur demonstrated the pleasure and excitement that could also be derived from big city life.

While the flâneur has been celebrated as a quintessential urban figure, a figure that embodies modernity, this positive appraisal has been balanced by critique. Implicitly, the flâneur is always a middle-class White man. His ability to move through the urban crowd anonymously, and his role as an observer rather than an object of surveillance, are dependent on his social privilege. Can women taste the delights of the city in a similarly detached way, or are they considered part of the delights to be tasted? Can ethnic minorities in White-majority cities wander anonymously or will their movements attract unwanted attention (see Chapter 4 on situated experiences)? While these questions prompt us to consider the flâneur in a critical light, Baudelaire's and Benjamin's work does point to a broadly shared appreciation of the excitement or enchantment that urban life and its diverse sensations offer.

Homeless people, whose urban pedestrian mobility might be contrasted to that of the flâneur, are generally considered a very different category of urban wanderer. As Emma Jackson (2012) found in her ethnographic study of youth homelessness in London, young homeless people were highly mobile but their mobilities were not necessarily voluntary. Rather than experiencing mobility as freedom, these young people could become 'fixed' in mobility. Their movements through the city often resulted from displacement and surveillance: they moved around the city by foot or by bus in an effort to find safe and affordable shelter and to escape the gaze of the police, local authorities and their peers. Their constant mobility could also serve as a tactic to stay safe and gain knowledge. Jackson shows how mobility could be a resource as well as a burden.

In his study of homeless men in post-Communist Bucharest, Romania, Bruce O'Neill (2014) found a similar sense of being fixed in mobility. He emphasizes the pervasive sense of boredom that the street homeless experienced, a boredom they associated with continuous wandering and with their lack of access to the urban landscape of consumption that emerged after the fall of Communism. As O'Neill (2014: 10, 14) explains, 'for Romania's newly minted homeless … boredom references their exclusion from an urban life that increasingly unfolds through practices of consumption', an exclusion compounded by a sense of 'being downwardly mobile in a neoliberal era of supposed ascent'. This relationship these men had to urban consumption marks another contrast with the flâneur: where the nineteenth-century flâneur found stimulation in the consumerist spectacle of the city, for twenty-first century homeless people it portended exclusion and humiliation.

Various authors have compared urban ethnographers to the flâneur, with the ethnographer moving around the city and observing urban residents in a somewhat similar fashion, as a familiar stranger, an insider/outsider. While this comparison may resonate with the experience of some urban anthropologists, it is evidently open to the same critique as that of the flâneur more generally: the detached interest of this type of ethnographic researcher also relies on a specific type of privilege. However, anthropological research based on urban walking can also be a more collaborative venture. In their collection on ethnography and walking, Tim Ingold and Jo Lee Vergunst (2008) offer examples of how walking with one's interlocutors, while remaining mindful of existing power relations, can enrich our anthropological practice.

Urban automobility

Automobility is another form of urban mobility that has received increasing scholarly attention in recent years. Where walking has been an important form of urban mobility as long as cities have existed, cars only appeared on the urban scene about a century ago. Yet it is hard to imagine a present-day city without this type of transport. As Mimi Sheller and John Urry (2000: 738) point out, the rise of the car in the twentieth century has had an extraordinary impact on social life, and especially on urban life, involving 'distinct ways of dwelling, traveling and socializing in, and through, an automobilized time-space'. They suggest that the analysis of automobility must take into account a range of components, including the manufactured object of the car, its status as an item of individual consumption, and the constitution of a machinic complex in which the car is linked to other industries from petrol refining and road construction to urban design. Other components of automobility include its dominant form of quasi-private mobility that sidelines more public mobilities, a hegemonic culture that valorizes cars, and its impact on environmental resource use (Sheller and Urry 2000: 738–739).

Moving around a city by car is not just a matter of speed and comfort. In many contexts, it is connected to forms of social distinction, to identifying yourself with a specific social category. In cities across the world, car ownership has been, and still is, associated with modernity and social mobility. Automobility is associated with modern virtues such as speed and freedom. It offers an individualized, encapsulated way of experiencing the city, characterized by privacy rather than an engagement with the urban public (Lutz 2014). While the automobilization of cities and societies is driven as much by political economic factors as by individual desires, being 'automobile' remains an important aspiration for many people.

Of course, automobility is not just about driving a car. What kind of car you drive makes all the difference. Different types of cars are associated with classed, gendered and ethno-racial identities. In many North American cities, the minivan is associated with a specific type of affluent suburban woman who spends a lot of time driving her children around town, sometimes characterized as the 'soccer mom' or the 'hockey mom'. Meanwhile, sports cars, classic cars and low-riders feature in different classed and raced performances of masculinity. In recent years, another type of car linked directly to social distinction has been the 'environmentally friendly' but also very expensive (hybrid) electrical vehicle. In North American and European cities, driving such a vehicle is not just an expression of one's commitment to sustainability; it has also become a marker of elite status (Griskevicius et al. 2010). This expression of socio-economic status through automobility points towards the broader connections between mobility and urban inequality.

Mobility and inequality

Mobility – and immobility – is connected to urban inequality in multiple ways. Inequalities in terms of physical ability or income limit urban residents' freedom to move as they desire. For instance, blind or deaf people often have a difficult time navigating urban traffic. By limiting access to public and private transport, a lack of income may equally constrain residents' ability to move beyond their immediate living environment. Such limits to urban movement can lead to social and economic exclusion: residents who experience barriers to being mobile often have less access to education, to work, to leisure opportunities and to political participation. In addition to how people move through the city, how quickly they move can also be an indication of underlying inequalities. Speed – driving a fast car, being fit and flexible enough to keep up with the pace of modern urban living – is often associated with a more privileged social position. However, the freedom to not be in a hurry, to be a leisurely flâneur who savors urban life, can also be a mark of privilege.

The ability to move freely and at one's own pace often intersects with gendered and ethno-racial hierarchies: women's movements, especially at night, are often inhibited by fears of sexual violence. Similarly, in many cities, members of ethnic or racial minorities are made to feel unwelcome or unsafe when they travel through certain areas. In New York City, for instance, a controversial crime control policy involved 'stop-and-frisk' searches, with New York City Police Department (NYPD) officers disproportionately targeting non-White pedestrians to check whether they were carrying weapons or illegal drugs. Somewhat similarly, throughout the United States, African-American motorists, and especially those driving expensive cars, are disproportionately pulled over for 'random' checks by the police. The term 'driving while black' has emerged in popular discourse to describe the experience of Black drivers of being subjected to this type of racial profiling and harassment. In this section, we discuss the relationship between urban mobilities and inequality, looking at two themes: physical disability and traffic.

Disability

There is a broad range of physical disabilities that may impact on urban mobility, including hearing impairments, visual impairments, intellectual disabilities and orthopaedic impairment. It is important to see disability not only as a matter of individual capacities, but as an interaction between these capacities and a person's physical and social environment. Many cities are planned and organized around the priorities of the dominant 'able-bodied' community. When cities are produced for particular kinds of 'normal' bodies, they – often unintentionally – exclude people whose bodies do not match this norm. Persons with disabilities are often unable to participate fully in urban life, and physical space and social space can work in conjunction in either limiting or enabling their participation in education, healthcare, labor markets and the political sphere. In this regard we might speak of 'disablement' rather than 'disability'. We also can look at cities and urban space and ask whether they consist of disabling environments (Imrie 1996). What types of urban spaces serve to lock people with disabilities out, and what types offer them more freedom and control over their everyday movements? How can government planners, architects and urban residents shape more universally accessible environments?

In his study of people with physical and visual disabilities in the Ecuadorian cities of Quito and Cuenca, Nicholas Rattray (2013) shows how their everyday social, political and economic practices took shape in the context of infrastructural and cultural barriers. Many of these disabled Ecuadorians experienced both spatial and social isolation, facing not only architectural and transport barriers but also stigma and shame. The ways buildings were constructed and transportation systems were organized meant that many urban spaces became inaccessible to them. Getting around by bus or taxi, for instance, required difficult or dangerous manoeuvres, such as trying to jump on a moving bus. Trying to use these forms of transportation also involved being refused service or suffering patronizing behavior from taxi drivers. In addition, many Ecuadorians saw disability as bringing vergüenza – shame – not only on people with disabilities, but also on their families. This stigma, which meant that family members often kept their disabled children hidden from public view, prevented people with disabilities from moving freely outside their own home. A disabling urban infrastructure, in combination with the fear, pity and shame many non-disabled Ecuadorians displayed, resulted in an experience of isolation and social exclusion.

Rattray describes how disability rights groups in Cuenca sought to improve accessibility through collective action, such as public rallies aimed at raising social awareness. In these mobilizations, they claimed their right to be part of a more inclusive city, critiquing urban design while also countering cultural attitudes towards disability. They employed spatial tactics such as marches through Cuenca's streets to claim their right to the city (see Chapter 9). These forms of activism, which utilized 'strategic transgression and other techniques aimed at contesting dominant practices that re-inscribe able-bodied space' (Rattray 2013: 41) asserted disabled Ecuadorians' rights to be not only mobile but also visible, rather than hiding in shame.

There are, of course, also cities that are more accessible, inclusive and empowering for people with disabilities. Various governments have adopted so-called 'universal design' standards (products and built environments designed with universal accessibility in mind) that take into account the diversity of urban people and their capacities. Interventions that improve access to roads and buildings, transportation, and communication and information can make a major difference in moving towards enabling environments. The Brazilian city of Curitiba, for instance, introduced a new public transportation system in 1970 that was designed from the start with the aim of providing full accessibility to disabled people. Buses were designed so that passengers with orthopaedic impairments could enter them easily, and a system of interconnected local and express bus routes facilitated continuity in the travel chain. In Malaysia, when new buildings are constructed, they must undergo an 'access audit' to determine their usability for people with disabilities. In addition, Malaysian university courses in architecture and urban design incorporate accessibility considerations, making 'universal design' more mainstream within professional education and practice (WHO 2011: 169–201). As the case of Ecuador shows, however, the relation between disability and inequality involves not only redesigning urban space to make it physically accessible; it also requires combating the social stigma that impedes the everyday movements of disabled people.

Traffic

Everyday motorized traffic is an important site for studying the links between urban inequalities, mobility and immobility (Figure 3.1). Historically developed political and economic relations shape the urban infrastructure of mobility, such as road networks and public transport systems. This infrastructure can facilitate or constrain the types of urban movement that are possible for different groups of people, promoting either public or private transport, and patterning both mobility and immobility. However, cultural preferences and prejudices also structure our everyday traffic experiences and encounters, often exacerbating social exclusion.

Daily traffic jams are a feature of many cities, and a prime example of urban immobility. In her ethnographic study of morning traffic on the Istanbul stretch of the Trans-European Motorway (TEM), Berna Yazıcı (2013) analyzed traffic as a social site where urban inequality is produced. Istanbul has developed on two peninsulas along the Bosporus Strait, with two bridges connecting the Asian and the European sides of the city. At the time of Yazıcı's study, over a million commuters, some 10 per cent of Istanbul's population, crossed these bridges every day. The city's traffic hierarchy included different types of commuters: laborers transported in the back of trucks meant for goods rather than people, low-income workers traveling on overcrowded public buses, wealthier employees transported in more spacious and comfortable company shuttles, commuters driving privately owned cars and affluent businesspeople traveling in the back of chauffeur-driven luxury cars. While all of these commuters faced the boredom and waste of time that being stuck in traffic entailed, those lower in the hierarchy tended to be more exposed to discomfort and traffic accidents. Class differentials intersected with gender, as sexual harassment and the threat of robbery presented larger concerns for female commuters. Looking beyond commuters, the highway

Figure 3.1 Traffic in Hong Kong, 2013 (photograph by José Carlos G. Aguiar)

was also populated by toll collectors and vendors selling drinks, snacks or flowers, for whom the highway was their workplace rather than the route by which they reached it. These workers were even more vulnerable to the health hazards of air pollution and accidents. As Istanbul's residential areas became increasingly segregated, the everyday reality of traffic congestion in the Turkish city created a zone of fleeting but close cross-class encounters, where elite residents could not avoid the presence of their poorer counterparts.

As Yazıcı shows in this 'anthropology of traffic', the physical proximity imposed by traffic jams underscored the social distance between these different groups. However, those at the extremes of Istanbul's class divide were exempt or excluded from this experience. The extremely wealthy resorted to traveling by helicopter to escape the city's daily gridlock. This exclusive form of transport is becoming increasingly common in cities suffering from congestion and insecurity; the Brazilian mega-city of São Paulo is another infamous example of elites using helicopters to avoid traffic and to display their social status (Cwerner 2009). In Istanbul, another forms of 'congestion exemption' was the clearing of highways so that national or international political leaders could move through the city quickly and safely, a strategy that created more gridlock for everyone else. A final, illegal form of avoiding the experience of being stuck in traffic was found in the phenomenon of ambulance-taxis: private ambulances hired to operate as elite transport. At the other end of the class spectrum were those Istanbul residents who did not participate in traffic because they could not afford any form of public or private transport. With low-income neighborhoods located far away from most workplaces, the city's poorest residents walked long and often dangerous distances to work. As in cities across the world, a lack of affordable transport could compound social exclusion, making it more difficult for the urban poor to access social networks, education and leisure opportunities.

Urban residents are positioned in traffic in different ways, not only through access to income, but also along lines of gender, race or age. In one scene in Paul Haggis's Oscar-winning movie *Crash* (2004), which emphasizes urban inequalities in Los Angeles, two African-American characters discuss why the city's buses have such large windows. Their ironic conclusion is that the windows serve to humiliate the (Black) passengers by displaying their poverty. The link between traffic, public transport and inequality goes beyond the discomfort of long, crowded commutes or health risks (in the case of Los Angeles, levels of carcinogenic diesel exhaust were found to be higher inside school buses than outside them). In many US cities, using public transport to get around the city is associated with poverty, stigma and shame. Access to private forms of transport, in contrast, is not just a matter of more efficient travel; it also symbolizes freedom and social mobility. Even in public transport, though, people may find ways to privatize their movements. Writing on the impact of the iPod on urban space and culture, Michael Bull (2008) points out that portable MP3 players allow people to move in their own personalized sound world. Even as they move through the public space of the city, MP3 players allow commuters to disengage by using 'sensory gating' to retreat into a semi-privatized space.

Writing on the historically shaped relationship between race, class and automobility in the United States, Paul Gilroy (2001) analyzes the importance of cars as a consumerist orientation amongst African-Americans. He suggests that car ownership and flashy public displays of customized cars have offered a form of escape and compensatory prestige against a backdrop of racialized violence and humiliations. While private motorized transport can be a claim to citizenship, the car-centric character of US cities has exacerbated urban segregation. Automobility enabled 'white flight' and racially homogeneous suburban sprawl – suburbanization itself has been associated with the erosion of the urban tax base, and deteriorating services and infrastructure for low-income, often non-White residents. On a more micro-level, car culture allows motorists to avoid encountering people with other ethno-racial or class backgrounds. The everyday traffic choices we make, then, can serve to contest or overcome urban inequalities, but they may also exacerbate them.

The cultural politics of mobility

Anthropologists have explored the meanings that are attributed to different types of urban mobility. We can understand this by studying the strong associations that mobilities carry, as is evident in a range of socio-cultural phenomena, from cycling activism to 'car cultures'. Because different ways of moving through the city can be highly contested, urban mobility can have a strong political dimension. Various forms of urban mobility have been seen as transgressive or emancipatory, from skateboarding to parkour. This section focuses on the cultural politics of urban mobility, discussing how specific movements – and the objects, designs and sensations associated with those movements – become both meaningful and politicized. It includes a discussion of first, low-rider car culture in Austin, Texas, and second, cycling in Bogotá.

Figure 3.2 Customized 'low-rider' car in Austin, Texas (photograph by www.flacosfotos.com)

Anthropological work on *car cultures* emphasizes the intimate and expressive relationship people have with cars (Miller 2001). Such an ethnographic approach understands cars as material culture and concentrates on the embodied and social experiences of automobility. Like other forms of globalized material culture, cars and car cultures are interpreted, appropriated and adapted differently as they gain significance in local contexts. In his work on the aesthetics and politics of 'low-riders' in Austin, Texas, Ben Chappell (2012) gives an extensive ethnographic analysis of one such 'car culture'. The low-riding scene revolves around customized cars, usually US models such as the Chevrolet Impala or the Oldsmobile Cutlass. These cars are modified according to a popular aesthetic that has been developing since the 1950s and that is identified with Mexican-American working-class barrios. Their owners install hydraulic suspension systems that allow the cars to 'bounce', repaint them with elaborate designs, replace their wheels with custom versions, and refit their interiors with distinctive upholstery, accessories and sound systems (see Figure 3.2). In US Southwest cities such as Austin, low-riders come together in cruising scenes, showing off their cars and socializing in parking lots.

Chappell makes a case for seeing car culture as not just expressive or representational. Low-riding should be understood as a material, space-making practice. He found that the cars themselves were quasi-private mobile mini-spaces, customized to suit their owners' desires. However, they also interacted with broader urban space, giving sites a particular classed and ethno-racial identity. As material objects associated with Mexican-American urban barrio communities, these cars affected and were affected by particular city spaces. Through their regular presence, both when cruising during the weekends and as part of everyday traffic, low-riders could (re)inscribe a neighborhood as a barrio. As Chappell (2012: 33) explains, 'Their presence can reinforce the spatial identity of an area as a barrio, or they can assert their barriological aesthetics in the public sphere beyond these boundaries.' Low-riders were also conducive to creating their own type of public sphere, a social space where conversation could take place. The customized cars were meant for public displays, and functioned as a site for owners and admirers to gather and talk – not just about cars but also about various issues affecting Mexican-Americans. While low-riders were often seen as transgressive (especially outside of barrio neighborhoods) because of their association with Mexican-American gangs, the public sphere this urban car style could create demonstrated its emancipatory potential as well.

Car cultures are not the only types of mobility associated with urban transgression. Depending on the context, urban mobilities may be fully accepted, or they may 'bump' against mainstream forms of movement. Skateboarding, like the newer phenomenon of parkour (or urban running), is a form of mobility that challenges our ideas of how urban space ought to be used. These mobilities are playful performances of artistry, skill and bodily discipline but, in their subversion of 'normal' uses of urban space, they can also be understood as critiques of urban planning and consumerism (Chiu 2009; Caldeira 2012). Yet in recent years, both skateboarding and parkour have been embraced by corporate sponsors, who draw on the transgressive image of these mobilities to enhance the appeal of their brands.

A similar form of ambiguity can be seen in the case of motorcycles. In many contexts, they are considered a noisy nuisance and associated with deviance and membership of 'biker gangs'. In Ho Chi Minh City, however, motorbikes have been a marker of freedom, autonomy and middle-class status in liberalizing Vietnam (Truitt 2008; see Figure 3.3). And in Bangkok, where motorcycle taxi drivers have the ability to slow down or block traffic, this form of transport became central in political protests (Sopranzetti 2014). These examples show how the same type of mobility can have a wide range of cultural and political meanings within and across contexts.

Studying the role of the bicycle in urban mobilities from a cross-cultural perspective, Luis Vivanco (2013) also focuses on its multiple meanings and associated 'bicycle cultures'. In many places, people tend to associate bicycles either with children's toys or with sports. Cycling social movements, however, seek to rebrand this form of mobility. By contesting its meaning, they hope to convince both urban residents and municipal governments that bicycling can transform city life in a positive way. In the Colombian city of Bogotá, for instance, the municipal government embraced cycling as a tool for social inclusion, investing in the Cicloruta, a 350 km cycle route. However, investing in urban infrastructure that caters to non-motorized forms of transport will not necessarily result in an immediate decrease in automobility. Vivanco points to the 'build-it-and-they-will-come' logic, a form of technological determinism that assumes that constructing bicycle lanes and related infrastructures will automatically result in drivers getting out of their cars and hopping onto their bikes. While bicycle-friendly material conditions and traffic policies are important, the preference for cycling is socially and culturally constructed. This type of preference is often harder to change than urban infrastructure. Like all urban mobilities, the meaning of traveling by bicycle is connected to cultural context, and any meaningful transformation of mobility will involve engaging in the politics of meaning.

Figure 3.3 Young women on motorbikes in Ho Chi Minh City, Vietnam, 2015 (photograph by Steve Estvanik via Shutterstock)

Conclusion

Movement is an important feature of social worlds. It an important expression and constituent element of distinct urban identities and inequalities, as well as an important site for cultural politics. Urban anthropologists have tried to understand why we move the way we move, by focusing on shared meaning-making and on social distinction and differentiation. They have studied the way we find our way around town, using different strategies to navigate through confusing streets or public transport systems. They have also analyzed the material and aesthetic attributes that accompany different forms of mobility, from customized car design to accessible urban infrastructures. This focus on materiality and design has also involved paying attention to the role our (young or old, able or physical impaired) bodies play in shaping our experience of urban movement. Urban anthropologists have asked what different mobilities mean to different people, in different times and across different cultural contexts. They have analyzed movement as productive of social life and social identities, as conducive to shaping solidarity as well as inequality. Since movement is a product of socio-cultural worlds as well as structural political-economic configurations, it can also be used to examine the complex, lived performance and negotiation of inequalities. Mobilities is a rich, new field for studying our intersecting cultural, political and built environments, and cities offer some of the most exciting sites for this kind of research.

Discussion questions

1   How has social science research changed as a consequence of the 'new mobilities paradigm'?
2   What are the differences and similarities between Kevin Lynch's early work on urban navigation and more recent approaches to urban mobility?
3   Do you feel the figure of the flâneur is still valuable to urban anthropologists, or do you think the critiques of this figure make it less useful for our analyses?
4   How does automobility affect urban life both negatively and positively?
5   What types of mobility are considered transgressive in your surroundings?

Further reading

Cresswell, Tim (2006) *On the Move: Mobility in the Modern Western World.* New York and Oxford: Routledge.
Ingold, Tim and Jo Lee Vergunst, eds. (2008) *Ways of Walking: Ethnography and Practice on Foot.* Aldershot: Ashgate Publishing.
Priya Uteng, T. and Tim Cresswell, eds. (2008) *Gendered Mobilities.* Aldershot: Ashgate.

Further viewing

Crash (2004), directed by Paul Haggis. Feature film about urban mobilities and social and racial tensions in Los Angeles.
Tokyo Godfathers (2003), directed by Satoshi Kon and Shôgo Furuya. Anime about the lives of homeless people in Tokyo.

Chapter 4

Social life in public space

In open city spaces, people have many fleeting encounters. Such ephemeral meetings are often taken to be a hallmark of urban social life. But how does such social life in public work? This chapter discusses the concept of *public space* (see Box 4.1), an important theme in urban anthropology, and explores how people relate to one another within this type of space. Anthropologists have studied the material characteristics that make public spaces 'work', the cultural politics that shape their production and use, and the *emplaced* and *embodied* encounters that urban residents have in the public spaces of the city.

Urban public space is often seen as a space of freedom and anonymity where individuals can reinvent themselves, engage in new types of encounters and develop new forms of sociability. However, urban anthropological studies have emphasized that cities are often characterized by an ongoing struggle to realize this potential. Many public spaces do allow for positive experiences and encounters, and in so doing they contribute to people's enjoyment of city life. Nonetheless, feeling free, anonymous and comfortable in public space is not a given, and not all encounters between strangers are convivial.

Urban encounters do not take place in neutral spaces or between neutrally positioned strangers. The identities we assume and those that are ascribed by others influence how we are positioned in the urban landscape. Our positioning in the urban landscape is based on intersecting social characteristics that are performed and read through the body. These characteristics include various identity markers, from hair and skin color to clothing and modes of transport. Because these different positionings influence urban encounters, people experience the city and its public spaces in divergent ways.

In every city, some users and types of behavior will be seen as legitimate, and others as suspicious. Such identifications and prescriptions often resonate with public discussions about national society and moral dimensions of citizenship. Anthropologists have explored how public debates on national belonging and 'proper behavior' play out in fleeting urban encounters between differently positioned city dwellers – for example, between men and women, or between working-class youth and urban elites.

The chapter starts with a section on the cultural and historical diversity of public space, contextualizing the politics and imaginations that shape these spaces. It then moves on to examine how different people are positioned in intersectional and embodied ways, focusing on the mutual constitution of the identities of people and places. Next, we discuss how the urban landscape can be understood as a tapestry of everyday spatial regimes that regulate social life in public space, by differentiating social spaces as appropriate for particular publics and activities. The chapter ends by examining how the micro-encounters

Box 4.1　Public space

What is public space? As an ideal-type, the term refers to shared, common spaces that are accessible to anyone, where everyone can participate in social life. Urban scholars have tended to see these open common spaces – places where strangers mix and meet – as part of the essence of the city (Young 1990; Sennett 2010). In addition, with discussions going back to Ancient Greece, public space has been associated with an ideal of urban political life. Many urbanists see the existence of public space as a precondition for the existence of democratic politics and of 'the commons' (Mitchell 2003; Casas-Cortés et al. 2014).

Actually existing urban public spaces are often contrasted with this ideal and found lacking. However, 'publicness' is only one aspect of the urban landscape. Open city spaces have many functions other than the ideal-typical ones of the meeting ground or the democratic forum. For most people, most of the time, these are the spaces in and through which their everyday life unfolds, spaces they traverse quickly or inhabit more leisurely, with more or less attention paid to the urban scenes of which they find themselves both spectators and participants.

Public space is a relational term, defined in opposition to the private. While the boundary between the two types of space is not always clear, 'public space' refers to more open, accessible, collective urban spaces, while 'private space' refers to more bounded and restricted home spaces. Understanding public–private as a spectrum rather than a sharp dichotomy helps us understand how public space can also include common spaces that are less than fully accessible. Cafés or shopping malls, for example, relatively open spaces – nominally accessible to anyone who can afford to consume – facilitate encounters between strangers and participation in urban social life. They are, however, privately owned and have numerous explicit and implicit entrance requirements. In this sense, they differ considerably from open public spaces like streets or parks. We can, then, think of publicness as a quality that is differentiated and graded. It is a potential inherent in urban spaces that is not always fulfilled.

that constitute this social life may be shaped by and express larger social hierarchies and political contestations.

Contextualizing public space

Across different disciplines, many urban scholars have sought to understand the particular character of what we call public space. Anthropological studies have highlighted the fact that the abstract concept of public space can take on a very different character across cultural and historical contexts. The meaning of public space in nineteenth-century Paris was quite distinct from that in contemporary São Paulo. In addition, anthropologists have focused on the everyday encounters that take place in public space, and how differently positioned people negotiate such encounters. They show that even as the ideal of public space requires openness, in practice certain categories of urban residents tend to be denied access. Rather than assuming the existence of an implicitly homogeneous, universal public space with openness as its main quality, ethnographic research compels us to ask what different kinds of public spaces exist in various socio-cultural settings. How are they produced as social spaces? According to what rules do they operate? What kind of social life unfolds in them? And how do they privilege some people and disenfranchise others?

Sociologist Erving Goffman (see Box 4.2) has provided us with important insights into the foundations of social life in public. Goffman analyzed the minute rules that allow for the smooth functioning of public social life. Building on Goffman's symbolic interactionism, William H. Whyte sought to connect these observations of public sociability directly to the material environment of the city. In his book *The Social Life of Small Urban Spaces* (1980) and the accompanying documentary (1988), Whyte analyzes why some urban spaces are 'successful' public spaces and others less so. Why are we attracted to some public spaces and actively seek them out, while other public places remain empty as most people avoid them?

Based on long-term, detailed ethnographic observation and time-lapse filming of social life in New York City parks, playgrounds, plazas and streets, Whyte and his colleagues at the Street Life Project tried to understand why some spaces 'worked' better than others. In addition to studying micro-interactions and encounters in public space, they studied how the built environment and urban design shaped urban sociability. The research project resulted in a series of concrete zoning and design guidelines for planning authorities seeking to establish successful public spaces, with detailed recommendations on types of lighting, seating, accessibility, plants and trees, and physical proportions, orientation and location. In addition, the Street Life Project eventually grew into the Project for Public Spaces, an organization aimed at ensuring that public spaces functioned as community spaces.

Box 4.2 **Goffman's symbolic interactionism**

Sociologist Erving Goffman (1922–1982), renowned for his work on the sociology of everyday life and the social construction of self, provides an important inspiration for analyzes of public social life. In his *Behavior in Public Places* (1963), he drew on observations in a mental hospital, where public norms are flaunted, transgressed or reversed. He also used etiquette manuals and anecdotal observations to uncover dominant norms for behavior in public places. He stressed that our ability to accomplish unremarkable everyday interactions is vital in the construction of our sense of self. Failure to accomplish basic everyday tasks, such as taking the bus or walking down the street, marks one as 'crazy' or 'unfit'.

Goffman's work provides important insights into the naturalized yet deeply social nature of public life. He analyzed the minute, tacit rules for everyday interaction that he saw as essential to the maintenance of an ordered public social life. Most famous among these ground rules of public social life is the courtesy of *civil inattention*: paying just enough attention to someone to signal an awareness of their presence, while refraining from engaging in more elaborate interaction that would make the other feel uncomfortable or out of place (1963: 83–85). According to Lyn H. Lofland (1989: 462), such civil inattention 'makes possible co-presence without mingling, awareness without engrossment, courtesy without conversation. It is perhaps the absolute sine qua non of city life.'

Public social life in context

Both Goffman and Whyte tend toward universal ideas of how public spaces work, leaving limited space for the socio-historical specificity and multiplicity of urban life that anthropologists see as crucial. Anthropological studies emphasize the need to locate urban scenes in time and space. In addition, they have paid more attention to the politics of how public spaces are created and used. While some of these studies follow Whyte in explicitly emphasizing the concrete, material dimension of public spaces, much anthropological work has tended to concentrate more on the symbolic aspects of social life in public space.

Ajay Gandhi (2011) evocatively demonstrates the need for a historical and contextual analysis of public space and urban social life. Public spaces and their use are not only specific to particular cities or historical eras, but may even vary quite strongly within cities, for instance between 'old' and 'new' parts of town, or wealthier and poorer urban areas. In post-colonial cities, such differences may echo colonial divisions between a new, modernist colonial city that was built adjacent to the older, pre-colonial town (see Chapter 8).

Gandhi discusses the streets of Old Delhi, contrasting them with the archetypical experience of public space conveyed by the Parisian *flâneur* (see Chapter 3). 'The Indian city's street … is not the same symbolic ground on which the storied flâneur of nineteenth-century Paris roamed', he argues (Gandhi 2011: 210). In Western cities, spaces like the pedestrian sidewalks, commercial areas and residential spaces are often clearly demarcated. Although such logics of separation and distinction were also part of Indian attempts at regulating urban life, Delhi's old city did not conform to such modernist ideals of order. There, the streets were uneven and broken up, and large parts were taken over by entrepreneurs. An appearance of chaos masked a relatively fluid internal logic, with the space of the street allocated to different occupants, such as cigarette seller, public phone vendors and other enterprising figures (see Figure 4.1).

In contrast to the modern city of New Delhi, where separations were enforced by walls and police surveillance, Old Delhi was also a very democratic space that welcomed both rich and poor. However, these streets were not places where one could wander around undisturbed, as Walter Benjamin's *flâneur* did, taking in the sights urban life had to offer. 'The Indian street, for ethnographer and resident alike, involved involuntary intimacy and exchange, a total immersion of seeing and doing in which one could not, like the Parisian flâneur, forget oneself' (Gandhi 2010: 210).

Focusing more specifically on the changing character of public spaces over time, Setha Low's (2000) classic study *On the Plaza* analyzes the material and symbolic dimensions of two plazas in San José, the capital of Costa Rica. The plaza is a standard element of public sociability in Latin American cities, but one that is also undergoing major transformations and, like public spaces elsewhere throughout the world, is a site of significant contestation. The plazas that Low studied were the Parque Central, a park constructed during the colonial era, and the Plaza de la Cultura, a twentieth-century creation intended as a symbol of modernity. Low highlights the politics through which public spaces such as these plazas come into being. These are not neutral spaces, but carry with them histories of domination as well as resistance.

Following the French social theorist Henri Lefebvre (1991), Low speaks of the *social production of space* to refer to the histories and political-economic conditions that shape planning, design and their material outcomes. She contrasts this with what she calls the *social construction of space*, its embodied and symbolic experience. To understand the development

Figure 4.1 Traders in Khari Baoli, Old Delhi, 2007 (photograph by Ajay Gandhi)

of San José's two main plazas, she studied the specific historical processes that shaped them, including a superimposition of Spanish colonial urban design on earlier indigenous spatial arrangements. Such histories resulted in specific, creolized material outcomes that reflected both the political ideals of different eras and the everyday contestations of those ideals.

Combining this historical approach with ethnographic research, Low compares the perspectives different groups of Costa Ricans had regarding these plazas. Everyday users, urban planning professionals involved in their renovation and politicians championing these renewal plans all had different perspectives, based on their diverse interests, imaginations and memories. These diverse positions, often connected to gender, age and income, shaped their preferences for specific material features and informed the uses they deemed appropriate, whether whistling at women, shining shoes, shopping or dealing drugs. Everyday social interactions and contestations over design and use served to rework the existing plazas so that they evolved continuously.

Low shows how public spaces such as these plazas remained important democratic forums, where social movements and other organizations could engage in political debate and express public dissent both verbally and non-verbally. In such central public spaces, socio-cultural, economic and political conflicts could become visible. The plazas offered concrete sites for people to work towards the resolution of these conflicts and towards political and social alternatives. However, Low also points to the threats to this civic potential of public space. Not only did state actors such as politicians and planners seek to limit the possibilities for citizens to use these spaces for the purpose of critical protests. In addition, the encroachment of global capitalism and consumerism had also begun to change the type of sociability that previously characterized plaza life.

Using the example of a Kolkata city park, Sudipta Kaviraj (1997) similarly demonstrates the particular genealogy and socio-cultural specificity of notions of public space. He traces understanding of what is 'public' to ideas about 'commonness' that emerged in the West in the course of the eighteenth century. These ideas emphasized universal access and a public sphere of exchange among citizens (Kaviraj 1997: 86). The park itself was a colonial invention, he argues, which introduced a particular idea of common space. These new common public spaces served as sites for the colonial bourgeoisie to perform their class position, while 'natives' were largely excluded. Colonial European ideas contrasted public space – the space of modern bourgeois self-presentation – with the familiar and sheltered privacy of the home. This division between public and private differed quite strongly from Hindu distinctions between a threateningly unruly 'outside' and a purified, controlled 'inside' of the home (Kaviraj 1997: 99).

Even after India's independence, parks long remained a space where the middle class could perform its modernity and respectability, for example through their daily 'constitutional', an early morning stroll around the park, for which one dressed accordingly. Kaviraj argues that lower-class users 'acted as interlopers ... without the right to remain there or to develop any proprietary stance' (1997: 101). Eventually, against the background of severe urban crisis, middle-class conceptions of public space, with their performances of middle-class respectability in public, lost out against notions of the public among Kolkata's poor, homeless and destitute. '"Public" came to mean that which is not private, spaces from which [the poor] could not be excluded by somebody's right to property' (Kaviraj 1997: 104–105), and to which they felt they had some degree of right since it concerned publicly owned property. The park was taken over by the city's poor, who starting using it as a place to live, work, play football and socialize.

As the cases of Old Delhi, San José and Kolkata demonstrate, the concept of public space, as well as the material outcomes and behavioral norms associated with it, are specific to particular times and locations. Powerful actors structure public spaces in order to encourage use by particular publics and discourage the presence of others. This involves allowing certain forms of self-presentation, and prohibiting a whole range of other behaviors, especially intimate behaviors, such as sex or defecating, which are seen as more appropriate to the privacy of enclosed spaces.

Intersectional positioning

Urban spaces are clearly highly differentiated. There is no such thing as a generic public space: there are specific streets, squares, residential and shopping areas, cafés and many other kinds of public hangouts. Public space can be an orderly environment, where people try to manage a respectable public presence, showing that they know how to behave in the public eye. In many cases, however, people experience public space as a less scripted social domain, where rules are unsure and interactions may be dangerous. Cities have long attracted people for exactly that reason: many search out the freedom and anonymity, heterogeneity and unexpected encounters that urban life can offer. Streets may also evoke the sense of an unpredictable urban jungle full of threats and pollutants, particularly for women (e.g., Phadke 2007). Urban anthropologists are often interested in grasping people's conceptions and mappings of urban space and the associated spatial rules, norms and social identifications.

Our understandings of certain spaces as suitable for certain publics at certain times are shaped by specific socio-cultural conventions and political-economic interests. Gender is an important lens for understanding such differentiations. As discussed in Chapter 2, public space has often been seen as a male domain, and the home as a predominantly female space. In many places, women's public presence remains haunted by the specter of prostitution. Elizabeth Wilson's discussion of the 'public woman' in nineteenth-century European cities is instructive of the way gendered notions of respectability pervade everyday social life in public (2001: 74):

> [T]he prostitute was a 'public woman,' but the problem in the nineteenth century urban life was whether every woman in the new, disordered world of the city, the public sphere of pavements, cafés and theatres, was not a public woman and thus a prostitute. The very presence of unattended – unowned – women constituted a threat both to male power and a temptation to male 'frailty'.

This ambiguity continues to provide the central backdrop to women's negotiations of public space in numerous settings. Public visibility can be taken to suggest (immoral) availability, and therefore has to be carefully managed.

However, there are long histories of contestations of gendered restrictions and women's claims to public space continue to cause heated debates across the world. In European and North American cities, feminist activists put women's right to public space on the agenda through actions like take-back-the-night marches or 'lactivist' demonstrations claiming the right to breastfeed in public. In many cities in the global South, the stakes of being in public have similarly been high, and activists in Brazil, India and Singapore have also organized 'slut walks'. Notwithstanding the common threads in such contestations, gendered definitions of social space differ markedly across urban landscapes.

Feminist scholars have contributed to our understanding of the spatial construction and expression of gendered identities and inequalities. As geographers Liz Bondi and Mona Domosh describe, with the appearance of feminized consumer spaces in late nineteenth-century New York City, certain parts of the city became associated with bourgeois definitions of femininity. Urban public spaces that had been off-limits for 'respectable' women were converted into spaces of consumption, and thereby became acceptable and welcoming spaces to them. These spaces reinforced the bourgeois identities of female shoppers, and their presence, in turn, marked these spaces as part of a bourgeois world. 'Definitions of femininity became interwoven with delineations of certain spaces within the city,' Bondi and Domosh conclude (1998: 279–280). Spaces help constitute social identities, and, in turn, the presence of particular persons helps construct the social definitions of specific spaces.

The case of nineteenth-century New York demonstrates the entanglement of gender and class in the social definition of particular spaces, and highlights the need to go beyond simple male/female binaries in understanding the gendered marking of city spaces. As feminist scholars such as Patricia Hill Collins and Floya Anthias have pointed out, markers of identity and inequality like class, race, age and gender intersect to position people in highly particular ways in society (see Box 4.3 on intersectionality). When analyzing the social construction of (public) spaces as appropriate for some groups of people and not others, an intersectional perspective is indispensable.

People's positioning in urban space also influences their embodied experiences of the city. In her work on the 'male gaze', geographer Gillian Rose emphasizes that experiences of space are gender-specific. While women are constituted as explicitly embodied, located

> ## Box 4.3 **Intersectionality**
> The concept of *intersectionality* draws attention to the way in which various forms of oppression, particularly those of race, class and gender, interact. The term was first introduced by Kimberley Crenshaw (1991), who drew inspiration from Black feminist critiques of White feminist assumptions about commonalities in women's experiences. Patricia Hill Collins (1993), a prominent Black feminist sociologist, has played a crucial role in elaborating an intersectional framework. An intersectional framing emphasizes that one is never simply a woman or a man, and is never positioned socially on account of one's gender alone. One's position in society is defined by the interaction between identity markers and systems of social hierarchy related to race or ethnicity, class, religion and sexuality.
>
> Critics of an intersectionality framework have argued that it easily leads to an add-on understanding of very different forms of inequality, or a matrix understanding of individual positioning (Black, heterosexual, middle-class Muslim women; White, working-class, bisexual, atheist men). They argue that this entails a fragmented vision of society and results in a potentially endless list of positions and groupings (Anthias 2013). Floya Anthias (2013) argues for a processual understanding of intersection, which does not approach intersections as the crossroads of various lines, but as the shifting articulation of various dimensions of inequality in social life.
>
> These insights are crucial for urban anthropology. Intersectional positioning informs what places in the city people can access, and how they are seen in various urban places – whether they are positioned as legitimately present or out of place, as a potential victim or a potential offender.

subjects, most men, in contrast, enjoy a masculine illusion of freedom from the body and its inevitable locatedness. Rose (1993: 145–146) argues:

> The threatening masculine look materially inscribes its power onto women's bodies by constituting feminine subjects through an intense self-awareness about being seen and about taking up space. … [I]t is a space which constitutes women as embodied objects to be looked at.

In this important early work, Rose drew attention to the radically different ways in which particular people are placed in and experience the urban landscape. However, this work did not consider the complex intersectional combinations of gender with other social markers such as class, race, age, sexuality and religion (see hooks 2003). The illusion of freedom that Rose discusses is often restricted to those who embody a dominant position in the social hierarchy. In Europe, this might apply to White, middle-class men between thirty and sixty, and then only in those spaces in which their privilege is unchallenged. This privilege might be contested in, for instance, a Parisian *banlieue*, where a middle-class White man might well experience physical unease and become uncomfortably aware of his own embodiment. He might feel out of place, with others possibly positioning him as a representative of the dominant order and as a target for abuse.

Cecilia McCallum (2005) examines the embodiment and emplacement of race and class in the Brazilian city of Salvador de Bahia. The urban landscape of Bahia is saturated with classed, gendered and racialized meanings, many of which can be traced back to its history of colonialism and slavery. In Bahia, as in Brazil more broadly, people of European descent often occupy a more privileged class position than those of African or indigenous descent, and a lighter skin color is often read as denoting a higher elite social status. McCallum (2005: 107) argues that certain types of public spaces are associated with certain types of bodies and vice versa:

> Euro-Brazilian whiteness is visually hegemonic in the districts of the city where the better off live and work. Blackness and brownness are patently normal, unmarked, elsewhere, a visual effect of the multiplication of bodies seen in public spaces. Crowds are colored distinctively and, thus, the spaces that they inhabit acquire their own hues. … Yet … the meanings that attach to spaces feed back on the inhabitants as they move through these spaces. Thus, when bodies of all sorts move through a space that situates them in relationship to a hegemonic Euro-Brazilian whiteness, they are engulfed … by the signifying force of that space. … [A] person may be whitened and placed higher up along the social scale, or may come to stand outside the social scale, as Other.

McCallum emphasizes the dynamic nature of the co-constitution of spaces and bodies. She illustrates this with reference to buses. While, in general, she found that riding the bus in Bahia 'darkened' passengers, bus stops and buses in central areas of the city were associated with Whiteness at those times of the day when they were crowded with students and office workers. However, in the early morning and later in the day, bus stops filled up with poorer and darker-skinned people commuting to or from work. The same 'coffee-colored' woman traveling by bus through the city center in the early morning might be seen as part of the poor, Black working class, possibly a domestic servant. Her presence on the bus at other times of day might serve to 'lighten' her and lead to her being perceived as a middle-class office worker.

Everyday spatial regimes

Urban social life is structured through a range of more or less tacit, embodied social norms and rules regarding appropriate presence and behavior in different public spaces. Not only do these norms and rules differ across the urban landscape, they also apply in varying ways to different persons. The socio-spatially differentiated ways in which social life in public space is regulated can be understood through the concept of *everyday spatial regimes*. These regimes are varying sets of norms, rules and social identifications that define the social life of public spaces. Urban landscapes consist of many such everyday spatial regimes, which shape our ideas and norms about comportment, propriety and who belongs where.

These spatial regimes, which vary across the urban landscape and according to the time of the day, organize how urban inhabitants interpret people and behavior and ascribe them with social identities. The spatial context and time of day may determine, for instance, whether an unaccompanied young woman is read as a prostitute or as a middle-class professional. Everyday spatial regimes also guide expectations regarding social interaction in public space: the spatially differentiated ordering of how we recognize and ascribe social identities enables certain interactions and inhibits others.

Think of a group of young men hanging out on a street corner in a city like Brussels, dressed in outfits that identify them as streetwise, precarious youths, very likely from minority backgrounds. Some passers-by may change their routes to avoid these young men, and their presence may attract police attention. Much will depend on whether this street corner is located in a more central or peripheral part of the city, an area that is defined as a 'White' or 'Black' neighborhood. If these same young men move to sit on the terrace of a nearby café, their presence will be interpreted differently, and will elicit different social interactions, since the way they occupy place, by consuming rather than hanging out, legitimizes their presence.

Another example relates to women's veiling. Working in Istanbul, Anne Secor (2002) found that the urban landscape was a tapestry of contrasting 'veiling regimes': spatially specific sets of dominant rules and norms regarding women's veiling. In Turkey, veiling or not-veiling represents an important fault line between staunchly secular sections of society and more Islamist, devout sections. These divisions also reverberate with other forms of social differentiation: rural versus urban, provincial versus cosmopolitan, and working class versus elite.

Secor found that the presence of veiled women across Istanbul's urban landscape was framed in varying ways. Depending on the specific context (city center or suburb, elite or working-class area, established urban or newly built-up migrant area), women's choices to veil or not to veil took on radically different meanings. In the city center, a woman's veil was more likely to be read as an indication of the invasion of migrant ways, while a bareheaded woman might feel less comfortable moving through neighborhoods where the majority of women covered their heads. The presence of veiled women was read as an indication of larger societal processes: for secularists, the influx of backward migrants into cosmopolitan urban spaces, or, relatedly, the rise of Islamists threatening Ataturk's secular Turkish state. Conversely, within Islamist discourse, these same veiled women might signify the reconquering of the immoral city. It is clear that such veiling regimes influence women's opportunities to inhabit and traverse different spaces freely and comfortably (see Figure 4.2).

Such veiling regimes are not restricted to cities where the majority of inhabitants are Muslims. They are also at work in European cities, as John Bowen (2007) shows in his analysis of French attitudes and policies with respect to headscarves. The French 'national value' of *laïcité* (secularity) plays a crucial role in the way the French state has acted with respect to such Islamic head coverings. Bowen notes that the French word 'public' brings together three distinct meanings: it can relate to the state and state institutions, to shared social space, and to an abstract general interest. Politicians emphasize the idea of a neutral, secular public space, which would allow people to meet on an equal footing. This helps explain the heated nature of public debates about headscarves, and the support for a ban on wearing headscarves in public schools, which was effected in 2004. Many French people interpreted wearing a veil in public schools as an intrusion of religion into an ostensibly neutral institution that was supposed to raise children to embrace an undivided, secular Republic. Headscarves were framed in terms of the intrusion of radical Islam and of gender violence. French urban veiling regimes became increasingly Islamophobic, curbing women's religious and social freedom.

Greg Noble discusses a political climate in Australia where particularly Australians of Arab and Muslim background were marginalized. He argues that they experienced forms of what Carol Gardner has called 'uncivil attention', the inversion of Goffman's civil

Figure 4.2 Young women in Istanbul, 2007 (photograph by Paul Prescott via Shutterstock)

inattention (see Box 4.2), in the form of stares, insults and other small acts that indicated they were not accepted as part of the legitimate public.

The notion of 'uncivil attention' draws attention to the importance of recognition to experiences of public life. It demonstrates that 'the opposite of recognition is not invisibility, but the active, affective regulation of the inappropriate existence of others – a constant reminder of inadequate existence'. Alya, one of Noble's interviewees, described that she went from feeling fairly invisible before 11 September 2001 to feeling 'noticeable', 'alien' and 'that people were looking at me' (Noble 2005: 115). Noble concludes that 'Our ability to be comfortable in public settings … rests on our ability to be acknowledged as rightfully existing there: to be recognised as belonging' (2005: 114).

Some categories of urbanites can legitimately claim a public space as their own, while others, in contrast, are made to feel out of place. The ambivalent reading of (classed, aged and racialized) women's presence in public spaces around the world presents an example of the relation between legitimate presence and being comfortable. In recent years, planners working in the context of neoliberal urbanism (see Chapter 8) have been trying to make cities safe and attractive for consumers. This means that people who are able to 'look like' and act like consumers will be seen as legitimate users of public city places, and will likely feel more comfortable in them.

The micro-politics of social life in public

The social life that unfolds in urban space is not only structured through complex and shifting everyday spatial regimes. It also manifests social hierarchies and political contestations. James Holston's discussion of the micro-politics of democratization in São Paulo, Brazil, demonstrates how minute social interactions in public are expressive of shifting political realities. Holston (2008: 278) examines how, despite movements toward democratization in Brazil, 'a pervasive regime of social differentiation … continues to structure the embodied habits and spatial practices of everyday life'. However, the micro-spatial routines of differentiation through bodily practices of distance and deference are contested rhetorically and in practice.

This mixture of continuities and challenges to old formations of inequality results in a tense social life. Holston (2008: 278) notes an 'awkwardness for most of the new proximities of … different bodies in everyday space'. Rather than taking the servant elevator in a building, a Black cleaning lady may now insist on taking the patron's elevator, a previously unassailably White, elite space. It is not so much that these bodies did not share spaces before, but rather that 'they must now do so on terms they cannot dictate … terms that upset assumptions of place' (2008: 279).

The upsetting of these spatialized social norms results in a strong sense of displacement on the part of São Paulo's elites, Holston observes. Their sense of displacement is caused both by the faltering of the previous spatial order of privilege that kept people from the peripheries at bay, and by the erosion of symbols of status distinction in everyday life (Holston 2008: 279–280). This elite sense of displacement has accelerated tendencies toward material segregation in São Paulo's urban landscape, primarily in the form of defensive elite enclaves (see Chapter 10). Teresa Caldeira notes that the propensity to give spatial and material form to social distance is connected to 'the inability [of more privileged inhabitants] to impose their own code of behavior – including rules of deference – onto the city' (2000: 319).

Holston's work demonstrates how everyday interactions in urban space are structured by larger social norms and hierarchies, and how these are inscribed in and enacted through the body. It suggests that strong connections exist between physical place in the city and socio-symbolic place in society. The connections between social norms, hierarchies and social life in public might become most readily apparent when borders are transgressed or seemingly solid hierarchies start shifting, as they did in democratizing Brazil. In other cases, the study of this embodied and tacit realm of urban social life may require innovative methodologies, such as mobile ethnography and auto-ethnography (see Chapter 1).

While people navigate the various everyday spatial regimes that constitute the social landscape, they also project meaning on the urban scenes they encounter as observers and participants along the way. While much of this meaning-making remains limited to situational interpretations of urban scenes, some city spaces may also be read as indications of something bigger. The scenes that unfold in streets, squares, shops, parks or public transport then become larger than life, and may be read as illustrations of larger social dramas: a kiss in public may be taken as an indication of the demise of public morality. People's everyday experiences can become entwined with larger narratives regarding society or the nation. They come to speak to, question or confirm such larger narratives. Such explicit reading of urban scenes is, of course, done in a highly selective fashion. Only certain urban scenes are accorded special attention and attributed symbolic significance. The question is when and why a certain city scene, a moment in the streets, a certain encounter in a shop or a sight in a square, comes to stand for something larger than itself.

Secor's (2002) analysis of regimes of veiling, discussed above, provides a good demonstration of such larger-than-life reading of urban scenes. In Istanbul the presence of a veiled woman was interpreted as indicative of something larger: their presence in the city center (as opposed to the migrant-dominated suburbs) was interpreted as symbolic of the competition between Islamist and secularist views, as well as urban lifestyles and migrant ways. Such situated readings of the veil have their counterparts elsewhere. In the Netherlands, some people routinely refer to *hoofddoekjes*, headscarves, to describe not the veil, but the veiled women themselves. Many Dutch people, not least the leader of the anti-Islam, anti-immigrant Freedom Party, Geert Wilders, interpret their presence as a sign of a lack of 'integration' or even deficient national loyalty, or of 'out of place', problematic manifestations of Islam in the Netherlands (see van den Berg and Schinkel 2009).

Political discourses obviously impact the way spaces, people and interactions in public are read. They contribute to making specific differences comfortable or, in contrast, alarming (Noble 2005: 118). This larger framing of particular scenes politicizes certain iconic urban figures and scenes, turning them into objects of debate and contestation regarding urban life or even the fate of the nation.

Conclusion

This chapter has discussed how conceptions of public space are particular to specific times and spaces. Public urban spaces are constituted as particular spaces for particular audiences and types of behavior. While urban life may at first glance appear to be fragmentary and even chaotic, it tends to be the result of structural processes of social organization and meaning-making at various levels. At the smallest, most intimate level, public social life involves the embodied reproduction (or contestation) of social norms and hierarchies through micro-spatial practices.

Social life in public is structured by everyday spatial regimes, complex sets of identifications, norms and expectations that are mapped onto the urban landscape. These regimes suggest distinct identities, rules of conduct and evaluations for differently positioned urbanites on specific occasions and in specific sites. In addition, public social life is also informed by larger political discourses. Particular urban scenes may be politicized and become the site of tense interactions or overt dispute, since they are read as indications of contested social processes. Social life in public is thus decidedly personal and embodied, but it is also constituted through complex spatial regimes, and is open to both everyday and spectacular forms of political contestation.

Discussion questions

1 What is public space? Do you think it is more useful to think of public space as a universal concept, or as something that is always culturally specific?
2 Thinking of an urban public space you know well, do you have sense of the historical conditions and political ideologies that have shaped its material features? Does this public space serve as a democratic forum?
3 Why is an intersectional framework important for urban anthropology?
4 Why will someone's presence be interpreted differently in diverse locations?
5 In the society you live in, can you think of a type of micro-behavior in public space that has become politicized in recent years? What larger social conflicts can explain the politicization of this micro-behavior?

Further reading

Anthias, Floya (2013) Intersectional what? Social divisions, intersectionality and levels of analysis. *Ethnicities* 13(1): 3–19.

Goffman, Erving (1963) *Behavior in Public Places: Notes on the Social Organization of Gatherings.* New York: The Free Press.

Low, Setha M. (2000) *On the Plaza: The Politics of Public Space and Culture.* Austin, TX: University of Texas Press.

Mitchell, Don (2003) *The Right to the City: Social Justice and the Fight for Public Space.* New York: Guilford Press.

Further viewing

La Haine (Hate), feature film directed by Mathieu Kassovitz (1995). Shows the different ways in which three young men from a Parisian *banlieue* are positioned in and experience the more privileged city center and the underprivileged urban periphery.

The Social Life of Small Urban Spaces (1988), documentary by William H. Whyte, produced by the Municipal Art Society of New York.

Part II

Crafting urban lives and lifestyles

Chapter 5

Urban economies

Urban anthropologists have studied the relationship between economic production and consumption, cultural meaning-making and social differentiation in the context of urban landscapes. This chapter approaches urban life through a focus on urban economies, and specifically on production. It starts with a discussion of the major shifts in economies worldwide that have occurred since the Second World War, from national developmental models to neoliberal reforms and globalization, and from Fordism to post-Fordism. In urban contexts, such shifts have led to theorizations of *neoliberal cities*.

In the next section, we describe how city life changes, as certain economic sectors take precedence in the context of these larger shifts. The prominence of particular industries is visible in urban space and social relations. A well-studied type of city has been the mining town, where anthropologists have explored the associations between a dominant type of industry and specific types of labor and social life. Starting in the late twentieth century, researchers have begun to study *post-industrial cities*. Deindustrialization may be accompanied by rapid depopulation or urban agrarianism, or the urban economy may become restructured around leisure and entertainment industries, a shift often accompanied by the rise of new professional middle classes.

Next, we discuss the contested concept of the *informal sector,* which has long received significant emphasis in anthropological studies of urban economies. This chapter gives a brief overview of this debate, pointing to the opportunities and limitations presented by unregulated economic activities, and calling attention to the distinction between informal and illegal practices. In the final section, the chapter shows how anthropological studies have analyzed specific economic places in cities, from the factory and the market, to the street and often overlooked domestic spaces. It discusses the different types of social networks that are formed through these economic activities and places, and the forms of solidarity, competition and exploitation they involve.

From national development to neoliberal restructuring

In the decades after the Second World War, many countries in the global North and global South developed large-scale national projects that included programs to stimulate industrial development and to extend educational and health facilities and social security provisions to large segments of the population. Across the world, large industrial complexes were developed, from the car industry in Detroit and the Philips electronics factories in Eindhoven, to the large textile mills in Egypt and India. These factories were organized on

Fordist principles of rationalized, efficient assembly line production (see Box 5.1). Similar modes of production were implemented in large extractive industries, for instance in the field of mining.

Workers in such industries were often relatively well paid, in comparison to agricultural labor, and could count on relatively secure employment. Especially in the global North, relatively affluent working classes became important consumers of new mass-produced

Box 5.1 Fordism and Post-Fordism

Important shifts related to the organization of capitalist economies and the division of labor are often referred to by the terms *Fordism* and post-*Fordism*. These forms of capitalism and associated labor regimes have been linked with specific forms of urbanism. Fordism was named after the American industrialist Henry Ford, who revolutionized manufacturing by introducing the assembly line in his automobile factories. As a concept, the assembly line involved the rationalized breakdown of complex production cycles into smaller, simplified tasks that could be accomplished by low-skilled laborers working with specialized machines and tools, in processes designed and supervised by a higher-skilled stratum of engineers and managers.

The logic of the assembly line and the type of factory labor it produced were central to industrial capitalism as it developed in the early to mid-twentieth century. This efficient organization of production and labor into standardized, mechanized procedures and components enabled the mass production of manufactured goods, the decrease in prices for these goods, and the emergence of a relatively well-paid working class that formed a growing market for the same goods. These developments (including growing automobile ownership) also influenced urban life and city shapes, with new urban workers playing a central role in mass consumption and eventually suburbanization.

Post-Fordism is associated with the late twentieth-century restructuring of the global economy, the rise of the information economy and the deindustrialization of North American and European cities. From around the 1970s, the number of blue-collar jobs available in these cities decreased, as manufacturing companies outsourced these jobs to cheaper labor markets in the global South. From Detroit to Leeds, cities that had been economically dependent on factories went into a prolonged period of crisis, with widespread unemployment and a lack of public funds due to radically diminished tax income. This combined fiscal and economic crisis often resulted in a deterioration of urban infrastructure and services, especially in former working-class areas.

In some cases, the economies of these post-industrial cities revived as municipal governments and investors turned to leisure, tourism or the so-called creative industries (e.g., architecture, design and entertainment) as new economic sectors. This shift in economic emphasis tends to privilege middle-class and elite urban residents and is sometimes associated with the displacement of working-class populations. However, post-Fordist economies also have disadvantages for wealthier classes, and their sources of income have also become more precarious. Both low-skilled and high-skilled labor has become increasingly 'flexibilized' and impermanent, while the stable, life-long employment that characterized Fordism has become a rarity.

commodities, stimulating further economic growth. Many workers in these industries were provided with extensive secondary benefits, such as health care plans or scholarships for their children. More generally, the democratization of educational facilities in countries around the world opened the possibility for working-class children to pursue a tertiary education. This meant that workers could aspire to middle-class careers, if not for themselves, then for their children.

Starting in the 1970s, the extensive state investments in such national projects came to be questioned. In the global North, neoliberal ideologies gained influence against the backdrop of the economic recession of the 1970s. Geographer David Harvey (2005: 2) defines neoliberalism as follows:

> Neoliberalism is in the first instance a theory of political economic practices that proposes that human well-being can best be advanced by liberating individual entrepreneurial freedoms and skills within an institutional framework characterized by strong private property rights, free markets, and free trade. The role of the state is to create and preserve an institutional framework appropriate to such practices.

Neoliberalism celebrates the efficiency of market forces over state intervention and regulation, both nationally and globally. It sees extensive welfare systems and a strong state involvement in the economy as responsible for stifling economic growth. Advocates of neoliberalism see the state's primary responsibility as creating a healthy business climate, rather than securing the full employment and well-being of its citizenry (Harvey 2005). Harvey argues that neoliberalism, despite the emphasis its ideological discourse places on the benefits of the market, should primarily be seen as a class project that serves the interests of economic elites.

Harvey sees debt as a major technology for the enforcement of neoliberal reforms. The growing indebtedness of countries in the global South in the 1980s provided a major impetus for neoliberal reforms. A sharp decline in world market prices for raw materials, the most important export products in many low-income countries, combined with rising interest rates and economic recession, initiated the 'Third World debt crisis'. Governments of debt-ridden countries in the global South had no choice but to accept the stringent conditions imposed by the International Monetary Fund (IMF) and the World Bank in the form of structural adjustment programs. Such more or less standardized packages of structural adjustment measures generally involved the 'privatization of public assets, severely reduced social expenditures, wage reduction, currency devaluation, liberalization of trade and investment laws and export enhancement' (McMichael 1998: 107). These programs prescribed cutbacks in state spending on social welfare, a neoliberal deregulation of the economy and an opening up of national markets to free trade.

The 1980s and 1990s saw the emergence of a system of global production, in which different segments of production processes became spread across the globe. The development of this global economic system was aided by new communication technologies, neoliberal deregulation, which removed obstacles to global economic flows, and the increased dominance of the finance industry in the global economy. According to Saskia Sassen (2001), this situation can be characterized as one of spatial dispersal and global integration (see Box 7.2 on the global city). Fordist modes of industrial organization became unpopular; post-Fordist economies were increasingly organized in 'flexible' ways, with part-time workers on short-term or flexible contracts. This new labor regime allowed production to adapt to the rapidly shifting needs and desires of consumers across the world.

This globally dispersed production system ruled by financial considerations led to the export of industrial production from previous strongholds in the global North to countries with lower wages, less stringent labor and environmental laws, and tax benefits for foreign investors. It fueled processes of deindustrialization in the 'old' major industrial cities, and inaugurated an important shift in the basis of Northern economies toward the service sector and knowledge economy. Mass production increasingly takes place in export processing zones in the global South that offer the lowest wages and limited regulation.

Neoliberal cities

The political-economic shifts discussed above have led to changes in urban landscapes across the world. Service sector and knowledge-intensive industries increasingly become the basis of urban economies. This has been accompanied by the rise of new class formations. Highly skilled professionals have seen the demand for their labor rise, whereas manual laborers see their labor conditions, wages and job security decline. Many authors have observed growing urban inequalities, with luxury high-rises and gated communities adjacent to large, informally built areas that house the urban poor. In Chapters 6 and 7 we discuss the increased power of middle-class professionals to shape the urban landscape to fit their needs and desires. As we describe in Chapter 8, neoliberal policies have championed the entrepreneurial city, with local governments actively promoting their city to international investors and tourists. New forms of urban poverty in US cities and elsewhere testify to the underside of deindustrialization in the global North.

In many cities in Europe and North America, and even more so in the global South, neoliberal reforms led to shrinking employment opportunities in the public sector, a rise in unemployment and casual forms of labor, and the growing informalization of economic life. Education, health care and security, and basic utility services such as water, energy and garbage collection were privatized. Meanwhile, state funds were often diverted from collective consumption (such as public housing) to infrastructure and spectacular developments that first and foremost serve elite segments of society (Bayat 2012).

Asef Bayat (2012: 111) argues that neoliberal social and economic restructuring has led to 'neoliberal cities'.

> The 'neoliberal city' … is a market-driven urbanity; it is a city shaped more by the logic of Market than the needs of its inhabitants; responding more to individual or corporate interests than public concerns. It is marked by an increasing deregulation and privatization of production, collective consumption, and urban space.

According to Bayat, this drive toward deregulation and privatization triggers a process of 'inside-outing', a growth of informal economic activities in public space and a larger reliance on public space by impoverished residents. In tandem with these developments, neoliberal cities are characterized by a move towards social closure and self-segregation, particularly among the city's elites, who seek to escape the overcrowded and increasingly derelict public spaces (see Chapter 10).

Urban industries, labor and class formation

As national and urban economies change, certain economic sectors take precedence over others. The rise of particular sectors leaves its mark on the urban landscape. Specific industries – from car manufacturing to high-tech business and urban tourism – can shape the demographic make-up of cities by attracting distinct categories of migrants or enabling some segments of the population to play a more prominent role than others in urban life. Just as the life of some cities is dominated by their political functions, as is, for example, the case with Geneva, Brussels and Washington DC, certain cities are dominated by one particular industry or economic sector. Some of these cities may even be founded on account of one such industry. Factory towns with textile mills, such as Manchester in the nineteenth century, were the focus of early urban ethnographers who wanted to understand the impact of the industrial revolution on the lives of the new urban working class (see Chapter 1). Manufacturing towns such as 'Motor City' Detroit and its Italian twin, Turin, in the twentieth century, or the Chinese export-processing zone of Shenzhen in the twenty-first, have also been prime sites for understanding shifts in the social and economic order. Similarly, high-tech urban regions such as California's Silicon Valley or India's Bangalore are seen as exemplifying contemporary shifts in global labor regimes.

The ties between a specific industry and its laborers tend to manifest themselves in the built environment, for instance in company housing, and specific consumption and leisure facilities, but also in the imaginaries through which people think of these cities and their inhabitants. Below, we focus first on mining towns, a city type that has received considerable anthropological attention over the decades, and that has been linked in various contexts to the formation of the modern working class and labor movement. Next, we move on to consider the socio-spatial impact of the rise of the service sector in contemporary post-industrial cities and the associated formation of the 'new middle classes'.

Mining towns

A well-studied city type where one economic activity dominates urban life is the mining town. Early urban anthropologists studied mining cities in the African Copperbelt, such as Kabwe, Luanshya and Ndola, located in present-day Zambia (see Chapter 1). Mining towns like those in the Copperbelt tend to be strongly influenced by the specific demands and organization of their economic activities. These cities often grew out of the need to house workers, and their demographic composition, spatial layout and social hierarchies reflected the priorities of the mining company to a significant degree. The urban imaginaries of mining towns often emphasized modernity and social mobility, even if the reality of labor in extractive industries often proved arduous and exploitative. However, the collective experience of, and responses to, those working conditions in many cases have been central to the growth of the labor movement and the formation of a self-aware working class.

Mining labor forces tended to be overwhelmingly male, a demographic make-up that left its mark on the urban landscape. Such towns often catered to male bachelors, with a minority of women providing a range of services, from cooking and cleaning to sex work. The policies of mining companies (and the states with which they often cooperated closely) significantly impacted the types of family and sexual relations prevalent in town. In the early period, Copperbelt mining companies discouraged workers from bringing their families, thereby keeping the costs of living and wages down, and limiting the investments needed for more extensive town facilities. Following major strikes, the companies changed orientation, adopting a welfare orientation that gave workers many benefits, from decent subsidized family housing to sports clubs and cinemas (Mususa 2012a).

The mining companies hoped to stimulate the formation of nuclear families headed by male breadwinners. However, the actual family relations that emerged within the parameters established by the mining companies hardly ever corresponded to the imagined outcome of a stable nuclear family life with a male breadwinner. In the Copperbelt towns, for example, extended family relations remained important, the relatively wealthy miners continued to have sexual relations outside marriage, and wives often developed important economic roles as traders (Ferguson 1999).

Moengo, a mining town in the former Dutch Caribbean colony of Suriname, provides a good example of the intimate connection between economic activity and urban development (de Koning 2011a). In early twentieth-century Suriname, bauxite mining drew workers away from the rural sugar plantations and artisanal occupations in the capital of Paramaribo, to work in a massive, highly organized and orchestrated company-cum-social community in an isolated setting in the country's interior. Founded in the late 1910s, Moengo developed into a thriving urbanized enclave where the almost exclusively male workforce was housed in different neighborhoods according to rank of employment. The higher ranks had family housing, while workers in the lower ranks often lived in barrack-like housing that was hardly suitable for family life. In the immediate vicinity, informal settlements sprang up, which housed both company workers and a more casual labor force, and provided services and facilities not available in the company town proper, such as small eateries and bars. Moengo came to epitomize modernity in the Surinamese context; many Moengonese remembered how advanced the small town of a few thousand inhabitants was compared to the capital of Paramaribo (Figure 5.1).

Despite its modern feel and reputation, the mining enclave also had many of the characteristics of a revamped colonial order. Labor was highly stratified along lines of ethnicity, with a largely White, partially foreign professional staff living in a closed-off compound, while Surinamese laborers of African and Indonesian descent did most of the skilled labor and field labor, respectively. Housing was similarly segregated, with the lowest ranks of labuorers relegated to the informal settlements on the town's perimeter. Leisure also reflected company hierarchies: Moengo's staff club, tellingly named Casa Blanca, was off limits to all but the White management staff. In spite of such racialized and classed hierarchies, company employment came to hold the promise of promotion, as there were increasing opportunities for employees to move up through the ranks.

The controlled site of the bauxite town long worked to reproduce the colonial conflation of class and race – and the associated social hierarchies and authority structures – that were characteristic of Caribbean plantations. In contrast to the sugar plantations, however, where both men and women were employed in the fields, the mining company almost exclusively employed men. Its employment conditions and facilities were designed for nuclear families with a male breadwinner. Life in the mining town helped create male-headed nuclear families and moulded a modern, almost exclusively male working class, providing many with the means to make a better life for themselves and their children. The growth of this self-conscious labor force and the trade unions that were first established

Figure 5.1 Office personnel at the Suriname Bauxite Company, Moengo, Suriname, 1940 (courtesy Tropenmuseum)

in this town can be seen as important steps towards Suriname's political independence in 1975 (de Koning 2011b).

Post-industrial landscapes

When mines are depleted, mining towns – like those in Moengo, or those in the Zambian Copperbelt – may experience rapid impoverishment and out-migration and may even be abandoned. James Ferguson (1999), for instance, has examined the post-mining phase in the Copperbelt, where born-and-bred urbanites had no choice but to move back to the countryside in order to make a living. This return migration forced them to renegotiate their social connections and claims in the village, and to reconsider their expectations of modernity. Even where mines continued to function, mining operations were often organized in different ways from before, as disconnected niches for extractive processes, which required none of the 'thick' investments that characterized the 1980s Copperbelt (Ferguson 2005).

Patience Mususa documents the despondency that marked life in the Zambian Copperbelt town of Luanshya following neoliberal reforms and the privatization of the mines in the 1990s. Many residents lived with memories of the 'golden age' when they still could plan for a future: 'For Copperbelt residents the past was in the lived-in remnants of the town's dilapidated infrastructure and in the incongruity of a well-spoken and obviously highly-skilled person trapped in an emaciated body draped in tatty clothes' (Mususa 2012b:

Figure 5.2 Abandoned houses in Detroit (photograph by Ali Safarov via Shutterstock)

309). People had little choice but to try to make a living in precarious circumstances, missing not only the wages, but also the many recreational and health facilities that the mining companies once offered. Many townspeople opted to diversify their income; the houses and yards that miners had gained as part of retrenchment packages became important assets that allowed them to earn extra income. '[R]esidents who had previously competed to win a best-garden award, which the mines had put into place as an incentive to beautify the neighborhood, no longer grew poinsettias, gardenias and other flower-bed plants', Mususa (2012a: 580) writes. Many yards were used for urban agriculture, from growing vegetables to rearing chickens and pigs and fish farming, giving Copperbelt towns like Luanshya an increasingly rural feel.

Such dramatically changing urban landscapes are not only found in places like the Copperbelt towns, but also in former industrial cities like Detroit, where the collapse of the car industry led to massive depopulation (see Figure 5.2). Deindustrialization affects cities across the world in perhaps less spectacular, but equally significant ways. As industrial jobs disappear, many working-class people find it hard to find stable jobs that provide living wages, that is, a wage that is enough to meet one's basic needs. As Bayat (2012) pointed out with respect to neoliberal cities, such urban landscapes see the growth of informal economic activities carried out in public spaces. From the 1980s onward, anthropologists have documented the rise of new forms of urban poverty in the context of deindustrialization and state retrenchment in US cities (see Susser 1996; Morgen and Maskovsky 2003). A famous example is Philippe Bourgois' work on crack dealers in New York City, which we discuss later in this chapter.

The rise of the service sector and the 'new middle class'

While most cities have more mixed economies than mining towns or factory towns, they will also demonstrate socio-spatial changes in response to larger economic shifts. As many urban economies in North America and Europe shifted from a reliance on the manufacturing industry to an emphasis on the service sector, the composition of urban populations and the demand for specific types of laborers began to change. As discussed above, these changes took place against the background of processes of economic liberalization and globalization. Production chains increasingly stretched across the globe, outsourcing labor-intensive manufacturing to places, often to special economic zones, that promised advantages in terms of legislation and a cheap (and increasingly feminized) labor supply.

As manufacturing jobs have shifted towards the global South, post-industrial cities in Europe and North America have increasingly turned to the *symbolic economy* to generate income and create white-collar jobs. The symbolic economy refers to economic activities that concentrate on cultural production and consumption, such as those associated with the tourism, media and entertainment industries (Zukin 1995). This type of urban economy is concentrated on leisure and consumerism, and often involves the promotion of the heritage industry and high-profile museums, or the organization of events from music and food festivals to sports mega-events such as the Olympics. To stimulate the symbolic economy, municipal governments compete to attract a highly skilled and creative international workforce, an economically productive group of professionals that Richard Florida (2002) has dubbed 'the creative class'.

However, the restructuring of the global economy has also increased the demand for skilled and educated urban workers in Asia, Africa and Latin America. Economic liberalization and globalization have not only created new blue-collar jobs in industrializing regions, they have also led to the increased importance and visibility of a 'new middle class', particularly in India and China (Heiman et al. 2012). This new social class, made up largely of educated professionals who act as managers, administrators and so on, is often employed in sectors and companies with a global outlook or aspirations, for example multinational offices, agencies that provide business producer services such as consultancy or accounting, or the offices of (international) non-governmental organizations (NGOs). In many countries in the global South, the state promoted this new middle class as being able to mediate between the local and the global, not only in economic but also in cultural terms, thereby acting as the proof of a country's ability to live up to global standards and aspirations.

In her work on India's new middle class, Leela Fernandes (2006: xxvii) notes that

> the new middle class in late-developing countries such as Malaysia or India serves as a group that represents the promises of a new national model of development, one with a global outlook that will allow such nations to successfully compete with the advanced industrialized countries.

Young professionals have come to embody India's new national ideals, first and foremost through their consumption practices, which set the standard even for people far less privileged than them. However, Fernandes also points to the shaky economic basis on which the new middle class relies. In times of economic crisis, these professionals suffer from highly insecure labor contracts and steep competition from other middle-class professionals also scrambling to expand their professional qualifications and maintain their comparative advantage by acquiring additional international credentials.

The active promotion of the middle classes also impacts the urban landscape, for instance in the form of the development of upmarket housing areas. Municipal governments often seek to improve urban consumption and leisure facilities (such as upscale restaurant and bar scenes) to attract and maintain privileged segments of the population. As Fernandes' work in Mumbai shows, the active promotion of the new middle classes can also lead to 'spatial cleansing' and new forms of spatial segregation, with clean-up drives by civic associations and by governmental actors aimed at getting rid of the sight of poverty in the streets. Such developments are reminiscent of similar, colonial-era attempts to clean up the city (see Chapter 8).

Informality and formality in the urban economy

Many studies of the urban economy draw a distinction between informality and formality. Economic anthropologist Keith Hart (2010) introduced the term *informal economy* in the early 1970s to refer to those economic activities that are less regulated by the state and that often appear invisible to bureaucrats, regulators and economists. This lack of regulation presents opportunities to new migrants and other groups whose lack of social connections make it difficult to find urban employment or to navigate formal bureaucratic procedures for entrepreneurs. However, the fact that these are often unregistered, unlicensed and untaxed activities, means that labor is often unprotected and working conditions tend to be more precarious. In contrast, the 'formal sector' usually refers to wage labor and to economic activities that are more regulated, licensed and taxed, but also more protected through laws and bureaucratic procedures.

A significant number of urban anthropologists have studied informal economic activities, from street vending to small-scale, home-based enterprises, often with attention to the gendered dynamics of these activities. Faye Harrison (1988: 119), for instance, shows how the informal economic sphere in Kingston, Jamaica was feminized, and how this 'contribute[d] to the reproduction of a cheap, casual, and concealed workforce accessible to capital for performing its temporary and largely unskilled tasks'. While income from petty retailing or domestic service offered women a measure of independence and autonomy, the low status of these activities and women's exclusion from broader economic and political spheres made it difficult for them to improve their structural position.

Other anthropologists have studied unregulated labor and entrepreneurship in light of migration and transnationalism, and the spatial politics associated with these processes. In many cases, rural-to-urban or international migrants are overrepresented in unregulated economic activities. While this often reflects their weaker position in urban labor markets, it also shows how the cultural dimensions of economic practices travel and are reterritorialized in new urban contexts. In his study of African immigrants working in Harlem's informal street markets, Paul Stoller (1996) considers street traders' activities in relation to the spatial, social and religious practices that characterized West African markets, such as the allocation of vending space by ethnicity or country of origin. He also shows how efforts to regulate the market on the part of New York City's mayor and established local businesses were informed by an aversion towards 'such a cluttered, informal third-world space in a first-world setting' (Stoller 1996: 779).

The fact that many informal economic activities take place outside legal regulation sometimes leads to the conflation of informality and illegality. However, the term 'illegal economy' is usually used to refer to illegal goods and services (e.g., the smuggling and sale of illegal drugs and weapons). In the informal economy, in contrast, the goods and services involved are mostly legal, but the conditions in which they are produced and traded are often illegal. Itty Abraham and Willem van Schendel (2005) make a useful distinction between the concepts of legal/illegal and licit/illicit: where legality is associated with what is considered to be legitimate under state law, licit activities and goods are those considered socially acceptable by the people involved.

Where the formal and informal economies were initially seen as separate spheres, urban scholars soon realized that the two were closely connected through various types of linkages. Some of these connections may be harmonious and others more contested. Formal economic production is often dependent on informal activities, whether through subcontracting to unregulated producers or when formal products are sold through informal networks of traders and vendors. In addition, formal businesses also incorporate many informal practices in their day-to-day operations. As Alan Smart and Filippo M. Zerilli (2014: 228) emphasize, 'informality is not a distinct sector of the economy, but a different and ubiquitous way of doing things. Even the most formal institutions have informal practices'. Moreover, informal enterprises may be regulated through semi-formal, quasi-legal rules and agreements, if not through state bureaucracies.

Lynne Milgram's (2014) work on street vendors in Baguio City, Philippines, gives a clear example of this blurry relationship between formality/informality and legality/illegality in urban labor and the use of public space. In her research, she found that both street vendors selling second-hand clothing and city officials negotiated informality and legality, in search of mutual advantages: better livelihoods for vendors and more rental income for the municipal government. Street markets such as the Harrison Road Night Market (Figure 5.3), the city's popular second-hand clothing market, offered jobs to unemployed urban residents and low-income migrants from rural areas. However, middle-class and

Figure 5.3 Harrison Road Night Market, Baguio City, Philippines (photograph by B. Lynne Milgram)

elite residents of Baguio City pressured the authorities to 'beautify' the city by ensuring that the streets were clean and orderly, and that traffic was unobstructed by market stalls.

While vending in public spaces was officially prohibited in Baguio City, the municipality vacillated between banning and tolerating vendors, allowing some forms of street vending in certain places or at certain times of day, while cracking down on others. Meanwhile, vendors also utilized both legal and less legal strategies to make their claim on the city's streets. Despite the fact that their activities were illegal, street vendors organized into formal associations that lobbied municipal councillors, and these associations succeeded in getting the authorities to set new vending by-laws and regulations in response to their demands. Following successful advocacy, a legal night market, largely self-regulated by the street vendor associations, was established in a popular area of the city. However, the vendors continued to circumvent regulations to gain a competitive edge, for instance by mixing their stock of used clothing with new, mass-produced goods, or by opening up for business outside the night market's official opening hours. Such examples show the difficulty of disentangling the informal and the formal, or the illegal and the legal, as both state actors and low-income entrepreneurs employed these registers strategically for their own economic and political gain.

Urban economic places

An anthropological approach to urban economies often involves concentrating on specific economic places, socio-cultural sites where processes of production and exchange are especially visible. Here, we discuss work in a number of such places: the market, the factory, the street and the home. Of course, there are many other important urban economic places where we can study the intersection of economic transactions with socio-cultural and political processes (for instance, offices, urban agricultural plots or restaurants), but these four types of places have arguably received the bulk of anthropological attention.

The market

Urban markets, where many different types of people come together to exchange various types of goods and services, have been popular sites for anthropological research. Ethnographic studies of markets tend to emphasize that economic exchange is never just about economics; economic transactions are always structured by historically shaped cultural norms and political interests. Markets are embedded in local economic specializations and preferences, but they are also always connected to other places, through networks that link vendors, traders, wholesalers, brokers and producers. The example of Tokyo's Tsukiji fish market, discussed in Chapter 2 (Bestor 2004), highlights this combination of local cultural heritage and global connections.

In cities across the world, markets used to be the most important outlets for food provisioning and for the exchange of goods between the city and its surrounding rural areas. In many cities, particularly in the global North, supermarkets have become central sites for grocery shopping. Whereas supermarkets and 'big box stores' have depersonalized economic transactions, markets continue to be important sites of public sociality, where economic transactions remain wedded to social interaction (Black 2012: 4–8). Markets provide fascinating arenas for studying social life, offering lively social scenes where people of various backgrounds meet and interact. As Rachel Black (2012: 2) writes of the Porta Palazza open-air market in the Italian city of Turin,

While thousands of kilos of fruits, vegetables, and other food stuffs are sold here each day, friendships are made, families are reunited, ethnic and cultural tensions are negotiated, and local identities are constructed through the daily workings of the market.

In many cities, municipal governments and local elites consider open-air markets and street trade to be old-fashioned and at odds with modern urban life. They argue that these spaces are unhygienic, block traffic and pose unwanted competition to formal commercial enterprises. Such viewpoints often lead to policies that seek to displace markets towards the urban periphery, 'cleaning up' the city center for wealthier locals and tourists (Evers and Seale 2014). Urban regeneration programs, informed by ideals of modernity and backed by wealthier commercial stakeholders, seek to crack down on informal trade and promote formal shopping sites such as malls and supermarkets. Often such programs take on a repressive character, with municipal authorities destroying market stalls and confiscating vendors' goods.

In various Latin American cities, for instance, street markets tend to be dominated by indigenous vendors and traders, and stigmatizing discourses have fed into their depiction as 'traditional' or even 'dirty' (Swanson 2007). However, in other contexts, street markets are seen as a tourist attraction and a source of municipal revenues. This is evident in the case of Lynne Milgram's work on the night market in Baguio City, described above, where the city government recognized the economic advantages of this type of trade. In North American and European cities, street markets – and especially those selling organic, local or artisanal goods – are also increasingly recognized as contributing to a city's ambience and attracting a specific, moneyed type of urban consumer.

The factory

In the twentieth century, many urban economies were dominated by the manufacturing industry, and the factory was a central urban economic place. From the earliest instances of industrialization in Europe and North America, factories formed the urban spatial context for major social and cultural transformations including shifts from subsistence to wage labor, and from agricultural seasonality to clock time. Factory work symbolized many of the shifts that accompanied rapid industrialization and rural-to-urban migration, and transitions to capitalist modernity. As Lisa Rofel (1997: 158) notes, 'The factory is the icon par excellence of modernity'. In the late twentieth century, many European and North American factories closed, as manufacturing jobs shifted towards countries with cheaper, less unionized wage labor. In cities across the world, dramatic reconfigurations of social relations have been highly visible on the factory floor, and anthropologists have studied a variety of topics from factory architecture and trade unions to shop-floor flirting and the enduring rural ties of laborers.

In their study of factory work in the Dominican town of Santiago, Lauren Derby and Marion Werner (2013) focus on popular stories of spirit demons called *bacás*, to understand how factory workers interpreted shifts in labor regimes and the changing role of the Dominican Republic in the global economy. From the 1980s, garment assembly factories in the Santiago export-processing zone attracted tens of thousands of migrants from rural areas along the Haitian border, although by the 2010s many of them had shut down again as trade agreements with the United States ended. In the early 2000s, in one of the largest factories in the zone, a number of workers' deaths, both inside and outside the plant, gave rise to rumors that the owner or manager had struck a pact with the devil, exchanging workers' lives for quick wealth. Sightings of the *bacá* in the shape of a little black man, and stories of blood splattered across the garments and in the factory toilets, contributed to widespread panic.

The stories indicated some of the anxieties that rural migrants felt as they were incorporated into urban capitalist labor relations – while in the rural areas the *bacá* usually appeared as a sometimes playful animal demon, in the urban factory context it morphed into a blood-sucking dwarf. Repeated stories of such a vampire-like figure also suggested fears that Dominican Republic's lifeblood was being drained, as its economy became increasingly vulnerable to the whims of global capital. As Derby and Werner (2013: 296) propose, we can read the *bacá* narratives as revealing

> a glimpse of some of the unspoken rage and dread evoked by the experience of factory labor under neoliberalism, in response to its mysteriously abrupt arrival and departure, its use of machinery, its gendered transformations, and the industrial rhythm of labor on the shop-floor.

Jean and John Comaroff (2000) have suggested that such mysterious hauntings are part and parcel of global advanced capitalism, which presents itself as a gospel of salvation, promising redemption and unimaginable riches, but whose shadowy riches seem strangely divorced from actual economic activities.

The street

Urban streets are another important economic place, particularly for informal or illegal types of economic activity. Philippe Bourgois (2003), who did extensive ethnographic research amongst Puerto Rican crack dealers in the East Harlem area of New York City in the late 1980s and early 1990s, draws explicit comparisons between the street and other economic places. He sought to understand why Puerto Rican young men became drug dealers rather than seeking legal employment. Rather than looking primarily to psychological explanations, his analysis focuses on structural shifts in the US urban economy, where the manufacturing industry, a prominent source of low-level jobs for working-class men, had almost disappeared. As factory jobs were largely outsourced to Asia and Latin America, where labor was cheaper, in US cities the main type of jobs available to workers with limited education became concentrated in the lower tier of the service sector. Bourgois (2003: 8) draws connections between the different types of jobs and what he calls inner-city street culture: 'a complex and conflictual web of beliefs, symbols, modes of interaction, values, and ideologies that have emerged in opposition to exclusion from mainstream society. Street culture offers an alternative forum for autonomous personal dignity'.

In the earlier era of urban manufacturing, Bourgois argues, factories were characterized by a masculine workplace culture that was largely compatible with an oppositional street culture that valorized tough, macho behavior, and factory supervisors accepted it. However, in the type of office-based employment that is central to the service industry, managers see this type of social interaction and cultural style as unacceptable. Lacking the professional and social skills necessary in an office environment, the young men from East Harlem that Bourgois worked with felt 'dissed' (disrespected and humiliated) by their White, middle-class supervisors. In contrast, their cultural style of toughness served them well in pursuing street careers as drug dealers, and offered them more dignity and respect than the minimum-wage jobs available to them in the legal labor market. Bourgois understands crack dealers' illegal work as a form of resistance to the subordination they experienced in post-industrial New York's new, service-oriented economy. However, he also shows how this mode of resistance was ultimately destructive both to the dealers themselves and to their neighborhood communities.

The home

An important and often overlooked economic place is the home. Domestic space has often been regarded as separated from the economic sphere, as a female space of reproduction (such as childcare, cooking and cleaning) rather than of production (see the discussion on domestic space in Chapter 2). However, feminist scholars have challenged this distinction, pointing to the economically vital role of unpaid reproductive work. In addition to this unpaid labor, the household is also an important site of paid work. Many economic activities (from small-scale manufacturing to domestic work) take place in people's private homes.

A number of anthropologists have studied so-called home-based economic activities, which involve the informal production of goods and services from people's homes. These activities can range from the manufacture of baked goods or home-made clothes to informal childcare or car repair services. While both men and women engage in these types of income-generating activities, they are often especially attractive to women, since they can combine them with unpaid reproductive activities.

Where industrialization and Fordist economic production gradually separated the workplace from the home, in the context of post-Fordism, such distinctions are becoming more blurred. Information and communication technology make it possible for employees to work from home, rather than in an office or factory, while the flexibilization of labor has meant that many former employees are now self-employed contractors without a formal workplace. This has in turn given great rise to an expanding sector of coffee shops and flexible workspaces where these newly self-employed flex-workers create an office away from home.

The home is not just the site of self-employed workers or entrepreneurs. It also the main site of domestic labor, for those employed as nannies, cooks, maids or gardeners. Such domestic service is associated with both the transgression and reinforcement of class, race and gendered boundaries. Middle-class and upper-class employers depend on having lower-class servants in their homes to tend to their most intimate needs. However, their spatial and emotional closeness is also a source of anxiety, and (especially female) employers often police domestic workers' movements and activities strictly (Dickey 2000). Increasingly, domestic work is structured through transnational networks, with predominantly female migrants from regions such as Southeast Asia or the Caribbean providing the bulk of 'care work' or 'affective labor' in homes in wealthier regions, from Hong Kong and Singapore to Europe and the United States, allowing educated women who are normally White and middle class to build careers, while their own children are left behind in their own countries to be cared for by grandmothers (Parreñas 2001).

Conclusion

Urban anthropologists studying economic processes have examined how different industries and forms of economic organization connect to social differentiation and the politics of urban space. Some of these industries and forms of organization are associated with specific economic places: the factory has been an emblematic space for the industrial city, while the street is an important symbolic and physical space for what is usually considered to be the 'informal economy'. Conflicts within and over these economic places are often related to tensions stemming from larger economic shifts, such as industrialization or deindustrialization.

As urban economies change, new types of social relations and systems of meaning-making develop. Existing hierarchies are unsettled, but new socio-spatial inequalities may emerge, as mining towns replace plantation agriculture, or manufacturing is overtaken by tourism. These shifts gain meaning not only through attempts by municipal authorities to 'rebrand' their city and to create a more 'modern' or 'global' image. In addition, urban residents make economic change meaningful through their everyday narratives, from vampire stories signifying the exploitative nature of free trade zones to debates on whether street vending is a public nuisance or part of a city's consumerist appeal.

Discussion questions

1 What impact has the shift from Fordism to post-Fordism had on urban life?
2 Which specific urban economic industries have been influential in your society over the past century? Have they played a clear role in class formation, or in changing gender relations?
3 Do you think the distinction between the formal and informal economy is a useful one?
4 What important economic places can you recognize in a city you know well? Do any of these places function as sites of conflict over the city's image, or reflect broader tensions between different groups of urban residents?

Further reading

Evers, Clifton and Kirsten Seale, eds. (2014) *Informal Urban Street Markets: International Perspectives.* New York: Routledge.
Hansen, Karen T., Walter E. Little and B. Lynne Milgram, eds. (2013) *Street Economies in the Urban Global South.* Santa Fe, NM: SAR Press.
Heiman, Rachel, Carla Freeman and Mark Liechty, eds. (2012) *The Global Middle Classes: Theorizing Through Ethnography.* Santa Fe, NM: SAR Press.

Further viewing

Roger and Me (1989), directed by Michael Moore. Documentary examining the social and economic devastation caused by the closing of General Motor plants in Flint, Michigan.
The Wire, Season 1 and 2 (2004–2006), created and written by David Simon. Series set in post-industrial Baltimore.
Urban Roots (2011), produced by Leila Conners, Mark MacInnis and Mathew Schmid. This documentary tells the story of urban farming in former 'Motor City' Detroit, where empty lots and crumbling houses and factories are making place for urban agriculture projects started by local communities.

Chapter 6

Consumption, leisure and lifestyles

This chapter shows how an early anthropological focus on urban production has been balanced in recent years by increasing attention on urban consumption and the ways in which consumption figures in city-based leisure and lifestyles. It examines how people enjoy and consume the city, and asks how such choices reflect, and may subvert, social hierarchies. Many anthropologists have studied the role of consumption, specifically in connection to leisure, in shaping urban lifestyles and subcultures, from the inner-city dancehall scene in Kingston, Jamaica, to the middle-class coffee shop culture found from Seattle to Cairo. This chapter discusses how a focus on consumption helps us to understand urban difference and inequality as well as solidarity, and how consumerism often represents both a form of politics and a site of imaginative self-expression.

As we discuss in the first section of this chapter, consumption is an important aspect of what is known as *cultural capital* (see Box 6.1). As such, it is central in creating and maintaining social distinction in the context of class hierarchies as well as broader identity politics. It plays an important role in the reproduction of social and spatial divisions and, in many contexts, *citizenship* is increasingly defined in terms of consumption rather than democratic participation. The second section focuses on the connections between consumption and urban space. Shifts in consumption play a major role in transformations of the urban landscape, creating specific types of places for particular kinds of consumers. Specifically, urban consumption shapes and is shaped by *leisure geographies*, cognitive maps of the city that influence our understanding of who should consume what, where and when. In addition, in recent years, urban space itself has become an important object of consumption, as is especially evident in phenomena such as urban tourism and city branding. The chapter's final section discusses *scenes, lifestyles and subcultures*, pointing to the role of youth styles and popular culture in the creation of new urban identities. It highlights the many creative and potentially subversive possibilities for self-fashioning that cities offer.

Consumption and distinction

Urban anthropological attention to consumption is partially explained by shifts towards service-oriented urban economies, especially in the global North. It is also connected to a growing anthropological interest in consumption more generally. Starting in the 1980s, material culture studies and researchers studying 'the social life of things' (Appadurai 1986) began to examine how objects acquire economic and emotional value through their embedding in social relations, from capitalist relations of production and consumption to gift exchange. Across different cultural settings and over time, the same good can take on different meanings and be attributed with different measures of value, shifting from a raw material to a commodity to a unique, highly valued personal possession to trash.

Consumption is interesting to anthropologists as a social practice in which the private and the public, the individual and the social, and the personal and the political intersect. Decisions about what to buy, use and wear and where to engage in these forms of consumption may seem very individual; we often see these choices as driven by our personal preferences and desires, and as expressive of our individual identities. However, these decisions are shaped strongly by the social and cultural groups to which we belong (or to which we aspire to belong), and by larger political economic structures that determine what goods are available for consumption. Two ways in which such connections between consumption, belonging and politics have been studied are through the concepts of cultural capital and consumer citizenship.

Cultural capital

The ability to consume is, of course, related to purchasing power. Beyond being straightforward markers of economic capital, however, the things people consume and the leisure activities they pursue are important sources of social identification and social distinction. Pierre Bourdieu's work has played a key role in our understanding of consumption as a marker of social standing. Bourdieu showed how class status is not only related to economic capital, or the possession of economic assets, for instance the financial means to consume. A person's social position is also constituted by their cultural capital: knowing *what* to consume, what to appreciate and where to be seen (see Box 6.1).

Maintaining a particular class position requires a skilful command of diverse cultural competencies. In many cities across the world, having cosmopolitan knowledge and tastes is a prerequisite for belonging to the upper-middle class. In many settings in the global South, being knowledgeable about global trends and being able to comfortably mix the local language with English may provide access to upmarket jobs and function as an important way to signal belonging to privileged segment of society. Displaying particular consumption goods, such as the latest model cell phone or brand-name clothing, and being seen in particular leisure venues such as the US-style coffee shops that are now found in cities across the world, helps consolidate that claim of privileged membership (de Koning 2009).

However, such use of cosmopolitan consumption as a form of cultural capital is not limited to the wealthier classes. As Christien Klaufus (2012) shows in her study of architecture in marginalized neighborhoods in the Ecuadorian cities of Cuenca and Riobamba, the urban poor also draw on knowledge of international tastes to attain social prestige and counter the stigma of poverty. As they constructed their house or made improvements to an existing dwelling – often drawing on remittances sent home by transnational migrants – less wealthy residents consciously used imported materials or referenced global architectural styles. The cosmopolitan sensibilities that low-income residents sought to express in their housing designs and decorations were part of deliberate strategies to achieve self-esteem and social mobility.

The cultural capital derived from global or cosmopolitan tastes is sometimes countered by the cultivation of localism. In many cities, as the consumption of globally sourced

Box 6.1 **Bourdieu and cultural capital**

The work of French sociologist and anthropologist Pierre Bourdieu (1930–2002) has been highly influential in the way we have come to understand the social role of taste. Bourdieu argued that judgments of taste are in fact key in the creation of social positions and hierarchies. His work has had a lasting influence on consumption and leisure studies.

Bourdieu proposed to extend the notion of capital to domains previously not included in analyses of class, for which he introduced the terms cultural and social capital. Various forms of capital contribute to people's social positioning and they may use them strategically to improve their social position. Bourdieu distinguished three 'guises' of capital: 'economic capital, which is immediately and directly convertible into money and may be institutionalised in the form of property rights'. This is the most familiar type of capital, consisting for example of real estate or other property, which can be directly translated into money, and therefore represents economic power. Bourdieu also introduced the notion of cultural capital. Such cultural capital encompasses forms of knowledge, skills and education that give one an advantage in a social field. According to Bourdieu, 'cultural capital is convertible, on certain conditions, into economic capital and may be institutionalised in the form of educational qualifications'. It can take formal forms, as in the case of a diploma, or informal form, for example in taste or style. Social capital, in Bourdieu's definition, is 'made up of social obligations ("connections"), which is convertible, in certain conditions, into economic capital and may be institutionalized in the form of a title of nobility' (1986: 243).

To illustrate: a mother's economic capital can pay for an Ivy League education for her children, which will provide them with cultural capital of the formal (diplomas) and informal kind (particular kinds of knowledge and skills, for instance class-specific body language or sense of style). It will also offer them the social capital, the networks, they need to establish themselves in their careers. An Ivy League diploma can even be seen as a formal type of social capital: a modern-day title of nobility. These less material forms of capital may prove crucial in the reproduction of the family's class position, or may perhaps even allow for intergenerational upward social mobility.

In his well-known study *Distinction* (1984), Bourdieu analyzed the relation between judgments of taste and social class. He argued that 'taste' is first and foremost a form of class distinction. He demonstrated that cultural expertise such as an appreciation of highbrow art is part of a class culture and is in itself a source of power and hierarchy. Appreciating haute cuisine is another example of cultural capital through which one positions oneself as part of a particular social group with tastes that are distinct from and above the lowly taste for large portions of comfort food, and which bolsters claims of high-class status. As we indicated above, cultural capital may be converted into economic capital, for example when a sense of style, which according to Bourdieu is inherited from an elite upbringing, allows one to work as a well-regarded and well-paid stylist.

products becomes increasingly mainstreamed, upper-middle-class and elite residents have begun to privilege local goods. While 'acting local' has long been a slogan of environmental movements, in recent years localism has become fashionable and a marker of distinction. Examples are 'locavores' who insist on eating only local produce, often bought from farmers' markets or upscale supermarkets such as Whole Foods, or shoppers who choose to buy at locally owned stores rather than at big box retailers such as Wal-Mart. The proponents of localisms highlight the environmental, social and health-related benefits of local consumption. Such emphases on buying and consuming locally are now also an important element in processes of class distinction (Barendregt and Jaffe 2014).

Consumer citizenship

Consumption is not only significant in shaping classed and gendered belonging. Increasingly, scholars understand it as central to political inclusion. Partially displacing the state and formal politics, consumption and the market are becoming more important sites for political expression and participation in public life. Being recognized as a 'good citizen' is often implicitly premised on an individual's capacity to be a consumer (rather than, for instance, an individual's role as a laborer, soldier or parent). This development of 'consumer citizenship' means that our ability to consume – to own and display basic or luxury commodities, such as clothing, housing or transport – shapes our (informal) status as full members of a larger political community (see, e.g., Daunton and Hilton 2001; Johnston 2008). This has obvious implications in terms of citizen equality, with claims to belonging determined by access to economic and/or cultural capital. The exclusionary implications of the close connection between consumption and citizenship is evident in urban areas in the commercialization of public space, and the attempts by police to remove non-consumers such as homeless people and lower-class youth from these spaces.

However, consumer citizenship has also been heralded as broadening the scope of democracy beyond formal electoral politics. The connection between consumption and citizenship can also be seen in the politicization of the market: the idea of consumer citizenship is associated with 'political consumerism', a phenomenon that sees consumer choices – from boycotts to ethical consumption – become key sites of political action. The 'locavores' mentioned above are one example; other forms of ethical consumption that are visible in the urban landscape include eco-friendly architecture or the valorization of 'slow' products and activities in fast-paced urban environments (Barendregt and Jaffe 2014). While many academics and activists are optimistic about the potential of critical consumers to effect political change, it entails a move away from both electoral and contentious politics. Looking to consumers for social change, rather than to political parties or social movements, individualizes collective action and privileges those with higher levels of disposable income. It involves not only the politicization of the market, but also the marketization of politics.

Amy Porter (2008) draws out some of the complexities of the relationship between consumption and citizenship in her research in Havana. In a changing Cuba increasingly dependent on the tourism economy, the government developed certain facilities (for example golf courses or motor scooter rental) that were available to tourists but off limits to Cubans. In addition to this differentiation in consumer possibilities between local urban residents and tourists, Cubans with access to US dollars or convertible pesos also had a larger ability to consume than those who only earned *moneda nacional* (national money).

Many Cubans with access to foreign currency, which enabled them to buy imported foods and luxury products in Havana's special 'dollar stores', embraced conspicuous consumption, while those without this access felt like second-class citizens. Porter argues that this increasing differentiation among citizens based on their ability to consume led to a 'crisis of citizenship'. The revolution's emphasis on providing for citizens' needs was displaced by a tourist economy that created and catered to wants and desires. This shift resulted in the increased stratification between those who could and those who could not consume freely, and eroded the socialist ideals of equality that had previously been more influential in Havana. In this context, she suggests that Cubans' turn to the black market – the illegal purchase of goods outside official state stores – can be seen not only as a mode of fulfilling their needs and desires, but also as a political, subversive act.

Consumption, leisure and space

Consumption, leisure and urban space are connected in a number of ways. First, consumption and a shift in many urban economies towards leisure activities have transformed urban landscapes. As the identities of consumers change, new venues catering to these groups, and advertisements targeting them, become visible in public space. Second, like all other urban activities, consumption and leisure do not happen in a spatial vacuum – it literally takes place. The specific 'where' of these activities reflects and reproduces leisure geographies that often have a strong moral undertone, structuring our ideas about who is allowed consume what, when and where. Third, urban places themselves are becoming commodified as consumption focuses not only on products but on experiences and symbols, as is evident in the transformation of cities and neighborhoods into tourist attractions. Below, we give examples of these three different kinds of connections in a range of urban contexts.

Creating new spaces of leisure and consumption

In Chapter 5, we discussed how cities are shaped by their economies, noting that shifts in the urban economy can drastically change urban landscapes. Shifting consumption patterns and leisure lifestyles are an important way in which these economic and spatial changes may manifest themselves. Post-Fordist economies (see Box 5.1) have introduced flexible forms of labor, for example through temporary and part-time employment contracts, increasingly making a lifelong career with one employer a thing of the past. In addition, these new economies often see a shifting gender balance in the workforce, with more female professionals entering service sector employment. As the identities of laborers change, so do those of consumers. The shifts in the labor force and the associated increase in women's disposable income have impacted the consumer landscape. In many cities, working women have become a highly important consumer market, which, in turn, has often given rise to new strategies to tap into this market segment.

In her ethnographic study of Japan's urban night-time spaces, Swee-Lin Ho (2015) describes how late-night entertainment activities such as drinking and visiting clubs, which had been considered important extensions of the working lives of middle-class men, but not of women, also became acceptable for female employees. From the 1990s onwards, the rising number of female professionals in the Japanese service sector created an attractive market for the producers of alcoholic beverages and leisure venues. Marketing campaigns

Figure 6.1 Advertisements for host clubs in Kabukicho, Tokyo, 2013 (photograph by Swee-Lin Ho)

rebranded particular drinks as suitable for working women. For example, one campaign successfully promoted a whiskey–soda mix called *highball* as a fashionable drink for women by portraying a well-known actress as an independent, knowledgeable whiskey drinker. The cocktail became hugely popular and Japanese cities saw the proliferation of numerous *highball* bars. This resignification of liquor offered women new social opportunities, Ho (2015: 39) writes: 'Emboldened by the transformed symbolic association of alcohol with masculinity into "gender-neutral" products by consumer marketing, many women are strategically reconfiguring the meaning of different alcoholic beverages and actively utilize drinking as a site for negotiating new self-identities'. Using their financial clout and new images of acceptable female drinking, middle-class working women were able to explore nightlife activities that had previously been deemed acceptable only for men. This included visits to host clubs and other sensual venues where men provide 'intimate, playful services' to female patrons (see Figure 6.1).

The shift in employment patterns and consumption imaginaries enabled working women to more fully inhabit the status of *sararimen*, white-collar worker, a status that had always centrally included drinking and night-time leisure. In addition,

> many women also find it empowering to be able to reverse the gender order in the night-time economy by mobilizing their economic capabilities to pursue a diversity of activities in the urban night space that only men have historically been able to engage in.
> (Ho 2015: 46)

A wide range of venues, from restaurants and *highball* bars to host clubs, now provide middle-class working women with ways to publicly position themselves as sophisticated members of the professional middle class and to negotiate their position in Japanese society through their consumption choices. These places provide them with particular kinds of cultural capital (being seen as a sophisticated female professional) and social capital (providing spaces for socializing and networking with peers), as well as fun spaces to relax after a hard day's work.

Leisure geographies

The global spread of US-style coffee shops (with Starbucks as probably the most well-known example) provides us with a good illustration of the interaction between global fashions and trends and local norms, preferences and desires related to leisure. In a broad range of urban contexts, US-style coffee shops have taken up new positions within local geographies of leisure (Roseberry 1996). We use the term leisure geographies for the cognitive maps of the city that influence our understanding of who should consume what, where and when. The spread of this type of coffee shop introduced a range of specialty coffees – from *ristrettos* to *caffè lattes* and flat whites – to consumers across the world. In many locales, these spaces and the consumer habits they nurture are associated with young urban professionals who choose to remain in the city, rather than move out to middle-class suburbs, and have become signposts of gentrification (see Chapter 2).

The taste for cappuccino has become a potent global sign, signifying gentrified tastes in cities across the world. These coffee shops borrow much of their signifying potential prestige, and distinctiveness from their embeddedness in global flows (cf. Appadurai 1990). Yet the kind of social spaces that coffee shops constitute within specific urban contexts, and the distinction conferred by the taste for *caffè latte*, are eminently local matters. They have to be understood within local leisure geographies that contain moral maps of respectable and less respectable places and forms of consumption (for example, of specialty coffees, movies, alcohol, drugs or sex), which are seen as morally acceptable or, in contrast, suspect or even taboo (see, e.g., de Koning 2009).

As illustrated in the case of Japanese white-collar workers, such mappings are strongly gendered, with certain places and forms of consumption and leisure seen as appropriate for men but not for women, and vice versa. Such geographies are often also highly class specific, making particular kinds of leisure acceptable for some, and dubious for others. In Cairo, for example, mixed-gender socializing in upscale coffee shops seems perfectly natural and respectable for young people with privileged class backgrounds, whereas among their less privileged counterparts this may be associated with loose sexual norms and even prostitution (de Koning 2009). Such classed leisure geographies may also pit local venues and styles against international ones, connecting them to lower-class or elite forms of consumption. In this context, leisure choices become ways of positioning oneself in terms of class, moral outlook or, as the case below illustrates, political allegiance.

The highly local nature of such leisure geographies – despite ostensible similarities in café styles, menus and names – is well illustrated by Lara Deeb and Mona Harb's (2013) discussion of the emerging leisure sector in Shi'ite South Beirut. The Lebanese capital of Beirut was long seen as the most cosmopolitan and liberal city in the Middle East. However, South Beirut, with its predominantly Shi'ite population and the dominance of the Shi'ite political-religious organization Hizballah was seen as rural, less sophisticated and overly pious. As a consequence of Lebanon's civil war, which lasted from 1975 to 1990, Beirut's urban landscape became fragmented along sectarian lines, with particular areas of the city associated with specific sects and their associated political movements. After the end of the civil war, South Beirut saw the emergence of a café culture that balanced demands of both leisure and morality, for example with respect to mixed-gender gatherings and the playing of music. This particular café culture provided pious young middle-class Shi'ite Beirutis with respectable leisure options. Moreover, in times of sectarian strife, they were able to stay safely close to home in Shi'ite territory and show their political allegiance by patronizing local 'Shi'ite' cafés. Beirut's leisure geography illustrates the complex mapping of lifestyle, class, morality, sectarian and political identity, which reflected many of the fault lines in Lebanese society.

Consuming urban space

In addition to studying where consumption takes place within cities, urban researchers have also begun to study the process whereby urban space itself becomes the object of consumption. This is perhaps most evident in urban tourism, where experiencing a city and its various urban places is the main attraction to visitors. However, transforming urban places into consumable sites involves coordinated efforts to resignify 'normal' spaces of residence and work into tourist attractions. This process often includes city or neighborhood branding campaigns (see Chapter 8) that construct a place image or narrative intended to entice tourists to come and spend their money in that place. Such images and narratives tend to highlight attractive or spectacular sites, such as historical architecture, colorful ethnic markets or scenic waterfronts, but often ignore contemporary urban inequalities and the histories of conflict that have shaped these cityscapes.

Amsterdam and San Francisco provide good examples of such depoliticizing place marketing. Both cities are promoted as gay capitals through high-profile events such as gay parades, while particular neighborhoods are signposted as queer friendly through the display of rainbow flags and monuments commemorating the struggle for gay rights. While such statements were once liberating, they are increasingly financed by entrepreneurial city administrations and big business and serve to promote the city. The marketing strategies that present these cities as gay capitals glibly gloss over continuing discrimination and stigmatization of people from lesbian, gay, bisexual, transgender, queer, questioning and intersex (LGBTQI) communities in these same cities.

The marketing of ethnic neighborhoods can have similar depoliticizing effects. In her study of the transformation of New York's East Harlem from a low-income, marginalized Puerto Rican neighborhood into a gentrifying tourist attraction, Arlene Davila (2004) contrasts long-time residents' understanding of ethnicity as connected to history and struggle with economic developers' production of 'marketable ethnicity'. The latter discourse rebrands Harlem as a travel destination or a fashionable place to live, with Puerto Rican bars and African-American churches not so much historical and political sites of struggle or community solidarity, but hip attractions for outsiders to visit and enjoy. Focusing on multiple New York neighborhoods that are undergoing processes of gentrification, Sharon Zukin (2011) makes a similar point, showing how the search for 'authentic' urban places often involves the commodification of urban culture. Increasingly, educated urban residents have come to prefer older, ethnically diverse neighborhoods over bland, standardized suburban areas. The urban authenticity these wealthier residents seek is generally associated with the activities and lifestyles of immigrants, artists and working-class residents. However, the sense of place these less privileged residents lend to an area is eroded as the 'local culture' of a neighborhood becomes something to consume.

A specific phenomenon within the consumption of urban space is so-called 'slum tourism', an increasingly popular form of tourism that involves visits to Rio de Janeiro's Rocinha *favela*, Johannesburg's Soweto township or Mumbai's informal settlement of Dharavi. Wealthy tourists, predominantly from Europe and North America, travel to these low-income neighborhoods in search of authentic experiences, and sometimes out of a desire to engage in 'pro-poor tourism'. However, the development of these neighborhoods into tourist attractions and a type of urban spectacle means that spaces of urban poverty and deprivation become sights and experiences to consume. While slum tourism encounters can connect people from very different backgrounds, this type of tourism also involves the commodification of urban misery (Dürr and Jaffe 2012).

Urban lifestyles, scenes and popular culture

Urban lifestyles and leisure activities – from fashion, music and shopping preferences to how and where people choose to relax and socialize – are not only about economic processes or class distinction. They are also very much ways of expressing and negotiating cultural identities and political viewpoints, but, importantly, they are also ways of just having fun or even seeking an escape from everyday concerns of economy and politics. Cities are especially fertile sites for new lifestyles, scenes and subcultures. Lifestyles can be understood as collective forms of style and consumption that tend to be constructed around distinct preferences in consumer goods and leisure activities. They have a strong symbolic dimension in which language, music, and bodily adornment and dispositions (including fashion, hairstyles, make-up or ways of moving) are important elements. Media from advertising and magazines to television and YouTube videos play a major role in popularizing specific lifestyles, from punk to grunge to hipsters.

How to conceptualize such contemporary clusters of taste, style and sociability has been the topic of much debate. Anthropologists and sociologists have sometimes studied them under the rubric of 'subcultures' or 'scenes'. While the concept of subculture was popular amongst anthropologists and sociologists in the 1960s and 1970s (see Box 6.2), it has lost its popularity because it implies an understanding of identities as static, rather than constructed and dynamic. In addition, the term subculture was used primarily to refer to lower-class styles and taste, inadvertently presenting middle-class lifestyles as normal rather than subcultural. The concept of scene is often used to refer specifically to music scenes, as dynamic cultural spaces where musical collectivities form. These collectivities, which involve clusters of musical consumption and production practices, can be rooted in a specific geographical locality, connect different settings translocally, or be primarily Internet-based, virtual scenes (Bennett and Peterson 2004).

Urban youth in particular are major players in generating forms of popular music, fashion and language that are sources of meaning, inspiration and identity. Such forms of popular culture often go global. From hip hop and heavy metal to KPOP, they travel between urban sites where new youth groups appropriate and 'indigenize' them. Reggae music and the associated Rastafari movement, for instance, emerged amongst rural-to-urban migrants in the underprivileged neighborhoods of Kingston, Jamaica, but became popularized in British and North American cities with Jamaicans' international migration (Jaffe 2012). They have also been taken up among disenfranchised youth, especially young

Box 6.2 **Hebdige and subculture**

Much of the research on urban lifestyles, scenes and subcultures has been conducted within the interdisciplinary field of cultural studies. An influential theorist in this regard has been the British scholar Dick Hebdige (1951–). Hebdige was associated with the Birmingham school of cultural studies, a group of researchers tied to the University of Birmingham's Centre for Contemporary Cultural Studies (CCCS). The CCCS, led by the influential Jamaican-born scholar Stuart Hall (1932–2014), was pioneering in its approach to popular culture as central sites for the negotiation of power relations.

Dick Hebdige, one of Stuart Hall's students, is best known for his key text *Subculture: The Meaning of Style* (1979). Drawing on research on youth culture and consumption in Birmingham in the 1970s, Hebdige, following Stuart Hall and Tony Jefferson's (1975) earlier work on subcultures and resistance, argues that subcultures such as punk should be understood as responses to classed and raced power relations. He sees subcultural style as a signifying practice, used to construct and communicate difference between social groups. Punk was a way for White working-class youth in Britain to distinguish themselves culturally in opposition to both their parents' generation and non-White youth (such as Jamaicans). While scholars have critiqued the book for its masculinist bias – Hebdige largely ignores the gender-specific processes that characterized the punk scene (McRobbie 1980) – and the term 'subculture' for presenting cultural collectivities as overly static, *Subculture* remains an important touchstone for studies of popular culture and style.

men, around the globe (Moyer 2005). Below, we discuss two forms of urban sociability constructed around shared styles, tastes and popular culture. We focus first on hip hop as a translocal form of popular culture that has been enormously influential in the experience and communication of urban marginalization. This is followed by a discussion of the role of urban fashion in constructing and expressing modernity, focused on the case of *bluffeurs* in Abidjan, Côte d'Ivoire.

Urban popular culture, place-making and marginalization

Hip hop is arguably one of the most 'urban' forms of popular culture. Originating in New York City's deprived neighborhoods, this form of popular culture – encompassing rap music, graffiti, breakdancing and DJ-ing – has become one of the dominant forms of urban youth culture worldwide. Hip hop emerged in response to urban marginalization, translating and contesting experiences of racism, poverty and violence through the creation of a broad range of alternative narratives and imaginaries of urban life (Jaffe 2014). In addition to being preoccupied with raced and classed inequalities, hip hop has also always been concerned with place-making (see Chapter 2). Graffiti – often referred to as the visual element of hip hop culture – also plays an important role in this place-making, with graffiti artists using their spray cans to make their mark on the urban landscape. In addition, rappers' lyrics tend to show a strong concern with locality ('the hood') and socio-spatial belonging (Forman 2002).

More than many other forms of popular culture, hip hop has become a translocal scene. In US hip hop, local hip hop scenes have emerged that emphasize distinct urban identities, from Los Angeles' gangsta rap in the early 1990s to the 'Dirty South' style of cities such as Atlanta and New Orleans in the late 1990s and early 2000s. But the reach of hip hop goes much farther than the United States alone; anthropologists have studied its globalization from Tokyo (Condry 2006) to the Tanzanian city of Arusha (Weiss 2009). Through linguistic differences and local appropriations and adaptions, youth in a variety of cities rework hip hop's themes of race, class, gender and space to fit their own concerns, while still referring and connecting to its US urban 'roots'.

In his research on Brazilian hip hop, Derek Pardue (2008) studies this type of reworking, noting how a style that evolves through global connections is also rooted in specific localities (such as the *quebrada*, the neighborhood). He shows how, for low-income, racialized youth in the *favelas* of São Paulo, hip hop presents a form of cultural activism that allows them to resignify their marginalized position. It offers a cultural mode of responding to the idea of *periferia*, their spatially and socially peripheral position within the city. Pardue found that while Brazilian hip hop included racial discourses that tied it to national and international engagements with blackness and Afrocentrism, spatial and socio-economic discrimination and exclusion were increasingly dominant themes. Young people's struggles to claim or 'conquer' urban space (*conquistar espaço*) for hip hop events ties to the broader struggles of the *periferia*'s inhabitants to claim their right to the city (see also Chapter 9 on insurgent citizenship in São Paulo).

Urban fashion, cosmopolitanism and modernity

Urban cultural styles are not only used to contest a marginalized position within a city; they are also important ways of positioning oneself in relation to modernity and change, as James Ferguson (1999) has demonstrated in his work on urban styles in the African Copperbelt. He found that urban residents employed 'localist' and 'cosmopolitan' styles, clusters of tastes and orientations in domains such as clothing, food, language and music (see Figure 6.2). While his respondents conceptualized their preferences as expressing a cultural dualism between 'tradition' and 'modernity', Ferguson suggests that we should understand styles as performative competences that construct rather than express such different identities. Cultural styles, he argues, are neither fully 'free' individual choices, nor is their adoption rigidly determined by social structures – style can be seen as 'a cultivated competence … situated both within a political-economic context and within an individual life course' (Ferguson 1999: 101).

In more recent research, Sasha Newell (2012a) encountered a somewhat comparable deployment of style and self-fashioning in Côte d'Ivoire's capital Abidjan. He describes the fashion feats of *bluffeurs*, a group that is similar to and indeed was inspired by the 1980s Congolese movement of sapeurs (MacGaffey and Bazenguissa-Ganga 2000). Part of internationally renowned La Sape (*Société des Ambianceurs et des Personnes Élégantes*, or the Society of Ambiance-Makers and Elegant People), sapeurs were generally poor young men who fashioned themselves by wearing designer suits and displaying extremely sophisticated taste. Similarly, the Ivoirian *bluffeurs* discussed by Newell are generally unemployed young men who earn money through the informal economy.

Bluffeurs used style to fashion an identity that was both distinctly modern (as opposed to traditional) and urban (as opposed to rural), but their performances also played with,

Figure 6.2 1970s bar scene in Kafanchan, Nigeria (photograph courtesy of Ulf Hannerz)

and sometimes inverted, those dualisms (Figure 6.3). Their stylized presence presented a way of contesting their socio-economic positioning. Generally extremely poor, *bluffeurs* went to great lengths to perform as wealthy youngsters, securing a fashionable outfit with brand names and money to lavish on a single night out. This did not mean people actually believed the bluff; most knew these young men hailed from the low-income *quartiers populaires*. As Newell (2012b: 47) says, this public knowledge was beside the point: 'the bluff was … about demonstrating the taste, the connoisseurship, of someone who had the means to live that way all the time – and it was this facility with the symbolization of luxury for which they were respected'. The appearance of the Ivoirian–French music star Douk Saga on the Abidjan scene in 2002 suggests the sense of overstatement and the playful symbolic economy that became central to this urban savvy style:

> In his first music video Sagacité, Saga sang from within a Dolce and Gabbana label, and performed a bluff to end all bluffs, handing out money to white women outside of designer stores on the Champs-Elysées [the famous Parisian boulevard that is home to exclusive fashion stores].
>
> (Newell 2012b: 48–49)

The *bluffeurs* demonstrate how cultural capital can be used to create a social standing largely disconnected from economic capital. Their style was clearly aspirational, attempting to produce success through consumption. However, Abidjan youths were not trying to copy local urban elites, but rather used their style to challenge the prominence of this Francophile elite through their creative and rapidly shifting stylistic assemblages

Figure 6.3 Bluffeurs at home in Abidjan, Côte d'Ivoire (photograph by Sasha Newell)

of local and international styles and fashions. Consumption and lifestyle, and particularly the cultural capital that allowed them to determine (rather than follow) local fashions, constituted a form of success and social mobility in spite of their lack of economic capital, displaying a mastery of global modernity that mattered in its own right.

Conclusion

Consumption has become an important topic of anthropological research, in part in response to a shift in emphasis from production to consumption in post-Fordist economies in the global North. In this context, citizenship is increasingly framed through the right and the ability to consume. Consumption is understood as an important form of self-expression, which also allows people to distinguish themselves from others. Urban settings, with their large populations and great degrees of anonymity and diversity, can be home to a range of subcultures or scenes that provide a sense of belonging and identification, as well as a community that is often quite distinct from or even in opposition to the urban mainstream. By consuming we display our economic and cultural capital and position ourselves socially. Anthropologists have documented how some people deploy their sense of style (a form of cultural capital) to suggest and perhaps even realize social mobility.

Urban anthropologists have also examined how consumption shapes urban landscapes. Shifting consumption preferences and the rise of new capital-rich groups of consumers can drastically change urban landscapes, for example through the spread of shops and leisure venues that cater to the tastes and appetites of the growing prominence of these particular consumers. Entire neighborhoods may be transformed on account of such shifting consumption and leisure landscapes, for example when gentrifiers move into predominantly working-class areas, attracted by the authentic urban feel of such quarters, soon followed by hipster coffee bars and organic food stores. Even the city itself can become a product to consume, something cleverly promoted by city branding campaigns that are designed to boost urban tourist economies.

Discussion questions

1 In what ways do you position yourself socially through your consumption choices? And how do these choices position you in the urban landscape?
2 Can you explain why consumption is both personal and political, and both private and public?
3 Can you describe how shifting consumption patterns have transformed particular parts of a city that you are familiar with?
4 Why can taste be considered a form of capital?
5 Can consumption be subversive?

Further reading

Barendregt, Bart and Rivke Jaffe, eds. (2014) *Green Consumption: The Global Rise of Eco-Chic*. London: Bloomsbury.

Condry, Ian (2006). *Hip-Hop Japan: Rap and the Paths of Cultural Globalization*. Durham, NC: Duke University Press.

Jayne, Mark (2006) *Cities and Consumption*. Oxford and New York: Routledge.

Further viewing

Style Wars (1983), directed by Tony Silver. Classic hip hop documentary that captures the evolution of graffiti and breakdancing. It shows how these expressions became a vital part of the budding hip-hop culture spreading in the streets of New York.

The Great Happiness Space: Tale of an Osaka Love Thief (2006), directed by Jake Clennell. Documentary about Rakkyo Café, an Osaka host club. 'Glamorous host boys make beautiful young women laugh, feel good about their lives – and pay handsomely for their pleasure.'

Chapter 7

Cities and globalization

Cities have always been crucial crossroads for long-distance connections and these connections in turn significantly shape their social, economic and cultural make-up. Changes in such connections reconfigure urban lives. Cities are key sites where contemporary globalization manifests itself, and they are crucial for the organization of global networks and operations. Cities are important nodes for trade and transnational production chains, as well as important immigrant destinations. Urban landscapes often display large degrees of socio-cultural diversity and can become the focus of ethnic or cultural tensions.

From the 1990s onward, globalization became an important topic in urban anthropology (see Box 7.1). We can define globalization as 'the stretching and deepening of social relations across national borders so that everyday activities are more influenced by events at greater distances' (Smart and Smart 2003: 265). Forms of globalization have been evident at least since European colonial expansion in the sixteenth century, and large empires and trade networks existed before that time. Thomas Hylland Eriksen (2007: 4) argues that contemporary forms of globalization are characterized by increased trade and transnational economic activity, faster and denser communication networks, and increased tensions between (and within) cultural groups due to intensified mutual exposure.

This chapter discusses how the role of cities in global networks affects city life. Anthropologists have studied the impact of long-distance movement and connections on the city by observing the place-making activities of transnational migrants. Another set of studies has been inspired by a more political economic approach to the role of cities in processes of neoliberal globalization. The first section of this chapter discusses migrant place-making and transnational social fields. The next section examines the concept of the *global city*, zooming in on anthropological studies that discuss how the everyday forms of inequality that accompany global city formation are lived and negotiated. Anthropologists have also studied the spectacular glitzy urban landscapes that are constructed in the quest for global city status. We discuss why even people who are excluded from the benefits of these new landscapes and their consumerist possibilities may receive these spectacular manifestations of globalization with extraordinary enthusiasm. However, transnational connections are not limited to these high-profile global networks and spectacular architecture. There are numerous other less visible or prominent connections and networks that shape urban landscapes and place-making in cities around the world. This chapter ends with an examination of how such *globalization from below* manifests itself in the city, and transforms the urban landscape.

Box 7.1 **Globalization**

The term 'globalization' became popular in the 1990s to capture a sense of increasing interconnectedness in social, economic and cultural terms, and to underline the growing significance of global networks as compared to nation-states. The term was accompanied by much anticipation, trepidation and hype. Life seemed to have changed irrevocably with the Internet, fast-moving capital and mass tourism. Some observers predicted the 'McDonaldization' of the world: the standardization of social life and homogenization of culture across different societies. Anthropologists soon pointed out that there were few indications of the actual homogenization of culture. Rather, evidence pointed to the predominance of highly particular local appropriations of what was glossed as 'global culture' or 'global products'. Sociologist Roland Robertson popularized the term 'glocalization' to capture the mutual imbrications of the local and the global. Globalization thus seems to produce at least as much heterogeneity as homogeneity.

Another, related debate concerned the supposed farewell to essentialist, closed identities or cultures, and an increased openness to creolization and hybridity. Many anthropologists, instead, documented the rise of nationalist and ethnic movements across the world. In various contexts, people mobilized to protest and combat what they saw as the loss of identity, community and sovereignty due to global flows of people and ideas, as well as the leveling of borders. A related debate concerned the alleged decline of nation-states as organizers of social and political life in light of particularly economic globalization. Authors criticizing the idea that the influence of the nation-state was waning pointed to, among other things, the continued importance of passports and borders in regulating the movement of people across the world.

An important anthropologist in these debates was Arjun Appadurai, whose 'Disjuncture and difference in the global cultural economy', first published in 1990, came to dominate anthropological understandings of globalization. Appadurai argued that 'The new global cultural economy has to be seen as a complex, overlapping, disjunctive order, which cannot any longer be understood in terms of existing center-periphery models' (1990: 296). Instead, Appadurai proposed five dimensions – ethnoscapes, mediascapes, technoscapes, financescapes and ideoscapes – which combined in unpredictable manners to produce global cultural flows (ibid.).

Amidst debates about the far-reaching effects of the new global era, some scholars remained more sceptical. Both the newness and the comprehensive nature of today's world connectedness should not be overestimated, they argued. Colonial historian Frederick Cooper (2005: 92), for example, noted that in some respects the world was more globalized in the nineteenth century than it was at the start of the new millennium. Cooper argues that we should study the nature of connections *and* disconnections, taking account of, for example, the effects of deregulated financial flows *and* increasingly restrictive border regimes.

Migrants and transnational social fields

One way in which anthropologists have examined transnational or global connections is by studying migrant lives, mostly in urban settings. This focus goes back to the early Chicago School studies of Polish migrants in Chicago at the start of the twentieth century by Thomas and Znaniecki (see Chapter 1). From the 1950s onward, large population movements from the decolonizing world to the rapidly expanding economies of the United States and the former colonial metropoles in Europe drastically changed US and European urban landscapes. While they did not exclusively move to major urban centers, the majority of transnational migrants did eventually settle in cities.

In a 1990s overview of anthropological studies of globalization, Michael Kearney (1995) spoke of a global implosion that blurred the distinction between center and periphery, or what was known as First and Third World. This implosion manifested itself in many cities in the global North. Anthropologists started discussing 'the Caribbeanization of New York', and a city like Miami could justifiably be called the capital of Latin America, just as Paris had become the capital of West Africa. Such observations are suggestive of the drastic changes in these urban landscapes, with the rise of neighborhoods that house significant migrant or 'minority' populations, and offer a range of 'ethnic' goods and services, from supermarkets to restaurants, beauty parlors and medical and religious services.

Transnational migration plays an important role in the transformation of urban landscapes. In cities in so-called host countries, migrants endeavor to create temporary or permanent lives for themselves. As we discussed in Chapter 2, their efforts to belong, to make a home away from home, is an important factor in the diversification of urban landscapes in cities across the world. The presence of large numbers of migrants and children of migrants also points to the increasingly transnational character of such cities, with people living lives that connect places across national borders (see, e.g., Eade and Smith 2011).

Against this background it has become increasingly clear that the fit between nation, state and territory, a cornerstone of the idea of the nation-state, is not a neat one. The presence of large numbers of immigrants gives the lie to the idea of a homogeneous national society. National sovereignty is compromised by supra-national modes of regulation, for example of international institutions such as the World Bank, or the European Union. Meanwhile, states with large numbers of nationals who migrated abroad develop transnational forms of nationhood and citizenship in order to control the influential non-resident population that also presents an important source of revenue. The privileges extended to 'Non-Resident Indians', particularly the sizable Indian expat contingent working in the United States and other wealthy countries, is a good example of such attempts to stretch the nation-state beyond its national borders.

In their classic work on transnationalism, *Nations Unbound* (1994), Linda Basch, Nina Glick Schiller and Cristina Szanton Blanc developed the notion of *transnational fields* to capture such border-crossing social formations. Transnational social fields are constellations of networks that stretch across territorial borders, connecting various places, not only so-called sending and receiving countries, but often also many other places where family and friends, or co-nationals are to be found. As Levitt and Glick Schiller (2004: 1006) argue, transnational migrants live simultaneously within and beyond the boundaries of nation-state.

The notion of transnational social fields clearly implies that migration does not only affect the urban landscapes of 'receiving countries', but also those of 'home countries', and that migration trajectories connect these places in new ways. Anthropologist Farha Ghannam (2002) has documented how remittances from young male labor migrants lead to new housing production or remodeling and introduce consumption practices that may set new local standards of what is modern and desirable. She describes how parents in a low-income Cairo neighborhood kept up a constant flow of communication with their children who worked as labor migrants in the Gulf states in order to ensure that they remained focused on the goal of their sojourn away from home. They expected their children to remain abroad for the period of time needed to earn enough money to buy and furnish an apartment in order to marry and set up a new household.

Ghannam (2002: 148) points out that

> ensuring continuous communication with young men and encouraging them to buy housing units or remodel existing apartments are important techniques that secure the flow of currency and reinforce the attachment of labor migrants to their families and neighborhoods in Cairo.

These daily communications were meant to ensure that the migrant lives abroad remained focused on developments at home. In this case, labor migration helped reinforce attachment to the neighborhood of origin, and significantly shaped the urban landscape and social life 'at home'. These labor migrants and their families operated within transnational social fields that thoroughly and intimately connected parts of the urban landscape to other places across the globe.

Globalization and neoliberalism

Contemporary globalization is often discussed in tandem with neoliberalism, which, as we discussed in Chapter 5, is an ideology that sees the rule of the market as the best way to secure economic growth and welfare. Globalization is shaped by the neoliberal emphasis on the (global) market, a rollback of the welfare state and the promotion of free trade. Neoliberal ideologies proclaim the superiority of the global market as an allocating and regulating force in economies and societies around the world. The free reign of the global market is said to bring about higher affluence for those who dare to brave global competition, while failure to do so spells inevitable economic slowdown. Such tenets become self-fulfilling prophecies as they influence the policies of state and non-state actors on a local, national and global scale. States around the world have rewritten their laws and redesigned their national budgets and economic policies to conform to global standards of neoliberal economics (see Chapter 5).

Processes of globalization that unfold within such a neoliberal framework diminish the importance of nations as containers of social, economic and cultural life, while they have promoted the importance of major cities. These processes have also contributed to changing class configurations in these cities, particularly the decline of working-class and middle-class living standards and the rise of a class of global winners: both global elites and certain sections of the professional middle class. These class divisions manifest themselves in the urban landscape in the form of new, flashy sites where the latest global fashions and trends are displayed, but that are often exclusive, out of reach and literally closed off to much of the urban population. Neoliberal globalization thus contributes to rising urban inequalities and forms of segregation in cities around the world. One of the most influential theories that has addressed these developments is Saskia Sassen's work on the global city (Box 7.2)

Box 7.2 **The global city**

Saskia Sassen's work on global cities (2001) has been highly influential in urban studies. From the 1980s onward, we have seen the rise of a global system of production in which the various parts of the production process are spread over the globe, with much of the primary production process located in countries with cheap labor (see Chapter 5). This global system entails both the spatial dispersal of economic production and global integration. This has created a new strategic role for cities. Besides their long-standing role as centers for international trade and banking, cities like New York, London and Tokyo have also become command points in the organization of the world economy and key locations for finance and business producer services, which have replaced (and displaced) manufacturing as the leading economic sector. An increasingly dense network of global cities harbors the material nodes of control for spatially dispersed production processes and are production sites for the specialized business services that make such control possible.

The urban sectors that are involved in such global coordination functions become increasingly disconnected from the surrounding landscape. London's City financial district is more closely connected to New York's Wall Street than it is to other London neighborhoods. This disjunction in the urban economy is accompanied by changing class configurations. Sassen and others have pointed to the sharp polarization of the occupational structure and income distribution. Global cities see the simultaneous rise of a high-end sector (professionals in the financial sector and related industries) and a low-end service sector (services to professional elites), and a withering middle class, whose former secure contracts and employment conditions are progressively dismantled. As a consequence, global cities feature increasingly disparate urban geographies and modes of inhabiting and consuming urban space.

Sassen's global city theory has also invited criticism. According to geographer Jennifer Robinson (2002), global city theory (along with similar world city theories) focuses on a limited set of economic activities and limited sections of a limited number of cities, yet such theories formulate grand claims of success or failure. Because of this narrow focus, cities that are crucial nodes in global networks in other ways fall off the map. Moreover, the image of the dual city, one part globally connected and the other part disconnected, does not capture the breadth of a global city's socio-economic landscape or translocal connections. The focus on command center functions, moreover, pays insufficient attention to the lasting influence of earlier patterns of global dominance and inequality. Global or world cities are often influenced by their colonial histories, and reproduce earlier colonial patterns (King 1990a).

Yet, the idea of the global or world city holds enormous appeal, Robinson argues. The global city has become a program, 'a regulating fiction' (Robinson 2002: 546). 'Global cities have become the aspiration of many cities around the world; sprawling and poor megacities the dangerous abyss into which they might fall should they lack the redeeming (civilizing) qualities of city-ness found elsewhere' (ibid: 548).

Inequalities in the global city

Sociologist Saskia Sassen (2000, 2001) argues that cities have gained importance as the nodes of coordination and control of dispersed global production (see Box 7.2). Cities contain sites that are deeply embedded in, and crucial to the operation of global networks, yet are increasingly disconnected from the rest of the urban landscape. The most obvious examples of such global sites are The City in London or New York City's Wall Street. This centrality of cities to global networks has created its own dynamic. Geographer Jennifer Robinson (2002) argues that the idea of the 'global city' has been translated into a regulating fiction that promises new urban prosperity, and threatens disbelievers with a global disconnect.

Sassen's work goes against the idea of footloose global flows that jet around the world without restraints or obstacles, unmoored from effective national control, leaving a hapless, disempowered populace behind. She instead argues that the new global economy relies on command centers that are located in a number of major cities, particularly London, New York and Tokyo. Sassen's work offers a way to study the global ethnographically, approaching globalization as something that not only manifests itself in cities, but is also literally *produced* in cities around the world.

Global professionals

As we discussed in Chapter 5, many postcolonial countries that pioneered large projects of state-building after independence, have, in the last three decades, turned to neoliberal reforms, often pressured to do so by international financial institutions. Their capital cities are the primary spaces where such changing political and economic orientations are manifested. Anthropologists have explored how such changing orientations have reshaped the urban landscapes of cities like Mumbai, Jakarta, Buenos Aires and Cairo.

In her study of Cairo at the start of the twenty-first century, in the years leading up to the sweeping uprisings across the Arab world, Anouk de Koning (2009) analyzes the effects of such neoliberal reforms in Cairo. She asks how the reforms affect Cairo's professional middle class, which had long been a prime beneficiary of state support. This professional middle class had been central to the 1950s and 1960s state-led development project that aimed to transform Egypt into a well-educated, modern country. In the 1990s, in the context of the structural adjustment policies agreed on with the World Bank and the IMF, the Egyptian regime initiated economic policies that aimed to create a liberal market economy integrated in global economic networks. Most of these new development programs were focused on the capital city Cairo.

At the start of the twenty-first century, Cairo's cityscape had acquired a spectacular global touch. The luxurious five-star hotels, high-rise office buildings, new and immaculately clean malls seemed to herald Cairo's status as a global city. The budding upscale gated communities, hotels, golf courses and foreign educational institutions in the desert around Cairo offered affluent Cairenes transnational products and experiences, as well as a seemingly perfect, affluent, socially homogeneous world that the city with its high poverty rates, crowdedness and pollution could not offer. This spectacular Cairo was one of the clearest expressions of three decades of economic liberalization. It bore the imprint of Egypt's new national project: the creation of a global city that could cater to transnational business and the lifestyles of affluent Cairenes.

Figure 7.1 Trianon, an upscale coffee shop in Cairo, 2004 (photograph by Anouk de Koning)

In this context, Cairo's large professional middle class became increasingly divided between a privileged upper-middle class that could staff upmarket workspaces and act as successful mediators between the 'local' and the 'global,' and a less fortunate middle-class strata. Cairo's upper-middle-class professionals were the equivalent of Sassen's stratum of high-income earners. What de Koning (2009) terms 'cosmopolitan capital' presented a crucial marker of these emerging divisions (see also Box 6.1 on cultural capital). Cosmopolitan capital comprised those forms of cultural capital that entail familiarity with, and mastery of, Western cultural codes, as well as local cosmopolitan ones. Such cosmopolitan capital consisted of fluency in English, as well as Western diplomas or degrees from educational institutes that were associated with Western knowledge, but also knowledge of Western or global consumer culture.

These divisions were also imprinted on Cairo's urban landscape, which saw the rise of a range of upscale consumption, leisure and housing options. In particular, the fashionable coffee shops that appeared in upscale areas of Cairo from the mid-1990s onward provided upper-middle-class professionals with new opportunities for socializing, finding partners, and other forms of networking and self-presentation (see Figure 7.1). Such coffee shops largely circumvented negative associations with Western leisure spaces, particularly alcohol and loose sexual norms. While they judiciously heeded religious sensibilities and gendered notions of propriety, they were also able to intimate a sense of First World inclusion.

A casual mixed-gender public and the presence of young professional women were among the most important markers of Cairo's globally up-to-date exclusive modernity.

Young male and female professionals spending time socializing after work marked these spaces as part of global circuits of leisure to be found in major cities across the globe. The casual mixed-gender sociabilities that characterized social life in these coffee shops were, however, confined to such class-specific, closed and exclusive spaces. In other spaces, men and women who engaged in such mixed-gender meetings would be seen as having loose sexual morals. Like the upscale coffee shops, Cairo's public spaces had become increasingly segmented as they mapped into a starkly polarized income distribution. Like in other global cities, the search for the global had resulted in an increasingly divided urban landscape and disjunctive matrices of belonging.

Poverty in the global city

Sassen (2001) argues that the global city is characterized by social and economic polarization, with the growth of a segment of high-wage earners and the expansion of a low-wage, increasingly insecure socio-economic segment, and the concomitant shrinking of the socio-economic middle that was made up of relatively secure, relatively well-paid blue collar and middle-class professionals. The city's most vulnerable workers, often (female) migrants, provide personal services to the global city's professionals – from dog walkers to nannies, massage therapists or sex workers (Sassen 1996). These seemingly marginal service providers form an integral part of the global city.

In a related argument, Kristin Koptiuch (1991) polemically argues that we are witnessing a 'third worlding at home', as global inequalities and hegemonic domination are being reproduced within the cities of the 'First World', for example in Philadelphia. Clear signs of such 'third worlding at home' are highly exploitative labor conditions, such as sweat shops, that had previously been banished thanks to the struggle for protective labor legislation, growing disparities in income and health between the dominant, White population and the 'minority' populations of the inner cities, and increasingly repressive and disciplinary forms of governance. Meanwhile, the impoverished areas where these marginalized and racialized populations live become a new urban frontier braved by a type of explorer reminiscent of colonial times: journalists and social scientists who produce images of a primitive, exotic Otherness that can now be found right outside one's doorstep.

In an anthropological rejoinder to Sassen's observations on the global city's contingent of nannies and massage therapists, Eileen Moyer (2004) describes an extremely marginal section of the urban population, which, nevertheless, forms an integral part of the city's global spaces. Moyer focuses on the lives and urban trajectories of young men who work and live in the streets of Dar es Salaam, the capital of Tanzania (Figure 7.2). Many poor people like these young men were attracted to the new global spaces such as the Sheraton hotel, DHL offices and the Subway sandwich shop because of their wealthy clientele. They offered these wealthy patrons services ranging from car attendance and car washing, to food vending and sex work.

The spaces in which these young men work and live are also globalized spaces, Moyer argues, even if they only exist in the shadows of conspicuously global spaces marked by their 'gated and guarded entrances, immaculately kept shrubs, and neat appearance'. These shadow global spaces are to be found 'on the sides of the roads, or even right in the middle of them, on the sidewalks, and other unexpected and often in-between sites that are produced and re-produced by globalization' (Moyer 2004: 136). Moyer evocatively concludes:

Figure 7.2 Street vendors in Dar es Salaam, 2003 (photograph by Eileen Moyer)

Globalization in the North and the South has engendered a heightened awareness of difference and fostered the emergence of geographically divided cities. Excessive wealth juxtaposed with extreme poverty occurs with greater frequency and intensity as the gulf of economic difference widens. This juxtaposition is most obvious in the occupation and contestation of urban spaces. In Dar es Salaam inequality confronts. Poverty knocks on one's car window and tries to sell luxuries which the vendors themselves could never afford. Poverty sits on the sidewalk waiting to stand face to face with the privileged as they leave work. It washes and guards their luxury land cruiser bought to guarantee a safe drive home, where poverty will open their gates and guard their sleep. The continued existence of the poor provides services, safety and security. And threatens it as well.

(Moyer 2004, 137–138)

In part due to the concurrence of wealth and privilege with poverty and exclusion, the global city becomes a strategic site of contestation. Who has the right to the city, global capital or also those at the other end of the urban hierarchy? City governments and private parties go to great lengths to reduce this kind of conflict and, more generally, threats to the urban lives of the elites. As we discuss in Chapters 8 and 10, local governments in cities around the world try to keep such inequalities and poverty out of sight of more desirable inhabitants. Oftentimes their policies aim to create urban landscapes that are hospitable to the much-desired professional middle classes and elites.

The neoliberal spectacle

Global city formation can be seen as an effect of economic globalization, but it has also become a regulating fiction, for example, in the case of Cairo, discussed above. Jennifer Robinson (2002) has argued that the global city has been propagated as a recipe for success, a cure-all that is adopted by city or national governments desperate to participate in global networks. According to geographer Neil Smith, the concentration of production at the metropolitan scale has given rise to competition among city governments, who each seek to capture a share of global business and improve their city's ranking in global city hierarchies (see also Chapter 8 on the entrepreneurial city). This 'quest for the global' generally involves a major shift in resource allocation toward spectacular showcase projects and infrastructure, as well as subsidies to global corporations to entice them to locate or remain located in a particular city, subsidies Smith pointedly calls 'geobribes' (2002: 427–428). Such programs have changed the face of many urban landscapes in cities of the global North and global South. As Ayse Öncü and Petra Weyland (1997: 1) note, 'Office towers housing multinational corporations, transnational banks, world trade centers, and five-star hotels, once the exclusive hallmark of a small number of "world cities", now signify the integration of almost every major metropolis into global capitalism'.

Such showcase investments in cities are, however, not only related to competition for global business. As Abidin Kusno (2004) argues, life in capital cities is often made to stand for the life of the nation. Having a national capital that features the latest statements of global modernity, whether it is in the form of high-rise buildings, glitzy malls or retro-themed condominiums, signals that a country matters on the world stage. The obverse may even be more true, with the lack of a modern capital signifying absolute disconnection and underdevelopment. The resultant *nationalist urbanism* entails large investments in the urban landscape of these capital cities in order to represent national ambitions. Such showcase projects can for instance function to intimate a country's move from 'Third World' to 'First World' status. The high-rise provides the best example of such national imagineering. The temporary and ephemeral status of having the highest high-rise building (which only lasts until the construction of an even taller building) is used to convey a country's prowess on the global stage (King 2004). Asian countries in particular engaged in this competition for the highest tower in order to signal their global ascendency (see Figure 7.3 for an image of Kuala Lumpur's Petronas Towers).

Emanuela Guano's study of urban developments in neoliberal Buenos Aires (2002b) demonstrates that such projects are significantly informed by long-standing feelings of exclusion from and longing for First World affluence, sophistication and membership. In her urban ethnography of Buenos Aires in the years leading up to the 2001 economic crisis, Guano discusses the paradoxical attitudes of middle-class *porteños* (inhabitants of Buenos Aires) toward spectacular and highly exclusive urban developments. Against the backdrop of a mounting economic crisis, many once solidly middle-class inhabitants were reduced to poverty. Not unlike the Cairo case discussed above, Buenos Aires' middle class was sharply divided between a minority of upper-middle-class professionals who were able to profit from new service economy occupations, and an increasingly impoverished majority that suffered from the withering of state employment and public services. One of the features of the new neoliberal cityscape was a growing spatial segregation that offered a 'safe distance' from the increasing population of slum dwellers. As we discuss in more

Figure 7.3 Petronas Towers, Kuala Lumpur, 2010 (photograph Andrey Khrobostov via Shutterstock)

detail in Chapter 8, increased segregation in response to perceived security threats has been observed in many cities across the world.

Guano argues that this spatial segregation was accompanied by a transnational spectacularism, exemplified by opulent shopping malls and a redeveloped waterfront. According to Guano, these spectacles of transnational consumption were part of a bid for neoliberal hegemony. While they obviously catered to the affluent upper-middle and upper classes, they also addressed a less affluent middle-class public through a 'simulacrum of inclusion' (Guano 2002b: 185). Even those who could never consume in Buenos Aires' most exclusive malls felt that their city had finally regained some of its stature and could feel they were once more included in a global modernity.

In his discussion of a rather different city, Kinshasa, Congo, anthropologist Filip de Boeck (2011: 278) similarly argues that even people who were excluded from various spectacular projects that were intended to signal Kinshasa's modernity, shared the dreams of a modern or global city that these buildings invoked. Even though they understood that they would never be included in such projects and could even be displaced on their behalf, they reveled in the promise of a new and improved Kinshasa.

Guano argues that Argentina's neoliberal reforms fed into long-standing narratives of exclusion from and desire for a First World that many middle-class people felt to be rightfully theirs. The neoliberal promise to 'return' Argentina to First World standards was enticing to many middle-class inhabitants. While many were critical of the neoliberal program of the government, they also delighted in the new urban sites that were perceived as signs of a renewed inclusion into the First World. As Guano (2002b: 184) argues,

> Constructed in racial and cultural terms, this Europeanness posited middle-class porteños as displaced from a more 'civilized,' more 'modern' elsewhere to which they essentially belonged. … Even though they overtly resented neoliberalism for causing their fall from grace, many middle-class porteños were enthralled by [President] Menem's pledge of bringing Argentina up to First World standards.

These encounters with the promise of a transnational modernity allowed people otherwise excluded from this new First World Buenos Aires to engage in acts of imaginary consumption (Guano 2002b: 202–203). The power of malls and gentrified real estate lay in their suggestion of inclusion to an exclusive First World reality.

Globalization from below

The global city literature and the literature on spectacular neoliberal urbanism both focus on particular kinds of global connections that work to maintain globally dispersed production processes: the networks of high finance, the nodes of global coordination, and the role of global city elites. Urban anthropological studies that use notions of the global city tend to examine similarly high-end spaces and people, often at the expense of less visible or less prominent connections and networks. However, less spectacular low-profile networks may have an equally strong influence on the configuration of urban landscapes and place-making in the global city, whether in the shadow of, or far away from, corporate headquarters and five-star hotels. Low-level traders, who work with relatively small quantities of goods, pay in cash, and personally transport their merchandise with them on the airplane, provide a good example of what can be called globalization from below.

Gordon Mathews (2007, 2011) examines how low-profile trade routes from sub-Saharan Africa to China, via Hong Kong, shape the urban landscape in one notorious Hong Kong site: Chungking Mansions (see Figure 7.4). On an average night during his research, this dilapidated building in Hong Kong's main tourist district housed some 4000 people, providing precious urban space to numerous cheap guesthouses, restaurants, and retail and wholesale businesses.

Mathews' ethnography introduces us to the range of people who found themselves attracted to Chungking Mansions. The building's units were mostly owned by Chinese, who often employed South Asian men as managers. The most important group of users consisted of African traders, who sought to buy cheap Chinese merchandise. In addition to the traders who frequented the building, it also attracted asylum seekers from South Asian and African countries and tourists from mainland China, Europe and the United States. 'Chungking Mansions serves as a world center for low-end globalization[:] … the transnational flow of people and goods involving relatively small amounts of capital and informal, sometimes quasi-legal or illegal transactions, commonly associated within the developing world' (Mathews 2007: 170).

These people had various reasons to seek out Chungking Mansions, reasons shaped by global, national and urban structures. On a global scale, Hong Kong functioned as a gateway to cheap manufacturing in China and its relatively lenient visa policy allowed easy entrance for people with, for example, sub-Saharan nationalities, who in many countries

Figure 7.4 Chungking Mansions, Hong Kong, 2013 (photograph by saiko3p via Shutterstock)

could not count on such easy entry. At the scale of the city, the fragmented ownership of the building had forestalled its sale, demolition and the redevelopment of the site, creating a cheap, yet decrepit island in an otherwise expensive urban landscape. Mathews points out that should any of these conditions change, this alternate global site might very well disappear or be significantly altered.

Mathews argues that Chungking Mansions offers an intimate portrait of globalization, since it exemplifies the intensification of global interconnectedness on a human scale. He uses the everyday interactions in Chungking Mansions to give us a sense of the interplay between anthropologist Arjun Appadurai's disjunctive global flows (see Box 7.1 on globalization). Chungking Mansions' social landscape is made up of a highly particular mixture of people from all over the world who were allotted specific places in Chungking Mansions' local hierarchies. This ethnoscape seems to spell out a deterritorialization of culture, a loosening of connections between particular cultural views, habits or preferences and particular places, as people perforce interact with a wide range of people from various elsewheres. However, mediascapes in the form of satellite TV allow for a reterritorialization of culture, as 'individuals from different societies are reinserted into their own societies through the mass media' (Mathews 2007: 180).

The African traders in Chungking Mansions and Cairo's migrant laborers, discussed at the start of this chapter, both demonstrate that the prominent global networks and flows discussed earlier are not the only ones to reconfigure cities around the world. Low-profile global connections and movements of people, money and goods may be as important in shaping urban landscapes North and South.

Conclusion

Cities have long been important nodes for long-distance trade and spatially dispersed economic activity. They have also served as important migrant destinations and have often harbored highly diverse populations. These long distance networks have significantly shaped urban life by intimately connecting parts of the urban landscape with places across the globe.

Globalization entails an intensification of such networks and flows. In a globalizing world, cities are increasingly important as crucial nodes in global networks. The concept of the global city has drawn attention to the increased importance of cities as producers of the global and has highlighted the consequences of this role. Anthropologists have studied how changes in the urban economy of global cities have impacted social inequalities. They have shown that such inequalities resonate with earlier colonial hierarchies, and have argued that these inequalities are translated in minute patterns of socio-spatial segregation in the urban landscape. Others have pointed out that 'the global city' has also become a political program in itself, with governments around the world striving to attract business and portray their country as modern and up to date by copying signpost features that are meant to signal global city status.

Global city formation and neoliberal programs of economic liberalization, structural adjustment and urban redevelopment have often caused growing inequalities. Anthropologists have found that, paradoxically, the clearest manifestations of that neoliberal era, its high-rises and glitzy malls, have contributed to a neoliberal hegemony, as even those excluded from such developments revel in the promises of the rejuvenated city up to date with global trends. However, it is not only through such prominent global networks or high-profile urban developments that globalization shapes city life. There are myriad low-profile connections and flows, made up of small-scale trade, migration, cash flows, cultural exchanges and religious networks, that similarly shape urban landscapes and lend them a worldly, cosmopolitan air quite different from that of the five-star hotel or spotlessly clean mall.

Discussion questions

1 Why has urban research taken on an important role in studies of globalization?
2 What is a transnational social field, and how do such fields impact urban landscapes? Can you identify the existence of such transnational social fields in your environment?
3 Why would Saskia Sassen's theories regarding the 'global city' be useful to urban anthropologists? Why are critiques of Sassen's work equally relevant for anthropologists?
4 Why would people who are by and large excluded from the benefits of neoliberal globalization still support neoliberal programs?
5 How is the study of 'globalization from below' distinct from many mainstream studies of globalization?

Further reading

Eade, John and Michael Peter Smith (2011) *Transnational Ties: Cities, Migrations, and Identities*. New Brunswick, NJ: Transaction Publishers.

Mathews, Gordon (2011) *Ghetto at the Center of the World: Chungking Mansions, Hong Kong*. Chicago, IL: Chicago University Press.

Sassen, Saskia (2005) The global city: Introducing a concept. *Brown Journal of World Affairs* 11(2): 27.

Smart, Alan and Josephine Smart (2003) Urbanization and the global perspective. *Annual Review of Anthropology* 32: 263–285.

Further viewing

Bread and Roses (2000), directed by Ken Loach. Feature film about the struggle of Latino migrant workers who work as cleaners in Los Angeles offices to unionize.

The Vanishing City (2009), directed and produced by Jen Senko and Fiore DeRosa. Documentary about the changing urban landscape of New York City, a global city par excellence, due to the dominance of the finance sector. Documents how subsidized luxury developments catering to the city's elites jeopardize the social fabric of neighborhoods.

Part III

Politics in and of the city

Chapter 8

Planning the city

This chapter examines the top-down structuring of the social life of cities through urban planning, and the way ordinary people engage with such top-down efforts to shape the city. Urban planning is a crucial form of managing urban populations and spaces. From the colonial to the postcolonial era, national and municipal governments have sought to realize their visions of an orderly, sanitary, modern or egalitarian society through planned interventions into urban space. An anthropological approach to urban planning focuses on the gap between envisioned utopias and actual everyday lives in these planned spaces. Such an approach contrasts the ideologies and socio-cultural prescriptions that characterize urban design with the ways in which residents subsequently appropriate and transform their new environments.

Historical anthropologists have studied how urban planning and design functioned as technologies of rule in *colonial cities*. In the first section of this chapter, we discuss how the racial segregation of neighborhoods and other planning interventions, for instance in the name of public health and sanitary reform, contributed to the legitimization and reproduction of colonial hierarchies. Anthropological studies of twentieth- and twenty-first-century cities have explored the often more progressive urban imaginations that inspire planning, and the social engineering such blueprints involve. These studies have sought to understand how such projects of the imagination work out on the ground, from the postcolonial *modernist utopias* of Brasília and Chandigarh to *post-war* and *post-disaster reconstruction* in cities such as Juba and New Orleans. Slum-upgrading projects present another common form of social engineering through urban planning, as they often try to remove the urban poor from central parts of the city, and uplift and civilize the urban poor through a makeover of informal living environments. Anthropological studies of urban planning often document how local populations engage with and rework such urban plans.

The final section of this chapter pays specific attention to recent anthropological discussions of *neoliberal urbanism*. It focuses on the everyday ways in which neoliberal plans and policies – favoring markets, privatization and the development of business-friendly, globally competitive urban environments – have transformed urban landscapes and produced new social cleavages. We discuss the emergence of the *entrepreneurial city* as a form of urban governance and the industries, images and infrastructures this has engendered.

Colonial cities, urban planning and sanitary reform

As Anthony King (2004: 82–83) argues, many urban landscapes bear the mark of colonization, war and conquest, processes that disrupt cities' existing demographic, socio-economic, cultural, architectural and spatial features. While these forces may destroy the 'old' city, they have more frequently led to a duplication of the city by building a 'modern' new center or quarter alongside it. Such modern aspirations also inspired many nineteenth- and twentieth-century governments to drastically redesign their capitals or other significant cities, following the latest imaginations and technologies of modernity. Downtown Cairo, for instance, was built in the late nineteenth century and modeled after Haussmann's Paris. The city plan with wide streets and the Parisian architecture signaled the ambitions of Egypt's ruler Khedive Ismail to create a modern city (see Figure 8.1). The same process might occur when revolutionary forces come into power and use the city to signal and enable their new aspirations, as was the case in Mao's Beijing.

All such interventions introduce a break in the urban texture and produce a resignification of the urban landscape, now divided between the old and the new, the traditional and the modern, and the indigenous and the foreign. The most studied example of this type of 'dual city' has been colonial cities. They tended to be marked by a strong degree of racial, social and spatial segregation, and their dualism was most evident in spatial arrangements that directly expressed relations of power.

Paul Rabinow's classic urban anthropological study *French Modern* (1989) was one of the first to examine modern urban planning in colonial contexts. Rabinow was inspired by Foucault's work on power (see Box 8.1). He argues that modern urban planning emerged in the early twentieth century in the context of French colonialism. Urban planning was

Figure 8.1 Downtown Cairo, 2009 (photograph by Hossam Fadl, courtesy Anouk de Koning)

Box 8.1 **Foucault on space and power**

The work of philosopher Michel Foucault (1926–1984) on power has exerted a strong influence on anthropological studies of urban planning. Foucault considered power to operate through particular regimes of truth: understandings of society that are held to be true in particular time and places. Such forms of power structure society through ideas about what is true and what is false, and what is normal and what is deviant.

Foucault saw space as important aspect of the operation of power. In line with Foucault's work on knowledge and power, the layout of colonial cities can be seen as instrumental in creating a particular understanding of the colonial situation. In many places, the distinction between the modern, European town and the traditional, native quarters contributed to the establishment of clear distinctions between colonial and colonized. It stipulated their place in the city and regulated contact. It also propagated a particular discourse about that colonial relation, portraying the colonial presence as a form of benign paternalism, bringing modernity and development to backward, stagnant societies.

In his influential study *Discipline and Punish* Foucault demonstrated the importance of space to the control and surveillance of individuals. The most famous example of such disciplinary spatial design is the Panopticon, devised by philosopher and reformer Bentham. The Panopticon consists of a tower with windows ringed by cells. The tower allows a supervisor to watch the adjacent cells without being himself being seen. Inmates are aware of the constant possibility of surveillance, but are not able to know when they are being observed. Foucault (1977: 201) argued that this induces 'in the inmate a state of conscious and permanent visibility that assures the automatic functioning of power'. Inmates behave as if they are being watched, even when the watchtower is empty.

Another example of disciplinary design is found in the replacement of Paris's crowded medieval streets by wide boulevards, in order to facilitate repressive action against the city's restive working classes (Harvey 2008). Haussmann's designs were copied in cities across the world, for instance in Cairo (Figure 8.1). In the twenty-first century, closed-circuit television (CCTV) cameras and other modes of surveillance proliferate in urban space, creating new levels of surveillance and control.

an integral part of the colonial project. It allowed for the establishment of military control, the regulation and separation of populations and activities and the establishment of a colonial order, both in a political and in an aesthetic sense. Colonial cities developed as hubs of colonial governance and colonial economic activity.

Colonial urban spaces represented not only a colonial dominance, but also a modernist aspiration that set these new urban spaces apart from what became imagined as the old, 'traditional' city. As King (2004) notes, such colonial spaces structured how encounters between colonizers and colonized, local and European culture, or 'tradition' and 'modernity' were understood. It was through modernist architecture that colonial government posited the European presence as civilized and modern, set against the traditional outlook of older parts of town (see also Chapter 2 and Box 8.1). They thereby shaped the aspirations of not only the colonial elites or servants, but also the local population, and especially the emergent middle classes.

Recent studies have questioned the extent to which colonial cities actually functioned according to imperial principles of duality in everyday life. These newer accounts emphasize the fluidity, hybridity and ambiguity of colonial urban landscapes. William Bissell, for instance, points to 'the incompleteness or intangibility of dual city projects' and 'the way that colonial aspirations to refashion space in a comprehensive manner across a huge swath of territory plunged colonial regimes into conundrums that they often could not comprehend, let alone resolve' (2011a: 226). Urban anthropologists and colonial studies scholars have focused on the tensions, anxieties and fragility of colonial relations and categories. Earlier approaches tended to create an overly simple and unidirectional understanding of colonial domination, but also privileged European actors, agency and views, at the expense of attention to indigenous agency, spatial practices and urban contestation. Newer studies, while still underlining the exploitation inherent in the colonial endeavor, have drawn our attention to 'in-between categories', such as mixed couples and mixed race subjects, or European inhabitants of native quarters (e.g., Yeoh 1996; Brown 2003).

Sanitary reform

A prominent concern within nineteenth-century colonial planning was sanitary reform. The sanitary reform movement emerged first in European and North American metropoles and was soon taken up in colonial cities. In cities such as Paris, Manchester and New York, rapid urbanization and industrialization had led to the growth of slum areas, where factory workers and their families lived in squalid, overcrowded conditions. Various epidemics, from cholera to typhoid, were especially deadly in these working-class areas. With advances in medical sciences that focused on the role of the environment in spreading disease, nineteenth-century governments and the wealthier classes began to view urban dirt and overcrowding as a public health threat, rather than as merely inconvenient or aesthetically unattractive. 'Contagionist' medical theories saw human contact as causing the spread of disease, while 'miasmatic' theories concentrated on the role of unhealthy locations characterized by 'foul air'. The understanding of disease as transmitted through place only shifted to focus on pathogens with the ascendance of microbiology and germ theory in the late nineteenth century. Informed by both contagionism and miasmatic theories, sanitary reformers tried to improve the living conditions of the urban poor. The movement was concerned with environmental factors, but also understood unsanitary and immoral behavior as causes of disease. Accordingly, their interventions involved a combination of infrastructural improvements, legal and administrative measures, and moral and educational strategies (Jaffe and Dürr 2010; Dürr and Jaffe 2014).

Such policies and practices aimed at improving public health through sanitary reform also proliferated in colonial cities. As in Europe and North America, these measures did not necessarily reflect an altruistic impulse; they were also driven by the economic imperative of maintaining a healthy urban workforce. In addition, colonial urban planning drew on fear of infectious disease to legitimize racial segregation (Goldberg 1993: 48). Colonial Indian cities, such as Madras, Bombay and Calcutta, were planned and developed in a broadly dualist fashion, with a 'White Town' dominated by colonial elites, and an indigenous 'Black Town'. Sanitary efforts concentrated on protecting White Towns from cholera and similar diseases, while the 'native' sections were depicted as inherently dirty and diseased (Prashad 1994). In many African cities, colonial authorities implemented a *cordon sanitaire* between indigenous and European sections of town, aimed primarily at preventing 'African' diseases from affecting Europeans. In general, colonial attempts to curtail disease and cleanse cities of filth were often discriminatory in nature, reinforcing existing social, racial and spatial hierarchies and power structures. As Anthony King (1990a: 55) notes, 'the culture and class-specific *perception* of health hazards more than the actual health hazards themselves was instrumental in determining much colonial, urban-planning policy'.

As Rivke Jaffe (2016) describes in a historical anthropological analysis, colonial anxieties over disease, race and morality were also evident in a moral panic that developed in the early twentieth century regarding the 'sanitary condition' of Willemstad, the capital of the Dutch Caribbean colony of Curaçao. Willemstad was a booming port town, but, as reports began to spread about rampant venereal disease spread by local prostitutes, the colonial authorities and local elites became concerned this would threaten the harbor's regional competitiveness. They feared that the reputation of the city's prostitutes as diseased and disorderly might cause foreign ships to avoid Willemstad. In 1911, the island's governor appointed a Sanitary Committee to investigate the matter, connecting prostitution and venereal disease to the city's broader sanitary conditions including urban public cleanliness (*stadsreiniging*). The committee's resulting report (Centrale Gezondheidsraad 1913) offered a combined analysis of issues of prostitution, waste disposal and housing conditions. The fact that these rather divergent issues were grouped together under the heading of 'sanitation' demonstrates the reformers' conflation of physical and moral pollution. These conflations were mapped most closely onto low-income areas and Afro-Curaçaoan female bodies.

The Sanitary Committee's findings and recommendations show the intersection of the governance of sexual health with colonial hierarchies. In their discussions of sex and sanitation, colonial officials repeatedly associated certain bodies and places with disease and dirt. Ignoring structural inequalities, they generally drew on narratives of vice and uncivilized behavior to explain the association between Afro-Curaçaoans and polluted low-income areas. Measures aimed at preventing sailors from visiting specific neighborhoods, where diseased women were thought to live and work, demonstrated beliefs in the pathogenic effects of place. Addressing problems surrounding solid waste and wastewater management, the committee expressed particular concern over waste produced by Afro-Curaçaoans, which they apparently saw as more polluting than that of Europeans. In their consideration of substandard housing in Willemstad, colonial officials stressed the importance of improving dark and dirty residences, connecting them to immoral behavior, from prostitution to violent crime. Again, such discourses and targeted interventions meant that impoverished Afro-Curaçaoans and low-income areas bore the brunt of stigmatization in terms of dirt, disease and vice. However, as a closer reading of colonial documents shows, both the prostitutes and the sailors who sought out their services were remarkably successful in evading or subverting sanitary reform measures, underlining the ambiguity of colonial plans when actually implemented.

Modernist utopias and visions of urban improvement

Urban planning tends to be driven by ideas of social and spatial improvement, which in turn often reflect specific ideological constructions of what a 'good city' or a 'good society' looks like. James Scott (1998) uses the term 'high modernism' to characterize attempts to achieve dramatic societal improvement through rational, scientific planning (see Box 8.2). Such attempts include the development of *new towns* such as Brasília or Khandigar,

Box 8.2 **James Scott and high modernism**

In his classic work *Seeing Like a State* (1998), James Scott describes and analyzes a number of large-scale utopian schemes developed by governments in order to organize, control and improve both society and the natural world. He sees these social-engineering schemes as stemming from what he calls a high-modernist ideology. This ideology is geared towards 'scientific and technical progress, the expansion of production, the growing satisfaction of human needs, the mastery of nature (including human nature), and, above all, the rational design of social order commensurate with the scientific understanding of natural laws' (Scott 1998: 4). Adherents of high modernism have a strong, uncritical faith in science and technology and the possibilities they offer for the comprehensive planning of complex social and ecological phenomena, from cities to agricultural production.

Within this ideology, modernity is equated with rational, intentional planning on the basis of supposedly universal scientific laws. High modernists believe that progress lies in the rational redesign of society and the natural environment. This 'sweeping, rational engineering of all aspects of social life' (Scott 1998: 88) tends to involve a strong aesthetic dimension, with scientific organization associated with a visual order characterized by symmetry, straight lines and standardized forms. This aesthetic dimension is highly evident in the urban layout and housing projects designed by utopian planners and architects such as Oscar Niemeyer and Le Corbusier.

Many high-modernist schemes have failed miserably, with catastrophic social and ecological effects. Scott gives the Soviet collectivization and Tanzanian villagization as examples, but also points to urban planning schemes in Brasília and Paris. He argues that these plans ultimately fail because their assumption of universal laws means they are not suited to local socio-cultural and ecological circumstances and because they ignore practical local knowledge, which he terms *metis*. In addition, he notes that plans to radically redesign the social order have been especially disastrous when they are developed and executed by authoritarian governments and when civil society has a limited capacity to resist.

in which utopian visions of ideal cities come out perhaps most clearly. The planners and architects who design these entirely new cities, and the governments that authorize them, often see their construction as an opportunity to address social ills such as inequality. Often these attempts do not live up to the high expectations of their initiators and planners.

The vision of an entirely new town continues to entice governments and planners: just in 2015 the Egyptian government launched a plan to build a new Egyptian capital some fifty kilometers from Cairo. On a less grand scale, utopian technocratic plans continue to pop up in post-conflict and post-disaster urban reconstruction efforts, and in urban development projects that seek to eradicate or improve informal settlements. In addition, high-modernist ideals are still evident in urban plans aimed at solving environmental and security problems through 'rational', technocratic interventions. Various governments have announced their intentions to create scientifically designed 'smart cities' and 'eco-towns' that will be safer, cleaner, greener, healthier and more energy efficient than any existing city. As with older examples of planning that aims to radically transform society, the actual implementation of these designs, and the livability of the cities that result from them may differ considerably from the initial vision.

New towns

New towns as planned utopias are largely a twentieth-century phenomenon. Following a model developed by the British urban planner Ebenezer Howard, the garden city movement resulted in the construction of several new towns, planned specifically to diminish the perceived ill effects of big city life on residents' physical and mental well-being. In the early to mid-twentieth century, garden cities such as Welwyn Garden City and Letchworth Garden City were built as smaller satellite towns near London and other large metropolises. Envisioned as self-contained communities separated from other urban areas by green belts, Howard argued that garden cities would combine the strengths of the city and the countryside. Concerned that urban residents were alienated from nature, and prefiguring later eco-towns, he developed a socio-ecological model of planning (Figure 8.2), hoping to develop towns that would restore the balance between humans and nature (see Fishman 1982).

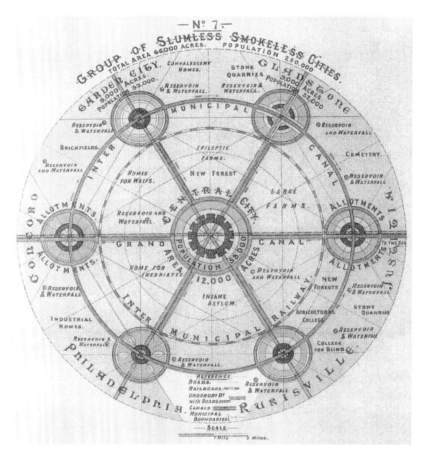

Figure 8.2 The Garden City concept by Ebenezer Howard, 1902

Towards the mid-twentieth century, even more ambitious urban plans were realized, as postcolonial nations from Australia and Brazil to Nigeria and India founded entirely new cities as national or state capitals, siting them on undeveloped land rather than redeveloping existing urban settlements. In various instances, the location of these new capitals was chosen symbolically to contest the colonial origin and function of previous urban centers. The new Brazilian capital of Brasília, for instance, was planned on an empty plateau exactly in the center of the country, representing a clean slate on which to develop a new and improved Brazil. The utopian visions of individual architects were often highly influential in the planning of these new cities. For instance, the Swiss modernist architect Le Corbusier was responsible for designing Chandigarh, founded in 1953 as the capital of Haryana, a new Indian state formed after the partition of Pakistan from India. Le Corbusier's vision of modernist urban planning and architecture was also influential in the construction of the Parisian *banlieues* (see below).

James Holston (1989) has studied the case of Brasília, built in the late 1950s following the designs of the architect Oscar Niemeyer and the urban planner Lucio Costa. Niemeyer and Costa, Brazilians who were strongly influenced by the modernist urbanism of European architects such as Le Corbusier, sought to create a city that was in everything the opposite of the colonial capital of Rio de Janeiro, with its class divisions, capitalist exploitation and polluted *favelas*. Their ideal drew on ideas of the city as a machine, a rational, technologically driven vehicle for social change. This machine metaphor and the modernist aesthetic of speed were evident in Brasília's layout, which from the sky resembles an airplane. Following modernist principles, the city was divided functionally, with residential neighborhoods, shopping areas and government districts all zoned separately. The housing developments were designed in a uniform manner as 'superblocks' rather than as houses on streets. Niemeyer expected this design to promote collectivism and do away with distinctions between poorer and wealthier residents. Buildings themselves were glass-and-concrete structures, bordering highways without sidewalks – architectural strategies intended to undo public–private divides.

Holston shows how residents experienced the city that grew out of these optimistic plans. Despite the desire to do away with unplanned low-income settlements, the original plans had not included accommodations for the construction workers who built the city in less than four years, and these workers ended up developing informal areas outside the borders of the formal airplane plan. The attempts to produce a collectivist, classless society by abolishing public–private divides also backfired. The absence of pedestrian-friendly streets, plazas and other public spaces translated into the 'death of the street', which residents experienced as a lack of human warmth and more broadly civic life.

Post-conflict and post-disaster reconstruction

The utopian impulse to radically improve cities through planning is a persistent one, and is now perhaps most evident in large-scale post-conflict and post-disaster urban reconstruction efforts. When cities suffer severe damage from natural disasters or wars, urban and national governments often seek to 'build back better', to borrow the Indonesian government's slogan for its reconstruction efforts following the December 2004 Indian Ocean tsunami.

Urban warfare often results in widespread destruction of a city's infrastructure and housing, while also severely affecting intra-urban social relations, especially in the context of ethnic conflict. In many cases, post-war urban reconstruction also goes hand in hand with state-building. As examples of cities such as Sarajevo, Beirut or Baghdad show, the reconstruction of built structures is generally more straightforward than the more intricate task of mending the urban social fabric or building political legitimacy. However, these infrastructural, social and political processes tend to be entangled, and those groups that emerge as dominant in the aftermath of the conflict often use planning as a way to legitimize and consolidate their position. The tensions that this produces has also led scholars to reconsider the term 'post-conflict', as it is often difficult to determine when exactly conflict ends.

Working in Juba, the capital of the post-conflict state of South Sudan, Naseem Badiey (2014) shows how disputes over urban development and land rights represent the state-building strategies of different groups of actors. Different visions of citizenship, rights and authority within the new state played out in negotiations over urban territory, land and property. The state of South Sudan was formed in 2011, following a decades-long civil war between the Sudanese government and the Southern rebel army, Sudan People's Liberation Movement (SPLM). Despite ambitious plans funded by international donors, the reconstruction of Juba was impeded by disputes over land and housing. Badiey argues that externally driven urban planning was unsuccessful because donors did not understand the complex dynamics, agendas and interests at stake in local land politics: 'the agents of reconstruction tasked with rebuilding imagined a town that was a "blank slate" waiting to be filled by the technological ideas of planners' (2014: 126). Political elites, long-time Juba residents, ex-combatants, internally displaced persons and returning refugees all sought to assert their claims to urban land and housing. These different groups articulated their claims to urban resources by appealing to customary ethnic land rights, their military contribution to the liberation movement or the suffering they had endured as refugees. These different types of claims evidenced different conceptualizations of citizenship rights within the new state.

Urban reconstruction efforts following disasters such as earthquakes, hurricanes or tsunamis share some of the tensions inherent in post-conflict reconstruction. Often, much of a city's infrastructure and housing stock is destroyed, and national or local governments and elites seek to use the opportunity of rebuilding to further their own interests. In some cases, the desire to build back an improved city may rely on preventing residents considered undesirable – often the urban poor and ethno-racial minorities – from returning to their homes. In addition, foreign governments and humanitarian NGOs often offer reconstruction aid that may be more geared towards audiences 'at home' than towards the actual needs of disaster victims. In the end, local people are often the main actors in remaking everyday urban life after a disaster, in a process that goes far beyond physical reconstruction and that has no definite end (Samuels 2010).

The rebuilding of New Orleans following Hurricane Katrina in 2005 is a good example of a city where post-disaster planning aggravated existing inequalities. Reconstruction programs run by private contractors redeveloped important parts of the city to cater to tourists and higher-income gentrifiers, while doing little to help displaced low-income African-American residents return. After two recovery plans had been critiqued for their lack of public participation, a 'participatory planning' program was established that was supposed to function as a model of shared governance, involving residents of the low-income neighborhoods affected most dramatically by the hurricane and including their visions for reconstruction.

As Roberto Barrios (2011) shows in his ethnography of post-Katrina planning, the original residents defined urban recovery in terms of re-establishing neighborly social networks and local forms of sociality, such as funeral parades and informal socializing in bars and on the streets. For them, attempts to restore the neighborhood's pre-hurricane social fabric meant rebuilding affordable rental housing so that displaced low-income tenants could return. However, the professional planners involved in this process wielded expert knowledge to instruct residents on what recovery 'really' involved, prioritizing capital over community and espousing a model of urban recovery that emphasized economic revitalization through private investment. Consequently, participatory planning worked largely as 'a pedagogical instrument for reeducating participants in neoliberal modalities of citizenship' (Barrios 2010: 8).

The 'problem' of informal settlements

Cities across the world have informal settlements where poorer, marginalized residents have made their homes. What these areas – variably called shantytowns, slums, *bidonvilles*, *favelas*, *gecekondus* or *'ashwiyyat* – have in common is that dwellings tend to be built without official titles or permits, or without regular connections to utilities like electricity or water. These informal settlements often provide one of the few options for urban dwelling to those who cannot afford formal, legal housing.

Many urban governments perceive such informal settlements as unsanitary and dangerous areas – in short, as problems. They may attempt to remove or improve them in order to improve the living conditions in deprived neighborhoods and offer their inhabitants a fairer share of urban resources. Such attempts may also aim at presenting the image of a clean, rational city inhabited by civilized and modern citizens, to compete as a city for business and visitors in a global market.

The now infamous housing estates in the French *banlieues*, built in the 1960s, were meant as improvements to the substandard housing of Parisian workers. They came to replace the *bidonvilles* or shantytowns that had sprung up around French cities to house migrant workers from Southern Europe and North Africa (Epstein 2011: 36–38). These shantytowns were considered health and security hazards, with inhuman living conditions, and were known as 'the shame of our cities'. They gave way to ambitious large state housing projects, *grands ensembles*, inspired by Le Corbusier's high-modernist vision of cities made up of skyscrapers set in green surroundings. These estates were to house a mix of working-class and middle-class residents. Before shantytown dwellers were relocated into regular housing, they were moved into *cités de transit*, transitory cities, where they would be educated about the requirements of 'modern living'. However, a mere decade later the *grands ensembles* design was abandoned; the *grands ensembles* were increasingly seen as an ultimate planning failure on account of their inhuman scale (Epstein 2011: 38, 55).

The more recent slum clearance projects are often part of neoliberal urban development schemes that try to make the city a safer and more attractive place for wealthier residents and global business. They frequently incorporate neoliberal development ideas that see the formalization of informal housing arrangements as a way to help poor people out of poverty. These ideas were championed by Hernando de Soto, who argued that providing poor people with secure housing tenure would allow them to qualify for loans, which in turn would allow them to develop or expand their entrepreneurial activities (De Soto

Figure 8.3 Jacarezinho *favela* in Recife, Brazil, 2004 (photograph by Martijn Koster)

2000; Rao 2013). Even as slum upgrading programs emphasize neoliberal ideas regarding individual responsibility and empowerment (rather than the collectivist ideas of Le Corbusier or Niemeyer), many continue to rely on modernist forms of planning.

Slum clearance programs may be executed in a harsh or even violent manner, with bulldozers destroying existing housing after inhabitants have been given short notice of their eviction. If alternative housing is provided, resettlement areas are often located in peripheral areas, and disadvantage former inhabitants whose livelihoods often depend on economic activities in the city center. In recent years, 'slum clearance' has tended to take the somewhat more benevolent shape of 'slum upgrading', which often involves a participatory approach, such as the one described in the case of Recife by Monique Nuijten et al. (2012).

The leftist government in Recife, Brazil, employed a participatory approach that sought to involve inhabitants in slum upgrading programs. In particular, these programs targeted *favelas* built on the city's riverbanks, where construction could cause flooding and presented health hazards. These areas were characterized by *palafitas*, barracks on stilts in the water (see Figure 8.3). The municipality sought to remove the *palafitas*, which they saw as symbols of poverty, and to project a more modern image.

The participatory approach did not lead the government to adjust their plans to the needs and aspirations of the targeted group – the fundamentals were clearly not open for discussion. Rather, echoing the case of participatory planning described above for post-Katrina New Orleans, the process was instrumental in having the inhabitants go along with the existing plans. *Favela* residents expressed limited opposition, believing that removal was unavoidable. In addition, the modernist aesthetics of the plan resonated with and fed the aspirations of the people who were to be rehoused in due time: 'The vision

Figure 8.4 New Prometropole housing project in Jacarezinho, Recife, Brazil, 2008 (photograph by Monique Nuijten)

of straight roads, canals and quaysides, and clean concrete houses, generated among slum dwellers strong aspirations for a better future and for social inclusion as citizens' (Nuijten et al. 2011a: 164) (see Figure 8.4).

However, the new housing project turned out a disappointment to many. The new houses were smaller than many of the riverside shacks that people had left behind. The lack of backyards, which had functioned as crucial extensions of the domestic space, meant that living conditions were even more cramped. The new spatial order left no room for the informal economic activities crucial to residents' livelihoods: there was little room for pushcarts, laundry and livestock; informal recycling, an important source of income for many, was forbidden. The regularization of utilities also meant that inhabitants had to pay for the water and electricity they had previously tapped illegally.

Some of the families never moved into the new houses, but chose to settle in informal areas elsewhere. Some rented out their new houses, while others sold off whatever they could, from the iron staircases to the washbasins. Those who stayed started transforming their houses, appropriating space adjacent to their houses by building porches or high walls. In a short period of time, little was recognizable of the modernist design of public space, with its neat, open spaces. As Nuijten et al. (2012: 165) note, 'In the view of the [project] representatives, the do-it-yourself (de)constructions changing the carefully designed model of the architects were turning the estate into a slum – for which they blamed the low moral values and cultural backwardness of the residents'.

The imposition of a modernist spatial order failed because it did little to address pressing problems related to unemployment, discrimination and violence. Nuijten et al. argue that such slum upgrading projects implicitly attempt to civilize the poor through changing their living environs, hoping to turn them into good citizens by creating a modern, healthy and civilized setting. However,

> instead of looking at what the poor need, [such projects] demand that they integrate into mainstream society and follow middle class norms of how to behave and use space – but without the jobs, money and other attributes for maintaining such a lifestyle.
>
> (2012: 166)

Such mismatches are thus built into the core of many slum upgrading projects, from Recife to Cairo (Ghannam 2002) and Delhi (Rao 2013); they often seem doomed to fail both their initiators and planners, and the people whose lives they seek to improve.

Neoliberal urbanism

As we discussed in Chapter 5, neoliberal ideologies have transformed states, economies and societies in the global North and in the global South. Visions of the good or desirable city and models for urban planning have shifted accordingly. Infrastructure is one of the domains in which this shift becomes apparent, with neoliberal attempts to privatize what used to be public amenities, like roads and water and electricity networks. The notion of the entrepreneurial city, discussed in the subsequent section, is another manifestation of the influence of neoliberal visions.

Urban infrastructure and neoliberalization

Infrastructure is an important determinant of city life and a crucial aspect of urban planning. It shapes how people relate to the city and each other. It regulates who has access to which basic services or forms of transport, whether people will choose to commute by car, bike or take the bus (see Chapter 3 on mobilities). It also shapes, as shown in our discussion of post-Soviet heat, below, whether people can be treated as individual consumers or only as part of a collective. Distinct assumptions and visions inform particular infrastructural designs, which distribute space, resources and amenities in specific ways, and may engender or mitigate urban inequalities.

Infrastructure can provide a particularly incisive window into how changing political regimes impact the design of urban landscapes, for example in the shift from welfare state to neoliberal regime. In their discussion of *splintering urbanism*, geographers Steve Graham and Simon Marvin (2001) point out that earlier forms of 'infrastructural modernity', with state provision of basic amenities to an entire population for a common, low price, were questioned in the context of neoliberal reforms. They argue that neoliberalism has led to the splintering of that infrastructure, resulting in important changes in the urban landscape and new forms of inclusion and exclusion.

Stephen Collier (2011) studied attempts to reform the collective heating system in post-Soviet Russia. In the Soviet Union, infrastructural modernity had an especially collectivist bend. Large boiler systems provided a number of companies and tens of thousands of inhabitants with heat according to externally set norms that were estimated to represent the needs of households. Heat streamed through kilometers of pipelines into tens of thousands of radiators without individual controls, warming all households equally according to those normed needs. The heating system linked companies to households and households to each other. As Collier (2011: 208) puts it, 'the heat apparatus "bundled" the Soviet social, not only linking the production, distribution, and consumption of heat in a common regulatory regime but also binding together the industrial enterprises, social welfare systems, and material conditions of habitation'.

Despite decades of neoliberal reforms in all domains of social life, little changed in the design and functioning of heating infrastructure. The particular features of the Soviet heating system made a shift to more individual consumption and pricing near impossible. Reform programs faced a major issue: 'How could heat systems be reengineered to transform subjects of need into sovereign consumers who suffer the costs and enjoy the benefits of the choices that they make?' (Collier 2011: 236). The answer was: largely no, these systems could not be reengineered. Despite some experiments with microeconomic incentives, heat continues to be provided through the collectivist logic of 'need' rather than the ability to consume. Thus, while infrastructures can bring about significant changes to the urban fabric and inaugurate new forms of inequalities, they also present a form of material thickness that cannot easily be changed to fit new ideological visions and power relations. Various historical layers of infrastructure perpetuate earlier economic, social and spatial arrangements, which entwine with new attempts to shape society through infrastructural plans.

The entrepreneurial city in the global economy

As we have argued in the previous chapters, cities must be understood in relation to their transnational connections, from global commodity chains to migrant labor. With the globalization of national economies, cities emerged as important hubs within the global economy (see Chapter 7). This prominence has also been linked to the rise of the entrepreneurial city, in which municipal authorities take on a new role as important economic actors. From around the 1970s, many city governments began to redefine their role as less about providing public goods and services to residents, and more about encouraging economic growth, development and employment.

Geographer David Harvey (1989) describes this shift in governance as a move from managerialism to entrepreneurialism, with municipal authorities placing increasing emphasis on efficiency, competitiveness and risk-taking. Urban entrepreneurialism is associated with inter-urban competition, as city governments compete nationally and globally with other cities for investors, tourists and wealthy residents. In the entrepreneurial city, the public sector behaves increasingly like the private sector: 'the city is no different from the corporation that must engage in image-building activities, promote its products, and be prepared to deal with change if it wants to maintain its competitive edge and grow its market share' (Spirou 2011: 47).

This entrepreneurialism and competition is evident in the city branding strategies that have become popular around the world. Urban planning increasingly involves thinking about place marketing: what interventions and investments in a city's image or infrastructure will help the economy grow? What strategies will help a city achieve the status of a 'global city'? Local governments employ marketing consultants to help them develop a unique image or brand that will help them 'sell' the city globally. In seeking to construct new urban identities that will turn their city into a 'world-class destination', they rely on slogans or signature architecture. Well-known examples of city marketing slogans include 'I♥NY', 'What Happens in Vegas, Stays in Vegas' or 'Hong Kong. Live It, Love It!' The Burj Khalifa in Dubai and the Centre Pompidou in Paris are examples of spectacular architectural projects aimed at raising the city's international profile (see Chapter 2 on the role of 'starchitects' in place-making).

The importance of urban image also points to the changing character of urban economies, as post-industrial cities have turned to the 'symbolic economy' (see Chapter 5). The pressure for cities to be globally competitive has not only changed the mode of urban governance, it has also changed the urban built environment and demographic make-up. Urbanization is increasingly oriented towards consumption and towards those residents and visitors who have sufficient means to be consumers (see Chapter 6). These processes, often associated with urban neoliberalism, tend to devalue or displace those whose skills or qualifications do not match up with the demands of currently dominant industries.

In Dubai, the entrepreneurial city model, with its embrace of urban image at the expense of residents' needs, has been taken to its extreme. Following the lead of neighboring cities like Kuwait and Jeddah, the ruler of the Maktoum dynasty decided to invite starchitects in an effort to position Dubai as a city at the cutting edge of global and urban modernity. The exclusivity that starchitects emanate is fed by a myth of exceptional architectural genius. As Ahmed Kanna (2011) argues, this myth helps to evade questions of politics. The authority of the architect bolsters the authority of the ruling elite, while the landmark buildings they jointly author become testimony to the stature of both starchitect and rulers. While drawing on a language of local culture and sustainability, the alliance of starchitects with the local ruling elite enables an exclusive focus on aesthetic concerns and the neglect of the

Figure 8.5 Dubai as construction site (photograph courtesy Shutterstock)

Figure 8.6 Construction workers playing cards in a labor camp near Dubai, 2006 (photograph by Rob Crandall via Shutterstock)

existing social fabric – it allows architects to imagine a clean slate that permits untrammeled architectural play (see Figure 8.5).

Concerns about whom the buildings will serve, whom they might displace and who will be exploited in the process of building them need not be asked, even though these are highly relevant questions in the context of an autocratic Dubai where large numbers of migrant laborers, mostly from Asia, work with few legal protections and no citizenship rights (see Figure 8.6). Kanna (2011: 80) concludes that

> A narrow focus on architecture as the exclusive concern with experimentation in aesthetic form becomes a means of collaborating in the erasure of local histories and reaffirmation of the claims local elites make on the politics, histories and spaces they already dominate.

Conclusion

Urban planning has often been used to express political claims or ideals, as was the case in the colonial sections of many cities within former European empires. These sections were meant to express European rule and dominance, as well as civilizational superiority or modernity. The new colonial spaces also changed the ways in which residents perceived and used what became the 'old town'. Modernist urban planning of the twentieth and twenty-first centuries was often informed by more progressive ideals, although large-scale plans to undo colonial structures and eradicate inequality were rarely entirely successful. In the first decades of the twenty-first century, urban designs are still made to carry particular political messages, but in the context of neoliberal urbanism they are increasingly geared toward the creation of urban assets that will help the entrepreneurial city in the global competition for business and visitors.

Urban planning can underline and exacerbate urban inequalities, but it also has the potential to combat them. Understanding the rationale and effects of urban planning involves attending to whose interests are taken into account. Who can influence the design and implementation of the plan? In whose image and to whose benefit is the city remade? Such plans affect the right to the city of different groups of people (see Box 9.1), impacting people's livelihoods, and involving different forms of spatially mediated inclusion and exclusion.

Anthropological studies of planning have often highlighted the mismatch between lofty, rational and modernist plans and the actual demands of people's daily lives. Urban plans often intend to change the prospective inhabitants or users of space, rather adapting to their needs and wishes. The divergence between such utopian visions and the realities of urban life on the margins is one of the reasons that many slum eradication and upgrading projects run into difficulties. Perhaps the most important contribution of urban anthropology to debates on urban planning has been this attention to the limits of the plan. Abstract urban plans may well be appropriated and subverted by the same people that these plans tried to reform.

Discussion questions

1   How do divisions in the urban landscape, for instance in the colonial city, influence the way people see themselves?
2   What parallels and differences do you recognize between colonial urban planning, high-modernist new towns and neoliberal slum upgrading?
3   If so many utopian urban plans fail, why do you think governments keep developing new ones?
4   Why is it that some urban reconstruction programs reproduce and aggravate social inequalities?
5   Can you recognize the effects of neoliberal urbanism in a city you know well?

Further reading

Bissell, William Cunningham (2011) *Urban Design, Chaos and Colonial Power in Zanzibar.* Bloomington, IN: Indiana University Press.

Holston, James (1989) *The Modernist City: An Anthropological Critique of Brasília.* Chicago, IL: University of Chicago Press.

Larkin, Brian (2013) The politics and poetics of infrastructure. *Annual Review of Anthropology* 42: 327–343.

Nuijten, Monique and Martijn Koster, eds. (forthcoming) Close encounters: Ethnographies of the coproduction of space by the urban poor. Special issue of the *Singapore Journal of Tropical Geography.*

Rabinow, Paul (1989) *French Modern: Norms and Forms of the Social Environment.* Chicago, IL: University of Chicago Press.

Further viewing

I Am Gurgaon: The New Urban India (2009), directed by Marije Meerman. Documentary on Gurgaon, a satellite city of New Delhi with 1.4 million inhabitants, which became a symbol of India's unparalleled economic growth.

If God is Willing and da Creek Don't Rise (2010), directed by Spike Lee. Documentary about New Orleans' rebuilding efforts in the aftermath of Hurricane Katrina.

The Pruitt-Igoe Myth (2011), directed by Chad Freidrichs. Documentary that tells the story of the transformation of the American city in the decades after the Second World War, through the lens of the infamous Pruitt-Igoe housing development. Pruitt-Igoe was a large public housing complex built in the 1950s to replace run-down neighborhoods with modern, public housing, only to be demolished in 1972.

Treme (2010–2013), created by David Simon and Eric Overmyer. Drama series about how New Orleans residents try to rebuild their lives, their homes and their unique culture in the aftermath of 2005 Hurricane Katrina.

Chapter 9

Cities, citizenship and politics

Cities, and capital cities in particular, are often extremely important political arenas and sites for the expression and experience of citizenship. Recent anthropological work on citizenship has emphasized the role of cities in shaping political communities and facilitating particularly urban forms of citizenship. In addition, various ethnographic studies have examined the unequal distribution of rights among members of a political community. This *differentiated citizenship* means that formally equal citizens are treated very differently in practice. Contestations of this inequality have been studied under the rubric of 'insurgent citizenship'. Both differentiated citizenship and insurgent citizenship have been especially visible in urban contexts.

In addition to this focus on citizenship, anthropologists have studied urban politics from a number of different angles. *Electoral politics* offer one way of incorporating city dwellers into the formal political system, through a range of mechanisms, such as clientelism or party politics based on class and ethnicity. However, more anthropological attention has gone out to urban politics beyond the electoral system, focusing on other modes of political engagement and contestation, in both democratic and authoritarian political regimes. This chapter places specific emphasis on less formal politics, discussing the *quiet encroachment* of the urban poor as an important type of informal politics. In addition, it shows the importance of more explicitly *political movements*, from the grass roots movements that emerge in inner cities and on the urban fringes, to cross-class social movements that mobilize around environmental issues or sexual rights.

In all these forms of politics, *public space* plays an important role. The strongly scripted and collective character of public space lends it its political character, and facilitates its functioning as a political forum. This chapter discusses this role in relation to different forms of political mobilization, with special attention to the recent, spectacular resurgence of urban-based movements and politics as evidenced in the Occupy movements and the massive uprisings in the Arab world.

Cities and citizenship

Although, historically, citizenship was tied to membership of the city, in the context of nineteenth-century and twentieth-century nation-building, citizenship has come to denote political membership of a nation-state. However, the city remains a key location for citizenship, 'whether it is viewed as a stage for national citizenship, or as a political community in its own right' (Lazar 2014: 67; cf. Holston and Appadurai 1999). Sociologist

T.H. Marshall's definition of citizenship (1950) has become the classical starting point for many discussions of citizenship. He defined citizenship as membership in a political community, a status that endows members with a particular set of rights and duties.

One of the main questions of citizenship is whom to include and whom to exclude as a member. This question can become particularly pertinent in cities, since they are often strongly embedded in transnational networks. They typically attract relatively large numbers of immigrants and their economies are often based on transnational economic networks, challenging the idea of political communities based primarily on the nation-state. As James Holston and Arjun Appadurai (1999: 10–13) point out, this raises the question of whether to grant rights to productive non-citizen urban residents, and produces new hybrid legal regimes that accommodate transnational networks.

Appadurai and Holston (1999: 4) make a useful distinction between formal and substantive citizenship, with formal citizenship defined as legal membership status, and substantive citizenship referring to 'the array of civil, political, socioeconomic, and cultural rights people possess and exercise'. They point out that 'although in theory full access to rights depends on membership, in practice that which constitutes citizenship substantively is often independent of its formal status' (ibid.). This may be the case because, despite formal equality among citizens, citizens enjoy very different rights within a nation according to their raced, classed, gendered or religious positioning. Conversely, non-citizen residents may enjoy many of the socio-economic and civil rights that formal citizens enjoy, often with the exception of the right to vote in national elections. The frictions between formal and substantive forms give rise to heated contestations about citizenship.

Differentiated and insurgent citizenship

One such contestation has been in the context of differentiated citizenship, the differential treatment of groups (by both the state and other citizens) of formally equal members of a political community. Political philosophers such as Iris Marion Young and Will Kymlicka have discussed differentiated citizenship as a way of recognizing that while citizenship implies a form of universalism, in practice it often entails dominant models and visions. These models implicitly discriminate against those who hold different beliefs and do not fit the dominant understanding of citizenship, for example women and ethnic minorities (Leydet 2014). These authors see differentiated citizenship – giving some sections of the larger political community different rights from others – as an approach that can contribute to righting historically developed wrongs.

In contrast, anthropologists, most prominently James Holston, have approached differentiated citizenship as precisely the outcome of historically entrenched inequalities. Holston (2008) documents the existence and contestation of citizenship regimes that distribute rights differentially among various categories of citizens. Such differentiation may be enshrined in law in the form of different categories of citizens, or it may be part of less formal, substantive elaborations of citizenship that discriminate against particular categories of citizens in everyday life.

Li Zhang (2002) discusses a striking case of such differentiated citizenship, and its contestation, in Beijing in the 1990s. The Chinese *hukou* system, a spatially differentiated system of household registration, registered people at birth as either rural or urban residents. This rural or urban status could not be changed, even if people did migrate from the countryside to urban areas. Urban residency status entitled people to a range of rights and entitlements, such as subsidized housing, free education for their children and medical care. The differentiated *hukou* system was meant to block rural-to-urban migration and to ensure that China's cities would not grow too rapidly. However, in the context of China's economic reforms, controls on people's movement were relaxed. In combination with strong economic growth in urban areas, this led to large-scale migration from the countryside to urban areas, which provided more opportunities than the meagre subsistence the countryside offered. This resulted in a sizable 'floating population' of urban residents with a rural *hukou*. Despite their urban presence and their contribution to the urban economy, these rural migrants were denied formal membership and a place in the city. Official discourses criminalized this floating population and portrayed the new residents as dangerous and a source of pollution.

Some migrants had developed into successful traders with transnational connections who earned incomes many times higher than the average city resident. Despite their success, as rural migrants, they had no right to housing and could be expelled when the authorities saw fit, while their children were denied access to education. Zhang describes various ways in which migrants created lives for themselves on the margins of this urban system, which resemble what Bayat describes as silent encroachment (see below). For example, migrants with more resources leased land from farmers to build their own housing on the outskirts of Beijing and other major cities like Guangzhou. These areas developed into 'urban villages', informally built, densely populated quarters that house thousands of migrant workers, yet are not recognized as part of the city and retain their rural status (see Figure 9.1).

Figure 9.1 Urban village in Guangzhou, China, 2006 (photograph by Ivo Bol)

In the Beijing case described by Zhang, the authorities eventually decided to get rid of an urban village that had grown into a community of some 40,000 migrants, demolishing their houses and expelling them from the city. The lack of urban citizenship eventually trumped the economic power of some segments of the migrant population, and the coalitions they had forged with farmers and urban residents. Zhang (2002: 320–321) concludes that:

> the social exclusion justified by urban citizenship has not diminished in the era of reform and mobility; what has changed is the specific forms of exclusion: Before, [those with a rural *hukou* status] were barred from the city physically: Today, even though they are allowed to leave their villages to conduct business in the city, they are kept as a disfranchised group by a state that merely tolerates their presence and denies them fundamental rights to permanent housing and use of urban space.

While in this Chinese case, differentiated citizenship was anchored in legal distinctions between categories of urban and rural citizens, differentiated citizenship may also exist without such clear categorical distinctions. James Holston's discussion of insurgent citizenship starts from a discussion of Brazil's differentiated citizenship regime, which 'uses social differences that are *not* the basis of national membership – primarily differences in education, property, race, gender and occupation – to distribute different treatment to different categories of citizens' (2008: 7).

A clear example of such discrimination was the historical restriction of political voting rights to propertied or educated citizens. Inclusion and exclusion from national membership were not central issues at the founding of the Brazilian republic. Echoing existing sharp colonial inequalities in wealth and status, it was the differentiation of various categories of citizenship that became the organizing principle, rather than inclusion and exclusion per se. This differentiated citizenship disenfranchised large swathes of Brazil's population, and absolved the state from the responsibility to redistribute wealth and provide basic services to its marginalized citizens.

In this context, marginalized Brazilians had little choice but to resort to the informal construction of housing and self-provision of basic services. Holston argues that the self-built or 'auto-constructed' areas that these disenfranchised citizens constructed on the outskirts of cities such as São Paulo provided the grounds for formulations of new claims, based on urban citizenship. What Holston terms 'insurgent citizenship' had its roots in voluntary associations, through which residents of the self-constructed peripheries demanded the regularization of their property and the delivery of basic urban services, as citizens claiming rights to the city (2009: 257).

These rights claims expanded beyond these initial efforts, eventually resulting in an expanded vision of social and economic citizenship that included social and economic rights, such as the right to health care, legal title or education, and fostered a democratic imagination that stressed social justice and equality. Beyond the gradual growth of insurgent citizenship on the urban periphery, these new conceptions of rights also became manifest in protests and demonstrations, and even in violent uprisings, in Brazilian cities in the early twenty-first century.

Even in countries where there are formal mechanisms in place to ensure that all citizens are treated equally, forms of differentiated citizenship may persist. Institutional policies and practices, notably those of the police, may discriminate against specific categories of citizens to the extent that this leads to an everyday reality of differentiated citizenship, as is the case in Europe and the United States with respect to racialized minorities (see Chapter 10). This came out clearly in 2014, with a number of highly controversial police killings of African-American men in US cities, including the fatal shooting of 18-year-old Michael Brown in Ferguson, Missouri, by a White police officer who was not indicted.

Formal and informal politics

As in the informal economy debate, many anthropological studies of politics have focused on the relations between forms of politics that are directly related to the state – such as electoral politics – and those that take place in a realm in which state laws and actors play a less important role. Just as with the discussion on formality/informality in the urban economy (see Chapter 5), we find that these spheres are also difficult to separate in urban politics. Elected politicians and formal state bureaucracies may rely on personal connections and informal or extra-legal practices to run the city. Similarly, city residents may actively seek to 'informalize' formal electoral politics in a range of ways, for instance by establishing personal relationships with political candidates and seeking to trade votes for favors. In addition, non-state organizations – such as trade unions, churches, NGOs, social movements or mafias – are often important urban political actors, and they may operate in a state-like fashion, as semi-legitimate forms of authority that rely on institutionalized procedures (de Koning et al. 2015).

One way of considering the relationship urban residents have to the municipal or national government is through the concept of 'mediated citizenship', where non-state actors function as brokers between citizens and the state (von Lieres and Piper 2014). In many cases, political parties, trade unions, religious organizations, neighborhood associations or even gangs act as intermediaries in state-citizen relations. These often collectivist non-state associations challenge liberal ideas of citizenship as a direct relationship between individual citizens and the nation-state. They show, instead, how people often relate to the state in more collective ways and via local, urban affiliations (Lazar 2008).

In many cases, specific, charismatic individuals within these mediating associations take on the role of brokers. Thomas Blom Hansen and Oskar Verkaaik (2009: 16) describe these figures as urban specialists,

> individuals who by virtue of their reputation, skills and imputed connections provide services, connectivity and knowledge to ordinary dwellers in slums and popular neighbourhoods. ... These figures are supposed to be in the know, supposed to have access to resources and knowledge that are not readily available to ordinary people. The magicality of these connections derives from their extra-local connections to centers of power.

These power brokers help the urban poor access state services and the political system, while also making these populations more legible and controllable to politicians. This intermediary position, Hansen and Verkaaik suggest, complicates clear-cut oppositions between governing powers and those who are governed.

These brokers who shape the connection between citizens and the state form part of what postcolonial theorist Partha Chatterjee calls 'political society'. According to Chatterjee (2004), 'civil society' is a bourgeois, Euro-American realm that has never been dominant in postcolonial countries. He argues that, while in Western Europe or North

America a majority of citizens may feel represented by the nation-state and be able to assert their rights by referring to the law, in countries such as India, only the wealthier classes can take part in civil society. Most of the world's populations, Chatterjee contends, are not so much citizens with rights, but 'governed populations' who can only take part in political society: the realm of everyday politics and rule-bending run by patrons, brokers, religious leaders and others who can mediate access to the state. While these populations cannot make rights claims, their successful negotiation of recognition and services does reflect their political agency. Below, we first discuss how electoral politics play out in the city, before we move on to discuss the less evident forms of politics that are part of the day-to-day practices of urban residents.

Electoral politics

Studies of formal urban politics tend to focus on how national and municipal elections play out in cities. In many contexts, residents have little faith in the possibility of achieving social change through party politics, and are highly sceptical of corrupt and self-interested national or urban politicians. Yet cities remain key sites for party political mobilizing and even sceptical citizens may get caught up in the excitement of election campaigns, or enter into clientelist relations with politicians to extract material benefits for their household or neighborhood community.

Elections are of course an important element in formal democratic citizenship, a key political right. However, the experience of voting goes beyond individual rights and should not be understood only as a singular, personal act. Many citizens do not see voting only or primarily as an expression of their individual political preference. They also understand elections as symbolic moments in which collective belonging to the state as well as other political communities can be experienced and negotiated. Anthropologists engaging in 'electoral ethnography' have begun to study voting not just as a political right, but as a central part of the symbolic performance of citizenship. Elections can be seen as performances in which experiences of the state–citizen relationship are reflected, reproduced and contested. Through the act of voting – through participating in this key ritual of democracy – citizens enact their ties to a political community (Banerjee 2014).

As Rivke Jaffe (2015) found in Kingston, Jamaica, for instance, many low-income residents were highly cynical about what they called 'politricks', and often expressed the sentiment that politicians were all corrupt crooks who did not care about anybody but themselves. Yet this cynicism was temporarily suspended around election time, when inner-city residents participated enthusiastically in campaign rallies. While their participation was partly explained by material benefits such as free food and drink, the festive events surrounding elections also engendered 'collective effervescence', a sociological term used to refer to intense experiences of joyousness, excitement and energy that encourage a feeling of shared belonging. Even the most sceptical citizens could temporarily suspend their misgivings and be part of this community – political belonging and the exercise of political rights are collective performances that can generate intense positive emotions (Jaffe 2015).

A number of urban anthropologists have focused on corporate clientelism: non-individual forms of clientelism in which political patrons seek relationships with blocs of voters, in many cases neighborhood communities. The collective nature of voting comes out clearly in such ethnographic studies. As Sian Lazar (2004) demonstrates in her study of election campaigns in the Bolivian city of El Alto, political clients are not necessarily passive, easily manipulated poor people but engage actively in electoral bargaining as a form of collective agency. In El Alto, this bargaining offered marginalized indigenous citizens a way to negotiate their relationship with the state, both instrumentally and affectively. It was a way for residents of low-income urban zones to lobby for investments in neighborhood schools and other public infrastructure, but it also offered citizens who were usually ignored a space in which they were seen and recognized by state actors and political elites, if only for the duration of the campaign.

Lazar found that the urban poor acted consciously and collectively to develop direct relationships with politician-patrons, because they saw the impersonal, 'rational' workings of delegative electoral democracy as unrepresentative and unresponsive. In so doing, they perpetuated 'personalist politics', but also enacted a collectivist citizenship that allowed low-income residents to negotiate a more intimate, emotional relationship with politicians.

In her study of Karachi, Pakistan, Tania Ahmad (2014) shows how the rejection of party politics and the conscious withdrawal from elections can also be understood as a form of political action. During a period of widespread political violence in the city in 2007, as campaign rallies escalated into armed altercations between political opponents, a moral discourse of indignation, denunciation and non-participation emerged among Karachi residents. This involved a call to retreat into domestic space and to withdraw from electoral politics: 'Residents articulated a rejection of party politics in favor of adamant claims for moral decency and compassionate humanity, set apart from the supposed filth of ostensibly democratic institutions' (Ahmad 2014: 412). From the spaces of their homes, residents remained in touch with each other and with the events going on outside through television live broadcasts and talk shows with viewers calling in, as well as communication by cell phone. These media enabled a tentative, emergent city-wide public that formed through the circulation of a discourse that was uncommonly critical and explicit for Karachi. Where the public space of cities is usually privileged as their main political arena (see the final section of this chapter on political mobilization and public space), Ahmad proposes that domesticity can also function as a political claim. In addition, she points out that this discourse shows how non-participation does not necessarily indicate depoliticization, but can be a political stance in itself.

Informal politics

In addition to studying the everyday workings and contestations of electoral democracies, anthropologists recognize an entire realm of urban politics beyond this domain, in authoritarian as well as democratic regimes. These can range from the insurgent citizenship described above or the self-help organizations that spring up amongst marginalized communities, to riots and revolutions, or the communication of dissent through graffiti scrawled on city walls. In addition, ethnographic studies have pointed to the role of non-state actors such as churches (O'Neill 2010) or gangs (Jaffe 2013) in shaping political communities.

Focusing on urban Iran, Asef Bayat (1997) draws our attention to how the silent encroachment of 'informal people' on city spaces and amenities also presents a form of politics, which he calls 'street politics'. Migrants and other disenfranchised urban populations squatting in empty houses or illegally constructing their homes on vacant plots of land, street vendors occupying sidewalks, the illegal tapping of water and electricity

– these ordinary, often unobtrusive practices of reclamation are strategies that the urban poor use to survive or get ahead. However, Bayat argues, they are also an important form of politics that is not always recognized.

While these activities are often counter-practices in the face of top-down planning and control, they should not necessarily be seen as resistance against the subordination of the urban poor by more powerful actors, as they actually often involve quietly offensive rather than defensive action. But neither does this silent encroachment entail a social movement: unlike most social movements, these informal politics are largely leaderless, and are driven by the self-generated action of individuals. Slowly and cumulatively, however, the actions of these disparate disenfranchised individuals can affect dramatic urban change, in terms of redistributing social goods and achieving autonomy from the state. Bayat suggests that this quieter form of communicating discontent may be especially salient in authoritarian states, such as Iran, where overt or spectacular political mobilization is often riskier than in democratic contexts. Bayat's street politics bear resemblance to what social theorist Michel de Certeau (1984) call 'tactics': the everyday practices of less powerful urban dwellers that slowly and surreptitiously undermine the 'strategies' of control developed by government planners and politicians.

In addition to street politics – these 'social non-movements' that are formed by the collective actions of fragmented, non-collective actors – Bayat (2013) also points to the importance of a symbolic realm of discourse that he terms 'the political street'. This realm consists of 'the collective sentiments, shared feelings, and public opinions of ordinary people in their day-to-day utterances and practices that are expressed broadly in public spaces – in taxis, buses, and shops, on street sidewalks, or in mass demonstrations' (Bayat 2013: 14). Street politics and the political street are interconnected, feeding one into the other. Particularly in illiberal settings, the political street may foster and circulate critical, oppositional discourses that can inform large-scale uprisings like those associated with the 'Arab Spring', which we discuss at the end of this chapter.

Social movements

A popular topic in urban anthropology, especially in recent years, has been social movements. Social movements encompass different types of collective action that seek to effect social change through means other than institutionalized, electoral politics, for instance through protests or occupations. Social movements have mobilized around a broad range of issues, from the abolition of slavery and workers' rights in the nineteenth century to sexual rights and environmental conservation in the twentieth. Studying social movements in the 1960s and 1970s, sociologists such as Manuel Castells (1983) emphasized the extent to which many important mobilizations were *urban* movements, which had grown in response to urban conditions and often targeted local rather than national governments. Castells (1983: 305) defined urban social movements as 'collective conscious action aimed at the transformation of the institutionalized urban meaning [in other words, the dominant mode of understanding the city] against the logic, interest and values of the dominant class'. While this definition emphasizes these movements' classed nature, Castells argued that the movements combined 'traditional' concerns over collective consumption (access to public services and infrastructure) with 'new' conflicts over local culture, identities and urban meaning. Many of these urban mobilizations could be understood as part of struggles over 'the right to the city' (see Box 9.1).

Box 9.1 **The right to the city**

In the 1960s, philosopher Henri Lefebvre (1996) developed the notion of 'the right to the city', a concept that was taken up by urban scholars, most prominently David Harvey (2003), to critique exclusionary urban landscapes and imagine a socially just city. According to Lefebvre, cities are crucial public spaces where different people mix and mingle. However, for cities to maintain this function, diverse people have to be able to inhabit the city and to struggle over how urban space and city life are shaped. These struggles create the city as an *oeuvre*, akin to a work of art, and they allow for the invention of new modes of living. As Lefebvre noted, in reality, much of the production of the city is done by and for elites. Lefebvre's notion of the right to the city, in contrast, stresses the right to appropriate the city, to inhabit and creatively shape the urban environments in which we live (Mitchell 2003: 17–20). As Harvey (2003: 939) stresses, 'the right to the city is not merely a right of access to what already exists, but a right to change it after our heart's desire'.

The right to the city was taken up as a rallying cry in the 1960s and 1970s by urban protest movements who critiqued bourgeois society and sought to realize a more creative, open and just society. More recently, the concept has also inspired urban-based activists, such as the US-based Right to the City Alliance and the Abahlali baseMjondolo (AbM), a South African movement of shack dwellers. In Brazil, the right to the city has even been enshrined in law, in the country's City Statute, which was passed in 2001.

One prominent type of urban activism has been around housing issues. Movements have mobilized in different ways to pressure governments or corporate actors such as slumlords and real-estate developers to provide or protect decent and affordable housing. Squatters' movements, such as the sizable movement that emerged in Amsterdam in the 1970s and 1980s, occupy buildings that are left empty while the owners choose to engage in real-estate speculation rather than converting their property to less profitable rental housing. Other squatters' movements, such as those that were common in Latin American cities in the 1980s and 1990s, may consist of collective land invasions, with organized groups of squatters occupying vacant land and constructing informal settlements. In line with Holston's discussion of insurgent citizenship in Brazil, these different types of squatters' movements often also develop new visions and cultural conceptions of political community (see e.g., Alvarez et al. 1998).

While focused on local housing issues, such movements are by no means parochial. The translocal network of Slum/Shack Dwellers International (SDI), for instance, connects informal settlement dwellers across hundreds of urban communities in the global South in their struggles for basic services and political inclusion (Mitlin and Patel 2014). Arjun Appadurai (2001) theorizes this type of cross-border activist alliance as a form of globalization from below. He sees it as indicating 'deep democracy', a form of politics that is characterized by both its rootedness in locality and its transnational networks. The strength of these movements lies in the horizontal forms of exchange and solidarity between activists, and the vertical partnerships that organized urban communities can develop with formal poverty reduction agencies.

In other housing movements, tenants mobilize in attempts to secure their housing from the threat of eviction or displacement following gentrification. Marianne Maeckelbergh (2012) gives an example of this type of movement in her work on New York's Movement for Justice in El Barrio (MJB). In the wake of the 2008 US housing crisis, MJB worked with tenants fighting to 'stay put' in the face of gentrification, and framed their struggle over housing as part of broader processes of disempowerment as a result of neoliberalism. This mobilizing frame allowed MJB to become part of a global network of social movements including the Mexican Zapatista movement.

Other urban social movements are less focused on issues that relate directly to collective consumption, such as housing, and concentrate more on citizenship rights related to identity politics. Indigenous or gay rights movements, for instance, are also in line with Castells' perspective on urban social movements as engaged in developing new ideals for city life and alternative visions of the types of urban social relations that are possible. The majority of urban anthropologists have focused on progressive movements and particularly those associated with low-income and marginalized urban residents. Some social movements, such as mainstream environmentalism in the United States, have been critiqued for their elitist membership and priorities. However, environmental justice movements mobilizing against urban pollution can foster cross-class, multi-ethnic coalitions (Checker 2001). The anthropological tendency to study left-leaning movements has also obscured the fact that not all urban social movements are progressive, as recent anti-Islam or anti-gay mobilizations in European cities demonstrate.

Political mobilization and public space

The various forms of urban politics discussed in this chapter – formal and informal politics, social movements – frequently center on public space (see Chapter 4). Cities harbor large concentrations of people, making it possible to mobilize large crowds. In addition, cities are often of strategic economic importance, and capital cities in particular house important political institutions and important symbolic sites that are tied to the nation, such as presidential palaces, parliamentary buildings and ministerial offices. These characteristics make cities important arenas for the display of state power, from political ceremonies and commemorative events to military parades. However, the same features facilitate the contestation of state power.

Monumental spaces and buildings, such as central squares, boulevards, national assemblies or courthouses, suggest particular relations between the state and citizens. While these sites are intended to convey and produce particular relations of power, their symbolic associations with the state and ruling elites also makes them important arenas for the contestation of dominant political representations. As Emanuela Guano (2002a) argues, such spaces allow for alternative performances that disrupt or contest official state spectacles. Large demonstrations with witty or rousing slogans, with a carnivalesque or sober and serious atmosphere, can become counter-spectacles that question, ridicule and undermine the legitimacy of powerful actors.

Visibility is a key aspect of the political potential of public space. It allows groups of people to present their political views and, often by the force of sheer numbers, position themselves as representatives of a larger collective. Pitching their views and concerns as those of a larger collectivity, most often the nation, allows protesters to question the legitimacy of state politics, which are oftentimes also formulated with reference to the will or the welfare of 'the people'. Public spaces in capital or major cities are especially effective arenas for this type of self-presentation, since these spaces are most readily associated with the nation.

The potential of urban space for political contestation was especially visible in 2011, the year of major urban uprisings across the globe, most dramatically in the Arab world. The political meaning of central squares became abundantly clear in the successive uprisings that started in Tunisia in December 2010, and were soon followed by similar mass protests in Egypt, Libya, Yemen and Syria against what had generally been considered authoritarian yet stable regimes. The hundreds of thousands of people who continued to gather in Cairo's Tahrir Square despite violent attempts to stifle the protests vividly demonstrated the importance of public space as an arena for mass mobilization and protest.

Various kinds of media play increasingly important roles in mobilizing such public protests and are crucial factors in their efficacy. Mass media like television and newspapers can report a protest or ignore it, thereby determining whether it becomes visible to a wider public. Their influence is also felt in their ability to frame particular demonstrations and protests as legitimate or ill-conceived, as large and lively or as having had a meagre attendance. In many cases, protestors suspect conservative or state media of intentionally playing down the impact of public manifestations. In contrast, the Internet and social media are seen as offering the possibility for an alternative public sphere from which to counter the messages of state-sanctioned media. They provide channels to report on protests and thereby ensure public visibility irrespective of coverage by mainstream media outlets.

Moreover, social media from Facebook to Twitter also increasingly represent crucial mobilizing tools. The power of social media has been considered significant to the degree that the uprisings in the Arab world were called 'Facebook revolutions', or 'Revolution 2.0'. However, in the case of Egypt, various authors have pointed out that much of the mass mobilization relied on other, less high-tech communication channels, and on existing social networks and histories of contestation (Ryzova 2012; Ismail 2014). These authors highlight the important role of young men from quite different worlds than those of the digitally savvy, technologically well-equipped men and women who acted both as organizers and citizen journalists. Young men from poor, informal areas of Cairo and well-organized soccer fans (known as 'ultras') who had developed a contentious history with state security forces were an important factor in protestors' ability to hold Tahrir Square despite violent state interventions (see Figure 9.2).

Another form of political mobilization that emerged in 2011 and combined a conscious spatial strategy with the extensive use of new media was the global Occupy movement (Figure 9.3). Jeffrey Juris (2012) studied this movement, which started with Occupy Wall Street in New York in September 2011 and soon went viral, leading to numerous other Occupy movements in cities across the world. Inspired by the uprisings in the Arab world, and the 2011 occupation of central squares in Spain by so-called *indignados* ('the indignant ones') in response to the financial crisis, the Occupy movement presented another instance of a protest movement that used the occupation of symbolically significant public places as a central political tactic. The Occupy movement urged people to stand up against the inordinate influence of 'the 1%', symbolically associated with Wall Street and corporate finance, over the lives of 'the 99%' – a numerical way of expressing their objective of representing 'the people'.

Like the protesters in the Arab world, the Occupy movement also relied strongly on the Internet and social media to organize and broadcast its activities. Commenting on

Figure 9.2 Young men dismantling downtown walls near Tahrir Square, Cairo, 2012 (photograph by Mosa'ab Elshamy)

the debate between techno-optimists who celebrate the radical potential of social media and sceptics who point to the crucial role of existing social networks and local political struggles, Juris (2012: 260) argues:

> It is clear that new media influence how movements organize and that places, bodies, face-to-face networks, social histories, and the messiness of offline politics continue to matter, as exemplified by the resonance of the physical occupations themselves. The important questions, then, are precisely how new media matter; how particular new media tools affect emerging forms, patterns, and structures of organization; and how virtual and physical forms of protest and communication are mutually constitutive.

Notwithstanding the important role of new media, the occupation of space was the key tool of protest in the #Occupy movement. Central spaces in cities were occupied by encampments that grew into self-organized mini-societies with working groups for various organizational tasks, from planning and budgeting to cooking and media outreach. The physical occupation sites were not only crucial in giving the movement a visible presence, but were also important as spaces where alternative communities and intense bonds of solidarity could be forged, and ideals of direct democracy and egalitarianism could be practiced in what has been called a politics of prefiguration. As Juris (2012: 269) points out, these occupations also contested the control of the state over urban space and its ability to define the uses and valuation of space: '#Occupy camps, particularly when situated near financial centers, sought to redefine urban space in ways that contrast with dominant socioeconomic orders, embody utopian movement values, and give rise to alternative forms of sociality'.

Figure 9.3 Occupy Wall Street, New York City, 2011 (photograph by Marcio Jose Bastos via Shutterstock)

Conclusion

This chapter has examined cities as important political sites, given that they are the location of vital economic and political activities and home to large numbers of people. The political significance of cities also derives from their symbolic function with respect to the nation, with important built structures that house national institutions or represent the nation in more symbolic ways, such as monuments or central public spaces like parks or squares. While citizenship is often understood to relate to formal membership in a national community, less formal, substantive forms of citizenship are often formulated *and* contested in urban space. This may be through the realm of formal politics, for example during elections, when poor city dwellers may opt to vote for a political patron as a way to secure some benefits for their community, or in more insurgent ways, when people claim rights to goods or spheres from which they feel they have unjustly been excluded. Many social movements have an urban basis and are fueled by experiences of unequal rights to the city. Urban anthropologists do not only study organized social movements or spectacular protests that involve the occupation of urban space. They have also examined more mundane forms of politics, such as forms of silent encroachment on the part of the city's poor that may not even register as political, but may eventually drastically change urban landscapes and shift the distribution of resources and power in the city.

Discussion questions

1 Can you recognize examples of differentiated citizenship in your own society?
2 Can you recognize instances of Bayat's 'street politics' and 'political street' in a city you know well?

3 Is it possible to separate such informal politics from formal politics?
4 What is the importance of public space in political mobilizations? Do you think this significance has diminished with the increased accessibility of information and communication technology?

Further reading

Bayat, Asef (2013) *Life as Politics: How Ordinary People Change the Middle East*, second edition. Stanford, CA: Stanford University Press.
Holston, James, ed. (1999) *Cities and Citizenship*. Durham, NC: Duke University Press.
Lazar, Sian (2008) *El Alto, Rebel City: Self and Citizenship in Andean Bolivia*. Durham, NC: Duke University Press.

Further viewing

The Slum, Episode 4: Vote for me (2014), produced by Paul Roy for Al-Jazeera. Documentary about election time in Manila's Happyland slum.
The Square (2013), directed by Jehane Noujaim. Documentary about revolutionaries and their protest activities on Tahrir Square, Cairo.

Chapter 10

Violence, security and social control

Violence, security and social control are three interconnected concepts that play an important role in the negotiation of urban order. In many contemporary cities, violence – whether armed robbery, sexual abuse, terrorist attacks or urban warfare – is a growing concern. Violence disrupts urban social order and is a threat to security. However, different social actors also use violence in attempts to maintain a certain type of order and to enhance the security of certain groups. Anthropologists have studied both the perpetrators and the victims of violence, emphasizing that the boundaries between these groups are not always clear. They have focused on the relations between marginalized residents, elites, criminal gangs, state security forces such as the police and military, and private security guards. This work underlines the destructive nature of urban violence and its horrific costs to lives, livelihoods and infrastructure. Anthropological studies have also explored the extent to which violence, in addition to being a force of destruction, is used 'productively', to pursue specific goals and shape social relations.

The first section of this chapter introduces anthropological approaches to violence, including reflections on the dilemmas associated with this type of ethnographic research. We discuss different typologies of violence and how these might apply to urban contexts, focusing specifically on criminal, ethno-religious and political violence in cities. In the second section, we look at how violence affects urban life. Anthropologists have studied how violence shapes narratives about urban space and influences people's trajectories through the city. In addition, their research has studied how the material form of cities changes, from urban infrastructure to architectural styles. The third section discusses the various strategies of control applied under the rubric of urban security, focusing on interventions by state actors such as the police. In a final section, we discuss the shift from 'police' to 'policing'. In addition to public security forces such as the police and the military, non-state policing actors such as security guards or vigilantes play a growing role in providing security to urban populations. A number of urban anthropologists have explored how we might understand these various non-state violent actors as sovereigns beyond the state.

Anthropologies of violence

Anthropologists working on violence have tried to understand different types of violence and how these form part of a continuum (see Box 10.1). While recognizing the interconnected nature of different forms of violence, anthropological studies often concentrate on one

Box 10.1 Typologies of violence

Violence can take on different forms that may appear quantitatively and qualitatively distinct, with different types of violent perpetrators and their motivations. Caroline Moser and Cathy McIlwaine (2004), for instance, propose a typology that distinguishes between political, institutional, economic and social violence. They define *political violence* as violence perpetrated by state or non-state actors in situations of political conflict, which may range from political assassinations to attacks by guerilla organizations or paramilitary groups. *Institutional violence* is enacted by state actors, or less formal institutions, in attempts to maintain or consolidate a specific form of rule and moral order. This type of violence can include extra-judicial killings by police officers, or mob justice. Moser and McIlwaine define *economic violence* as violence perpetrated with economic motives, including gang violence, robberies and organized criminal activities such as protection rackets. *Social violence* covers domestic, sexual and 'routine everyday' violence. In practice, these different forms may blur, as the motivations of perpetrators may be unclear or overlap – rape, for instance, may be used in contexts of political conflict, while institutional violence may involve economic advantages to perpetrators.

Nancy Scheper-Hughes and Philippe Bourgois (2004) take a more conceptual approach, speaking of a 'continuum of violence' rather than a typology. They note that 'violence can never be understood solely in terms of its physicality … alone. Violence also includes assaults on the personhood, dignity, sense of worth or value of the victim' (2004: 1). This leads them to emphasize the connections between physical violence and other forms of harm, foregrounding *structural violence*, those chronic forms of political and economic oppression, exclusion and inequality (see Farmer 2004). *Symbolic violence* involves the internalized legitimations of structural violence and its hierarchies, inequalities and humiliations. This concept, developed by Pierre Bourdieu, can be understood as the mechanism through which victims of structural violence blame themselves for their domination and in so doing render it legitimate (see Bourdieu and Wacquant 2004). *Everyday violence* involves the normalization and 'invisibilization' of suffering through institutionalized processes and discourses, which produce social indifference to violence that would otherwise be seen as shocking and unacceptable. Finally, *intimate violence* involves interpersonal forms of harm, including self-harm as well as physical injury in the context of delinquency and crime.

specific form, connected to a particular sphere of life, for instance violence in the domestic, economic or political sphere. In urban contexts, much attention has gone out to criminal, ethno-religious and political violence, as we discuss in the subsection below.

Anthropologists doing research in contexts of urban violence have also begun to reflect on the ethical and methodological dilemmas involved in this type of fieldwork. Conducting ethnographic research in these circumstances can increase the risk of physical danger, not only for researchers themselves, but also for their local interlocutors. In many cases, anthropologists can try to minimize the risks for everyone involved in their research project by thorough planning, and by ensuring that they counter the common distrust of researchers by adequately and honestly explaining their presence, especially in contexts where people suspect nosy outsiders of being spies (Sluka 2012). In addition, risk management often involves understanding and adopting local safety techniques: 'The strategies local people have developed to avoid and manage quotidian violence present options for how to organize one's own behavior so as to keep safe while conducting effective and productive social research' (Goldstein 2014: 14; see Nordstrom and Robben 1995).

Another type of dilemma emerges in writing up research on violence. Ensuring the anonymity of respondents is of utmost importance when the topic is on political or criminal violence. Beyond physical safety, writing about urban violence also involves ethical dilemmas related to representation in a broader sense. Like anthropological representations of poor neighborhoods (see Box 2.2), ethnographies of urban violence can inadvertently feed sensationalist narratives. Even carefully worded studies can end up reinforcing stigmatizing representations of particular people or neighborhoods as deviant and dangerous, and run the risk of being misinterpreted as indications of a 'culture of violence'.

Criminal, ethno-religious and political violence

While different forms of violence tend to overlap (see Box 10.1), we can make a broad distinction between urban anthropological work on criminal violence, and work on political and ethno-religious violence. The first body of research connects to a long tradition in literature and the arts of representing the city as a dystopia. This dystopian imaginary frames urban areas as hotbeds of deviance, crime and violence. A similar preoccupation (and sometimes fascination) with criminal violence has also been something of a tradition in the social sciences, including early urban anthropological studies, such as Oscar Lewis's *La Vida* (1966; see Chapter 2), that sometimes contributed to notions of cultural deviance.

More recent anthropological work on urban gangs and criminal groups has often taken a less culturalist approach, highlighting the relations between crime, violence and urban inequality. A classic study in this tradition is Philippe Bourgois' *In Search of Respect* (2003), which connects the practices of crack dealers to broader transformations in the political economy of New York City (see Chapter 5). Other anthropologists, also seeking to move away from ideas of gangs as a type of social pathology, have emphasized both the prevalence of gang-like social arrangements across the world and the cultural specificity of the diverse groups lumped under the category of 'gang' (Hazen and Rodgers 2014). Other recent anthropological work has connected gangs and criminal organizations to globalization, studying their role within transnational criminal networks and the global trade in illicit goods (e.g., van Schendel and Abraham 2005; Nordstrom 2007). As rates of homicides, armed robberies and rapes soared, especially in regions such as Latin America and the Caribbean, urban anthropologists began to explore residents' everyday negotiations of urban crime and fear. This focus on the broader impact of violent crime on city life has entailed a shift beyond gangs and comparable urban social groups, towards a closer study of the role and responses of more elite actors.

A somewhat distinct body of anthropological work has focused on ethno-religious and political violence. A number of cities, such as Belfast, Jerusalem, Beirut and Mumbai, have featured prominently in these anthropological studies. In addition to simmering tensions between different ethnic, religious and sectarian groups, these cities have also suffered years or decades of terror attacks and episodes of what Arjun Appadurai (2000) calls 'urban cleansing'. Anthropologists working on these more collective types of conflict have emphasized the need to understand the complex political dynamics that fuel inter-communal tensions and that provide justifications for violence. Moving beyond simple narratives of primordial inter-ethnic hatred, anthropologists have sought to understand the historical roots and contemporary catalysts of ethno-religious and political violence. For instance, narratives that frame different urban ethnic or religious communities as antagonistic and incompatible can feed inter-communal violence.

Analyzing the anti-Muslim riots that raged in Bombay/Mumbai in 1992/1993, for instance, Appadurai (2000) shows how, in a city with a long tradition of inter-ethnic commerce and cosmopolitanism, conditions emerged that made ethnic violence a possibility. He points to a complicated mix of factors, in which a deindustrializing urban economy, ongoing rural-to-urban migration, and extreme scarcity and speculation in the realm of housing led to the proliferation of informal dwellings and enterprises in every possible bit of free space: 'As struggles over the space of housing, vending and sleeping gradually intensified, so did the sense of Bombay as a site for traffic across ethnic boundaries become reduced' (2000: 644). The problem of spatial scarcity was reframed by the Hindu nationalist movement Shiva Sena as a 'Muslim problem'. Connecting notions of cultural purity to anxieties over political sovereignty and the military threat posed by Pakistan, they conjured a vision of Hindu Mumbai and represented 'the figure of the Muslim [as] the link between scarce housing, illegal commerce and national geography writ urban' (2000: 649). As this example of inter-communal conflict shows, spatial relations tend to play a significant role in legitimizing urban violence. In addition, these same spatial relations often change as a result of violent conflict, as we discuss in the following section.

Violence, fear and urban space

Violence and fear affect urban space and the built environment in multiple ways. They shape experiences of urban space, and result in physical changes to the built environment. In cities with high rates of violence, residents often respond by developing socio-spatial narratives to make sense of a frightening environment and by changing their everyday patterns of mobility. In addition, both residents and governments often develop material interventions in attempts to enhance safety, or at least a sense of safety. In this section, we examine the different impacts of violence and fear on urban space. We start with a discussion of the emergence of specific spatial narratives, moving on to examine the impact on urban mobilities, and ending with an overview of changes in urban form and the built environment. In many cases, comparable spatial narratives and effects appear to emerge regardless of whether the threat relates to criminal, ethno-religious or political violence.

Spatial narratives

In many contexts of criminal or political violence and fear, we see narratives emerging that emphasize social distance and create discursive boundaries between urban places and populations. As residents try to make sense of a scary city by distinguishing between 'good' and 'bad' neighborhoods and people, urban geographies of fear take shape that are based on spatial and ethnic 'othering' within the city. In some cases, new social categories of 'threatening' and 'threatened' urban places and people are constructed, while in others existing categorizations are reinforced. The discourses of danger that emerge in response to violent conflict and fear, can, in turn, instigate or legitimize violence against those seen as threats, as is evident in the case of anti-Muslim riots discussed above.

Another well-studied example of urban conflict is Belfast, where three decades of ethno-sectarian violence during the period known as the Troubles resulted in a socially and spatially divided city. The ethno-nationalist conflict between Irish Nationalists or Republicans (Catholics who supported the reunification of Northern Ireland with the Republic of Ireland) and Loyalists or Unionists (Protestants who supported its remaining within the United Kingdom) hardened the symbolic and spatial boundaries between Catholics and Protestants. During the conflict, both groups of residents were exposed to bomb attacks, targeted killings and torture by a range of violent actors, including the British security forces and paramilitary groups such as the Irish Republican Army (IRA) and the Ulster Volunteer Force (UVF).

In their study of 'post-conflict' Belfast following the ceasefire in 1994, Peter Shirlow and Brendan Murtagh (2006) underline the lasting effect of violence and polarizing narratives of difference and danger. They show how key narratives and symbols worked to reinforce territorial enclaving and the idea of the ethno-sectarian 'home' enclave as morally superior. Murals, flags and street parades all served to make socio-spatial divides between Protestants and Catholics seem normal and natural. Everyday narratives as well as political and media representations that depicted the two religious groups, and their neighborhoods, as incompatible and antagonistic lasted after the violence had ended. Even a decade after the Troubles had formally ended, Shirlow and Murtagh found Protestant residents who shopped at a locally owned supermarket in a Catholic area would repackage their groceries in other bags to avoid being identified as spending money on 'the other side' (2006: 100). Residents still distinguished between various parts of the urban landscape in sectarian terms, and oriented their actions according to their own allegiances.

Urban mobilities

Discursive categorizations and associated cognitive maps can lead to changes in how residents use space. In most cities, residents develop mental maps that distinguish between safe and unsafe areas and that guide their movements, but these maps become especially salient in cities marked by high levels of crime or political conflict. Protracted conflict affects urban mobilities, as residents seek to avoid what they see as risky locations or encounters. These cognitive maps intersect with material interventions in the urban built environment: physical security infrastructure such as walls, checkpoints and other barriers also work to impede some types of movements and facilitate others.

In their research on Beirut, Mona Fawaz, Mona Harb and Ahmad Gharbieh (2012) show how the city's securitization impacts residents' everyday lives. They describe how complex and overlapping fears – anxieties over threats ranging from political assassinations and riots to sectarian attacks and petty crime – redirected and restricted residents' movements. In some cases these changes to urban mobilities were voluntary, in other cases public and private security actors actively intervened to determine who could move where. As with urban mobilities in general, not everyone was free to move in the same way (see Chapter 3). As Fawaz et al. (2012: 191) explain:

> The actual experience of security and how it affects one's practices differs considerably from one person to another, depending on their position in social hierarchies that determine whether they will be constructed as a possible threat by a security group, rendering some groups more vulnerable than others. These forces eventually

reconstruct people's geographies of the city, paralleling the visible architecture of security with another divided geography in which city dwellers self-select themselves as able to move in particular neighborhoods, depending on how their presence will be interpreted and scrutinized.

In Beirut, urban residents' identifiable positioning in terms of categories such as gender, age, class, religion or political affiliation (see Chapter 4) influenced their movements, both through their own decisions and through that of state and non-state security actors. Everyday mobilities, then, both shape and are shaped by discursive categories of 'safe' and 'dangerous' people and places.

Urban form and the built environment

Beyond urban narratives, mental maps and mobility, the effects of violence and fear are often visible in material form, as they shape urban space and the built environment in a number of ways. Longer periods of violent political conflict, as in the context of urban warfare, often have a dramatic effect on city spaces. Ida Susser and Jane Schneider (2003) draw on organic models of the city, approaching the city as a 'body politic' to understand how war and other dramatic forces of destruction can result in 'wounded cities'. Responses to violence and fear may have an impact on urban form, modifying urban infrastructure and planning. The impact may also be visible at a smaller scale, with architecture reflecting fears or memories of violence. This material impact, which often takes the shape of material elements of separation and segregation, is difficult to separate from discursive and social responses. Violence-fueled narratives of antagonistic difference can lead to processes of urban fortification or 'disembedding', described below, creating so-called segregated cities in which urban 'others' seem all the more frightening. In general, the combination of material, discursive and social reactions to violence tend to exacerbate urban inequalities.

Drawing on her research on crime and segregation in the Brazilian megacity of São Paulo, Teresa Caldeira (2000) points to the emergence of 'fortified enclaves'. These are privatized spaces of residence, work, consumption and leisure, characterized by defensive forms of architecture from walls and gates to barbed wire and security cameras. Across the world, wealthier urban residents have begun to retreat into these enclaves, in response to increased levels of insecurity but also triggered by what Caldeira calls the 'talk of crime'. The latter entails pervasive discussions of crime and violence, through which residents seek to give order and meaning to a frightening reality. In practice, the talk of crime tends to reinforce social boundaries and reproduce fear by allocating blame to particular classed and raced urban groups, for instance 'the urban poor', 'migrants' or 'Roma'. The social and economic life of the wealthier classes increasingly takes place in gated communities and enclosed shopping malls, and this may lead to urban public space becoming devalued 'residual' space, a zone occupied only by those who have no other options.

Working in the Nicaraguan capital of Managua, Dennis Rodgers (2004) builds on Caldeira's work by focusing on the securitization of both places and mobilities. In addition to fortified enclaves, he identifies the emergence of fortified networks. These networks are created through an exclusive transport infrastructure that connects residential and economic enclaves. In Managua, a high-speed motorway was constructed that connected the city's elite areas, while carving up low-income neighborhoods into smaller, disconnected segments. While fortified enclaves are associated with urban fragmentation and segregation, Rodgers argues that fortified networks result in the disembedding of an entire layer of elite space from the urban fabric. As a result, the fate of the urban elite is less and less connected to that of other segments of the urban population, and to spaces other than the elite enclaves they inhabit.

Rodgers' emphasis on road networks also ties into recent anthropological work on infrastructural violence. This work understands infrastructure as an important material form that is 'ethnographically graspable' and that can serve to 'highlight how broader processes of marginalization, abjection and disconnection often become operational and sustainable in contemporary cities through infrastructure' (Rodgers and O'Neill 2012: 403).

Caldeira and Rodgers both direct our attention to the responses of elites to urban crime and violence, emphasizing how fortification and disembedding not only further marginalize the urban poor, who are already relegated to residual and undesirable city spaces, but also reinforce the view that they are the source of crime and violence. The residents of urban *favelas*, ghettos or *barrios bravos* are faced with forced removal or punitive measures if they transgress socio-spatial boundaries.

In addition to studying elite practices and their consequences, anthropologists have also done research on the ways that the urban poor cope with insecurity and fear, demonstrating that these practices also shape city life. In the Rio *favela* of Jacarezinho, for instance, neighborhood activists installed gates and cameras to turn their community into a gated 'favela-condominium'. In addition to being a practical intervention, this gating also served as a symbolic form of political communication, challenging Brazilian ideas about whose neighborhoods could assert agency and demand protection (Vargas 2006).

At the scale of neighborhoods and streets, architectural styles and elements can also be read as public forms of communication, which respond and give meaning to experiences of violence. Abidin Kusno, in his work on architecture in urban Indonesia, argues that both physical and symbolic violence find expression in the built environment. Violence, he argues, is 'produced, ignored or reinscribed through the production of buildings and urban spaces' (Kusno 2010: 9). This negotiation of urban violence through architecture takes various forms. A well-known form is the defensive architecture associated with fortified enclaves. Within such enclaves, the architecture is inward-looking, with imposing outer perimeters aimed at deterring unwelcome guests. The presence of fences, 'beware of the dog' signs or CCTV cameras all reflect a defensive type of urbanism.

In addition, as Kusno points out, architecture also plays an important role in memory work. Beyond immediate reminders of urban warfare – bombed-out buildings, bullet-scarred walls – architectural styles, visual elements and monuments can memorialize past conflict in more subtle ways. Such 'mnemonic practices' can include visual commemorations such as Dublin's peace walls, Cairo's martyr murals commemorating young men who died in clashes with the police (Figure 10.1; see also Chapter 9) or the memorial murals for residents killed by gang or police violence that are found in many inner-city neighborhoods in the United States. Small memorial shrines or signs commemorating violent incidents indicate to passers-by a potential for violence. However, architecture can also seek to obscure memories of violence. In the riots that took place in Jakarta in May 1998, the businesses and homes of Indonesians of Chinese descent were targeted for looting and destruction, while hundreds of ethnic Chinese were gang-raped or murdered. The post-1998 architectural reconstruction of the Chinese business district of Glodok completely ignored this painful history, suggesting the possibility of architecture to 'cover up' a violent past (Kusno 2010).

Figure 10.1 Martyrs mural in downtown Cairo, 2013 (photograph by Anouk de Koning)

Police, spatial governmentality and social control

In addition to researching violence and its effects on urban spaces and populations, anthropologists have paid increasing attention to state strategies aimed at producing urban security through policing and other forms of social control. A range of ethnographies has studied the role of the police in reproducing an often unequal urban order, for instance as certain population groups are subjected disproportionately to surveillance and police violence. Such studies show how differentiated citizenship (see Chapter 9) is produced in routine and spectacular encounters between urban residents and police officers, as police forces prioritize and 'recognize' certain types of threats in everyday urban life.

While policing can contribute to safer and fairer cities and societies, in practice police activities often target marginalized people and places (low-income neighborhoods, ethnic minorities) for surveillance and interventions. In so doing, they reinforce the criminalization of these people and places, reproducing an unequal social order. This policing of the status quo has long been evident in the punitive responses by security forces to labor organizers, political protests and strikes. It is also apparent in the context of neoliberal urbanism (see Chapter 8), where the police increasingly act to protect commercial spaces and interests. Often, the police focus on preventing or punishing 'disorderly' behavior or people in these spaces, targeting minority youth or the homeless. Meanwhile, elite crimes (such as financial fraud, corruption and other white-collar crimes) tend to receive much less police attention (Heyman 2014).

Neoliberal forms of policing link to what Sally Engle Merry (2001), following Richard Perry (2000), calls 'spatial governmentality'. This represents a new logic of governance, in which the urban social order is governed through spatial methods, rather than through punishing crimes or disciplining offenders. This concept builds on Foucault's work on governmentality, understood as 'the conduct of conduct'. Foucault distinguishes between sovereign, disciplinary and biopolitical rationalities of governance. These three different forms of governmentality work through mechanisms that act on the body (sovereignty), by reforming the soul of individual persons (discipline) and by managing populations (biopower). As a biopolitical form of governance, spatial governmentality achieves social order through spatial zoning and regulation. It seeks to diminish risks to broader populations by excluding or hiding 'offensive' persons and acts, rather than punishing or reforming them. Such spatial mechanisms often seek to promote security by minimizing risk to the general population or insulating groups seen as more vulnerable or valuable. However, these newer systems of spatial ordering co-exist with, and are backed by the threat of, punitive and reformist forms of power, such as the police, prisons and therapy.

The proliferation of fortified enclaves represents one form of spatial governmentality, separating wealthy consumers from 'risky' populations such as the urban poor – it 'works not by containing disruptive populations but by excluding them from particular places' such as shopping malls (Merry 2001: 20). However, Merry demonstrates that spatial governmentality goes beyond class relations. Her research in the Hawaiian town of Hilo focused on shifting approaches to gender violence. She found an increase of spatial measures that exclude batterers from their victim's physical space, such as temporary restraining orders and women's shelters. While punitive and reformist approaches continued to exist, the skyrocketing use of protective orders represented a new risk-based, spatial form of social ordering. More than punishing wife batterers or reforming them through therapy, Hilo courts resorted to spatial measures that diminished the risk to victims by spatially separating men and women.

Merry's research shows that spatial mechanisms of control need not be regressive or reinforce existing inequalities; they can also help to protect vulnerable populations such as low-income women. Temporary restraining orders are spatial measures that were developed through the long struggle of feminist activists, and are highly popular amongst victims of domestic abuse, many of whom 'do not want their abusers punished, but reformed or gone' (2001: 25). Merry did find, however, that the moderately progressive gendered logic of protective orders was connected to a classed logic, as low-income batterers were much more likely to be targeted by these spatial mechanisms of control.

The continued role of punitive, penal forms of power in backing up spatially exclusive mechanisms comes out clearly in Didier Fassin's (2013) ethnography of urban policing in France. Focusing on the anti-crime squad and its engagement with Parisian *banlieues*, Fassin shows how the day-to-day routine of the squad's activities in these marginalized areas was often quite boring, consisting of endless monotonous patrols. In part to alleviate this tedium, officers often provoked and humiliated ethnic minority youth during routine stop-and-search encounters, in order to justify an excessive response and assert their power performatively. As Fassin demonstrates, officers' encounters with youngsters contributed less to ensuring public order than to enforcing an unequal social and spatial order based on implicit racial categorization.

In recent years, anthropologists have also begun to pay attention to the impact of the 'war on terror' and broader processes of 'securitization' on city life. In many cities, the distinction between the police and the military becomes blurred. War-like tactics, technologies and aesthetics – from checkpoints and armed guards to security cameras and drones – have become so ubiquitous that urban landscapes take on a militarized character even in peacetime. The geographer Stephen Graham understands such developments as part of what he calls the 'new military urbanism', which includes the use of 'militarized techniques of tracking and targeting [to] permanently colonize the city landscape and the spaces of everyday life' (2011: xiv). Like previous forms of policing – including colonial policing – this new military urbanism draws on specific forms of spatial governmentality and tends to reproduce an unequal social order.

Security and sovereignty beyond the state

Traditionally, studies of security and policing have focused on state practices and discourses. However, neoliberal policies have seen state actors retreat from certain social spheres and city spaces, encouraging the privatization of formerly public services (see Chapter 5). This is particularly evident in the field of security; increasingly, urban residents are made responsible for safeguarding their own physical integrity and material belongings. A longer historical perspective on security and policing shows that the centrality of the police in maintaining urban order is a relatively recent phenomenon – various types of private security actors, from privately paid militias to voluntary self-policing bodies, have long played a role in protecting some urbanites and excluding others.

These insights have led anthropologists to take a broader perspective on security, and to develop ethnographic studies of security and policing actors beyond the state. Daniel Goldstein, for instance, calls for

> a critical, comparative ethnography of security [that] can explore the multiple ways in which security is configured and deployed – not only by states and authorized speakers but by communities, groups, and individuals – in their engagements with other local actors and with arms of the state itself.
>
> (2010: 492)

An important phenomenon in this regard is the rise of the private commercial security sector. In addition, less wealthy residents often turn to more informal forms of non-state security, relying on neighborhood watches or vigilante groups. We discuss work on these two types of security providers in the subsections below. Given that traditional definitions of 'the state' have been based on the idea of the monopoly of violence, these different types of non-state violent actors have sometimes been understood as 'sovereigns beyond the state'.

Private security

As state responses become increasingly repressive in many cities, wealthier citizens retreat into gated communities and other types of fortified enclaves, as noted above. In addition, they are often unconvinced of the ability of public security forces such as the police to protect them, and turn to private security companies. Ethnographies of private security guards show that these commercial actors often exacerbate inequalities between high-income and low-income urban neighborhoods and residents. As private security companies take on a range of duties previously associated with the police, urban anthropologists have also emphasized the role of private security guards as non-state sovereigns.

In his research in an Indian neighborhood in post-apartheid Durban, South Africa, for instance, Thomas Blom Hansen (2006) describes how, as the official police force became democratized and was supposed to incorporate human rights considerations, private security firms took over the 'old style' of violently racist colonial policing. Many private security officers were former policemen who were used to incorporating violent practices in securing Indian neighborhoods from the supposed threat of poorer African neighborhoods. Hansen suggests that in democratic South Africa, we might be witnessing 'a new form of sovereignty arising from communities, executed by former policemen now free of the injunctions regarding "correct" conduct and the rights of the detainees' (2006: 291).

Building on Hansen's work, Tessa Diphoorn's (2015) ethnographic study of armed response officers in Durban also emphasizes the shifts in power and sovereignty associated with the rise of private security. She studied the everyday policing practices of these officers and their interactions with the 'real' police and with citizens (Figure 10.2). She found that, increasingly, private security agents took on a public role within Durban's wealthier neighborhoods. Private security officers and their armed response officers mimicked and appropriated state police practices and symbols, for instance copying national and international police aesthetics in the design of their uniforms and patrol cars. In addition, they took on responsibility for ensuring order in public spaces, rather than restricting their activities to private spaces. Citizens reinforced this 'public' role: even residents who

Figure 10.2 Private security in Durban, South Africa, 2009 (photograph by Tessa Diphoorn)

were not a private security company's clients would flag down armed response officers on the street and command them to pursue thieves, treating them like police officers with a public duty to protect paying and non-paying residents.

Diphoorn analyzes this quasi-public role as what she calls 'twilight policing', punitive and disciplinary policing practices that are neither fully state nor non-state. In certain cases, the practices of armed response officers undermined the sovereign power of the police, but in other contexts, they partnered with police officers in ways that bolstered police authority. She also shows how the private security industry and its agents reinforce existing inequalities. Armed response officers relied on raced and classed constructions of the 'dangerous other' encapsulated in the term 'Bravo Mike', shorthand for (poor) 'Black male'. By constructing this exclusionary type of categorization and drawing on it in punitive performances, these officers sought to establish a moral order and claim a public form of authority. Yet their own low status, difficult working conditions and relatively underprivileged backgrounds meant that the officers themselves were also subject to exploitation, surveillance and exclusion.

Informal private security and vigilantism

Those urban residents who cannot afford private security, but cannot trust the police to protect them either, often turn to informal and sometimes illegal forms of security provision. While neighborhood watches are often a more or less innocuous form of informal self-help security, anthropologists have documented the global prevalence of violent vigilante groups that take on a policing role (Pratten and Sen 2007).

Working in urban Bolivia, Daniel Goldstein (2004) analyzes mob violence – actual and attempted instances of the lynching of thieves – as a performative practice. He argues that in the marginalized neighborhoods where these lynchings took place, mob violence was a spectacular public performance that serves a political function. In part, such violent performances could help to strengthen internal solidarity and reaffirm shared norms within the neighborhood. In addition, they could also serve as a medium of external communication, aimed at shaping perceptions of the neighborhood and its residents, communicating their sense of exclusion from the larger city and the nation-state. This work underlines the need to understand violence as a mode of performance or communication, used to pursue specific goals and shape social relations.

Rivke Jaffe (2012a) discusses another, more organized form of such extra-legal security provisioning in inner-city neighborhoods in Kingston, Jamaica. Here, residents also depended on private security arrangements, as they experienced the police force as ineffective, brutal or corrupt. However, their lack of income prevented them from accessing formal commercial security providers. In many cases inner-city residents could only turn to 'dons' (community leaders who are often linked to criminal organizations) for security and dispute resolution. Dons would hold informal court sessions, responding to different crimes – such as theft, domestic abuse, rape or 'informing' to the police – with a more or less institutionalized set of punishments, which could range from a warning or banishment from the neighborhood to a severe beating or even death. The informal, extra-legal don-based system of 'self-help' law and order, which generally relied on violent retribution, was relatively popular among marginalized urban residents, who felt that the formal justice system was biased and inaccessible. In addition, these residents often also benefited from the broader social provisioning role dons fulfilled. The most influential and wealthiest dons could provide or facilitate access to various forms of financial and social welfare and help residents gain employment, either within their own organizations or through their connections to politicians and the private sector.

Like the private security guards in Durban, Jamaican dons did not operate in isolation from the state. Their own origins lay in Jamaica's 'garrison politics', a form of political clientelism in which politicians used state resources to secure votes, and supplied loyal communities with material benefits such as housing or employment. These politicians used dons as brokers, surreptitiously channelling weapons and money to them. In exchange, dons would ensure favorable electoral outcomes in inner-city 'garrison' neighborhoods and suppress urban unrest. In addition to this historical connection to electoral politics, there were also various instances of the Jamaican police collaborating with dons. In various cases, the police would refer both victims and perpetrators to the dons' informal security and justice system. The effects on the urban social order also resemble those of private security in South Africa. While dons do enjoy significant local legitimacy, their violently punitive and authoritarian leadership means that 'the effects of informal security privatization on everyday lives in inner-city neighborhoods, and thus on the possibility of realizing a public, democratic urban landscape, are cause for deep concern' (Jaffe 2012a: 195).

Conclusion

This chapter has discussed how violence, and more broadly attempts to provide security and establish social control, impact the urban landscape. People create narratives about the city to make sense of frightening experiences, often blaming particular raced and classed groups for the city's troubles and labeling them as dangerous. Experiences of violence also influence people's mental maps of the city, which distinguish between safe and unsafe places and people. Such mental maps in turn influence people's orientations toward the city and their everyday urban trajectories. Urban landscapes bear the marks of violence, whether in the form of defensible architecture, visible security technologies or in memorials that commemorate violent incidences. These various reactions to urban violence often deepen existing inequalities, for instance by singling out particular marginal groups as culprits or by removing more privileged groups from common urban spaces, as is the case with practices of elite self-segregation in gated communities.

State and non-state actors develop various strategies to control the urban landscape. Neoliberal forms of governing cities include measures to spatially separate rather than discipline or reform offenders or potential threats. However, even with the rise of such spatial forms of governmentality, policing remains a crucial technology of control in urban landscapes. Anthropological studies have demonstrated that policing often reproduces existing inequalities by focusing especially on already marginalized populations and areas. They have also shown that the daily practices of police officers, private security guards and vigilantes may resemble each other and overlap, significantly blurring the boundaries between state and non-state agents in the field of security provision. Such blurring raises significant questions with respect to the rights of different citizens, both those who turn to vigilantes as a private form of security provision and those that may be targeted as likely perpetrators by state agents or private guards.

Discussion questions

1 Which of the different typologies of violence discussed in this chapter do you find most helpful in understanding urban violence?
2 In what ways does the occurrence (and fear) of violence shape the urban landscape? Can you recognize these changes in your own surroundings?
3 What consequences could the disembedding of elite spaces have for cities?
4 How do you think anthropological approaches to urban crime and violence differ from those developed by sociologists or criminologists?
5 What different types of public and private policing organizations can you recognize in a city you know well? When can these different organizations contribute to a more democratic city? And when do their forms of security provision and law enforcement contribute to differentiated citizenship?

Further reading

Caldeira, Teresa (2000) *City of Walls: Crime, Segregation and Citizenship in São Paulo*. Berkeley, CA: University of California Press.

Fassin, Didier (2013) *Enforcing Order: An Ethnography of Urban Policing*. Cambridge: Polity.

Goldstein, Daniel (2004) *The Spectacular City: Violence and Performance in Urban Bolivia*. Durham, NC: Duke University Press.

Nordstrom, Carolyn and Antonius C.G.M. Robben, eds. (1995) *Fieldwork under Fire: Contemporary Studies of Violence and Survival*. Berkeley, CA: University of California Press.

Susser, Ida and Jane Schneider, eds. (2003) *Wounded Cities: Destruction and Reconstruction in a Globalized World*. New York: Berg.

Further viewing

Cidade de Deus [City of God] (2002), directed by Fernando Meirelles. Feature film on drugs crime and violence in the *favelas* of Rio de Janeiro.

Ghosts of Cité Soleil (2006), directed by Asger Leth and Milos Loncarevic. Documentary on gang rule in Port-au-Prince.

La Zona [The Zone] (2007), directed by Rodrigo Plá. Feature film on vigilante violence in a gated community in Mexico City.

Tsotsi (2005), directed by Gavin Hood. Feature film on a young criminal in Johannesburg.

Chapter 11

Conclusion
The future of urban anthropology

After a peak period of interest in the 1970s and 1980s, urban anthropology has resurfaced in the twenty-first century as an important part of the discipline and as an original voice in the broader interdisciplinary field of urban studies. Urban anthropology has developed as a subfield that takes the spatiality of urban life seriously, that asks how specific characteristics of cities (including their density, heterogeneity and their political and economic significance) shape everyday social life in different cultural contexts, and that explores how these different dimensions of urban life are imagined and represented.

In this book, we have sought to present an overview of current themes in urban anthropology, relying primarily on this renewed urban anthropology that has developed into the twenty-first century. While themes such as place-making and urban inequality have remained central to urban anthropology, recent years have also seen a number of new concerns emerge. Current urban anthropology analyzes urban life in relation to processes of globalization, researching how migration, transnationalism and new communication technologies impact the city and its residents. More broadly, urban anthropologists have begun to focus more closely on how different technologies shape urban life, whether in the form of infrastructure, mobilities or the intersection of offline and online worlds. Recent studies have also focused on neoliberalization, as a political economic program transforming urban spaces, as a model of city governance or as a force shaping urban subjectivities. Urban anthropology has also paid increased attention to consumption, often in connection to a new interest in the middle class as a research focus. In addition, anthropological research on social movements has become increasingly attentive to the urban nature of many recent uprisings and protests, as these sprung up from Tunis and Cairo to Madrid and New York City.

Writing in the mid-2010s, we can identify a number of additional, emergent trends and developments within urban anthropology, which we sketch in the concluding pages to this book.

Post-neoliberal solidarities

One emerging interest within the subfield is *post-neoliberalism*. Urban residents, social movements and governments are increasingly active in signaling the shortcomings or failure of neoliberalism (see, e.g., Barber et al. 2012). In cities across the world, we see attempts to go beyond neoliberal visions and programs in imagining how to organize social, political and economic life. In line with prefigurative practices such as those used by the Occupy movement, discussed in Chapter 9, groups of urban residents are trying to create a new world by consciously reconfiguring everyday routines and choices. This involves trying to develop alternative modes of cooperation and exchange that diverge from those offered by neoliberal capitalism, for instance by experimenting with a wide variety of sharing economies or forms of communal farming (see e.g., Gibson-Graham 2014; Parker et al. 2014). As anthropologists turn to study such movements and their attempts to carve out spaces for alternative economic practices, we expect them to focus on the clash between idealistic intents, organizational obstacles and limits to mobilization potential. The danger of co-optation is also present, as new forms of participatory governance also claim the domain of community and try to reinvent mutual solidarity as a way to fill the gaps left by state retrenchment.

An issue closely related to such attempts to move beyond neoliberalism is solidarity. How are feelings and practices of solidarity created in today's mobile, neoliberal and media-saturated world? Earlier forms of solidarity often rested in imaginaries of the nation-state, or of a stable working class. Today, nation-state imaginaries often clash with the multicultural realities of transnationally connected cities and their mobile inhabitants. In many places this has led to exclusionary forms of nationalism that invoke urban dystopias peopled by migrant or minority 'others' (Modest and de Koning forthcoming).

Meanwhile, the urban working class has become increasingly fragmented and informalized, and the labor movement's historical appeal to class solidarity appears to have limited purchase in many twenty-first-century cities. Recent work on the *urban precariat* – a new group of workers in flexible, precarious conditions that has replaced the industrial proletariat – attempts to theorize this new form of exploited urban labor and its political potential, for instance in post-disaster Japan (Kindstrand 2011). In the US context, studies have also focused on the role of the penal state in disciplining and warehousing this urban precariat (Cunha 2014). Yet, the attempts to move beyond neoliberalism that we discussed above also entail efforts to define solidarity anew in a more inclusive manner. The same holds true for the recent urban uprisings, which have also led to transnational, intersectional alliances between different progressive movements.

Affect and temporality

Affect is another theme that is increasingly popular in urban anthropology, reflecting a broader affective turn in anthropology. Anthropologists have increasingly grown interested in exploring affect: embodied emotions and passions that are collective or intersubjective, rather than individual. Various urban anthropologists have started to examine affective registers of city landscapes and the urban aesthetic forms associated with them (Navaro-Yashin 2012; Schwenkel 2013). Such affective registers may primarily promote a modernist optimism, evoked, for instance, through an architecture of shiny malls and sleek high-rises that are part of the neoliberal spectacle discussed in Chapter 7. Urban landscapes may, in contrast, also invoke nostalgia for better days when people could plan for the future, as in the case of the Copperbelt town of Luanshya discussed in Chapter 5, where empty buildings and overgrown tennis courts reminded the residents of the perks of Fordist modes of production. Other recent studies have begun to focus on the role of emotion and affect in governance, where particular programs suggest the right emotional disposition for worthy neoliberal subjects (Muehlebach 2012; Ramos-Zayas 2012).

Such studies of affect often also touch upon another emergent theme, that of *temporality*. Modernist affective registers are oriented towards the future (de Boeck 2011), whereas nostalgic affective registers often concentrate on the ruins and remnants of bygone glory days. In addition to urban anthropology's more long-standing interest in spatiality, recent work in the subfield has demonstrated the potential of focusing on different forms of temporality. Sometimes this is related to popular understandings and uses of urban history, and widespread processes of heritagization of the urban landscape. In other cases, this interest in temporality concentrates on urban futures (Cunningham and Scharper 2014), studying how these are imagined and materialized, for instance in forms of 'anticipatory urbanism' that draw on urban risk as a governmental tool (Zeiderman forthcoming).

Ecology, sustainability and technology

The increased research interest in urban futures also connects to concerns over the environmental future of cities. As environmental problems at both the urban and the global scale – from solid waste and air pollution to climate change – become ever more pressing, urban anthropologists are also increasingly involved in studying *urban ecology and sustainability* in different cultural contexts, often with a strong focus on *environmental justice*. This recent work is seeking to understand how sustainability is imagined, implemented and contested in urban policies, programs and various forms of collective action (Isenhour et al. 2014). Such anthropological approaches to the urban environment have also involved new perspectives on urban nature, which interrogate long-standing culture–nature divides (Rotenburg 2014; Rademacher forthcoming). This type of research has included a consideration of the role of non-human species in shaping urban life, for instance in recent work on mosquito and urban health (Kelly and Lezaun 2014).

Studying urban ecology and sustainability often includes a consideration of the potential and problems associated with the rapid development of new *technologies*. Urban anthropologists are likely to be increasingly involved in studying the impact of ongoing technological innovations on urban encounters and politics. They study, for instance, how 'smart city' policy models are imagined as heralding cleaner, greener and safer cities. Careful scrutiny of recent smart city developments suggests that the rolling out of these models in a range of urban contexts reflects the influence of corporate actors on city governance, and is associated with increased surveillance (Zandbergen 2015). At the same time, other scholars are closely tracking the democratic potential of new digital technologies in facilitating urban mobilizations and enabling different forms of urban networking and solidarity (D'Andrea 2014).

Cities are socially and culturally dynamic spaces that produce, facilitate and respond to changes in ecology, technology, economy and politics. Urban socialities and cultures are always in flux, a fluidity that often translates more gradually in the built environment of cities. While urban anthropologists are also attentive to historically enduring urban (infra) structures, this fluid, changing character of urban social life will continue to be both a challenge and an inspiration to urban anthropologists into the twenty-first century. In addition to influences from broader anthropology and other disciplinary approaches to urban studies, city life itself will continue to prompt new conceptual developments and empirical queries in urban anthropology.

Bibliography

Abolafia, Mitchel Y. (2002) Fieldwork on Wall Street. In: George Gmelch and Walter P. Zenner (eds.) *Urban Life: Readings in the Anthropology of the City* (4th edition), pp. 179–185. Long Grove, IL: Waveland Press.

Abraham, Itty and Willem van Schendel (2005) Introduction. In: Willem van Schendel and Itty Abraham (eds), *Illicit Flows and Criminal Things: States, Borders, and the Other Side of Globalization*, pp. 1–37. Bloomington, IN and Indianapolis, IN: Indiana University Press.

Ahmad, Tania (2014) Socialities of indignation: Denouncing party politics in Karachi. *Cultural Anthropology* 29(2): 411–432.

Alvarez, Sonia E., Evelina Dagnino and Arturo Escobar, eds. (1998) *Cultures of Politics/Politics of Cultures: Re-visioning Latin American Social Movements*. Boulder, CO: Westview Press.

Anderson, Nels (1923) *The Hobo: The Sociology of Homeless Men*. Chicago, IL: University of Chicago Press.

Andrew-Swann, Jenna (2011) *Cafecitos y nostalgia:* Building transnational landscapes in the Cuban diaspora. *Anthropology News* 52(3): 12.

Anthias, Floya (2013) Intersectional what? Social divisions, intersectionality and levels of analysis. *Ethnicities* 13(1): 3–19.

Appadurai, Arjun, ed. (1986) *The Social Life of Things: Commodities in Cultural Perspective*. Cambridge: Cambridge University Press.

Appadurai, Arjun (1990) Disjuncture and difference in the global cultural economy. *Theory, Culture & Society* 7(2): 295–310.

Appadurai, Arjun (1996) *Modernity at Large: The Cultural Dimensions of Globalization*. Minneapolis, MN: University of Minnesota Press

Appadurai, Arjun (2000) Spectral housing and urban cleansing: notes on millennial Mumbai. *Public Culture* 12(3): 627–651.

Appadurai, Arjun (2001) Deep democracy: Urban governmentality and the horizon of politics. *Environment and Urbanization* 13(2): 23–43.

Asad, Talal, ed. (1973) *Anthropology and the Colonial Encounter*. London: Ithaca Press.

Augé, Marc (1995) *Non-places: Introduction to an Anthropology of Supermodernity*. New York: Verso.

Badiey, Naseem (2014) *The State of Post-conflict Reconstruction: Land, Urban Development and State-Building in Juba, Southern Sudan*. Woodbridge: James Currey.

Banerjee, Mukulika (2014) *Why India Votes?* New Delhi: Routledge India.

Barber, Pauline Gardiner, Belinda Leach and Winnie Lem, eds. (2012) *Confronting Capital: Critique and Engagement in Anthropology*. New York and Abingdon: Routledge.

Barendregt, Bart and Rivke Jaffe, eds. (2014) *Green Consumption: The Global Rise of Eco-chic*. London: Bloomsbury.

Barrios, Roberto E. (2010) Budgets, plans and politics: Questioning the role of expert knowledge in disaster reconstruction. *Anthropology News* 51(7): 7–8.

Barrios, Roberto E. (2011) 'If you did not grow up here, you cannot appreciate living here': Neoliberalism, space-time, and affect in post-Katrina recovery planning. *Human Organization* 70(2): 118–127.

Basch, Linda, Nina Glick Schiller and Cristina Szanton Blanc (1994) *Nations Unbound: Transnational Projects, Postcolonial Predicaments, and Deterritorialized Nation-states.* New York: Routledge.

Bayat, Asef (1997) *Street Politics: Poor People's Movements in Iran.* New York: Columbia University Press.

Bayat, Asef (2012) Politics in the city-inside-out. *City & Society* 24(2): 110–128.

Bayat, Asef (2013) *Life as Politics: How Ordinary People Change the Middle East*, second edition. Stanford, CA: Stanford University Press.

Becci, Irene, Marian Burchardt and José Casanova, eds. (2013) *Topographies of Faith: Religion in Urban Spaces.* Leiden and Boston, MA: Brill.

Bennett, Andy and Richard A. Peterson, eds. (2004) *Music Scenes: Local, Translocal and Virtual.* Nashville, TN: Vanderbilt University Press.

Ben-Ze'ev, Efrat (2012) Mental maps and spatial perceptions: The fragmentation of Israel-Palestine. In: Les Roberts (ed.), *Mapping Cultures: Place, Practice, Performance*, pp. 237–259. Basingstoke: Palgrave Macmillan.

Bestor, Theodor (2004) *Tsukiji: The Fish Market at the Center of the World.* Berkeley, CA: University of California Press.

Bissell, William Cunningham (2011a) Between fixity and fantasy: Assessing the spatial impact of colonial urban dualism. *Journal of Urban History* 37(2): 208–229.

Bissell, William Cunningham (2011b) *Urban Design, Chaos and Colonial Power in Zanzibar.* Bloomington, IN: Indiana University Press.

Black, Rachel E. (2012) *Porta Palazzo: The Anthropology of an Italian Market.* Philadelphia, PA: University of Pennsylvania Press.

Boeck, Filip de (2011) Inhabiting ocular ground: Kinshasa's future in the light of Congo's spectral urban politics. *Cultural Anthropology* 26(2): 263–286.

Bondi, Liz, and Mona Domosh (1998) On the contours of public space: a tale of three women. *Antipode* 30(3): 270–289.

Booth, Charles (1902–1903). *Life and Labour of the People in London* (17 Volumes). London: Macmillan and Co.

Bourdieu, Pierre (1973) The Berber House. In: Mary Douglas (ed.), *Rules and Meanings*, pp. 98–110. Oxford: Routledge.

Bourdieu, Pierre (1984) *Distinction: A Social Critique of the Judgment of Taste.* Translated by Richard Nice. London: Routledge.

Bourdieu, Pierre (1986) The forms of capital. In: J.G. Richardson (ed.), *Handbook of Theory and Research for the Sociology of Education*, pp. 241–258. New York: Greenwood Press.

Bourdieu, Pierre and Loïc Wacquant (2004) Symbolic violence. In: Nancy Scheper-Hughes and Philippe Bourgois (eds), *Violence in War and Peace*, pp. 272–274. Malden, MA: Blackwell.

Bourgois, Philippe (2001) Culture of poverty. *International Encyclopedia of the Social and Behavioral Sciences* 11904–11907.

Bourgois, Philippe (2003) *In Search of Respect: Dealing Crack in El Barrio*, second edition. Cambridge University Press.

Bowen, John (2007) *Why the French Don't Like Headscarves: Islam, the State and Public Space.* Princeton, NJ: Princeton University Press.

Brenner, Neil, David J. Madden, and David Wachsmuth (2011) Assemblage urbanism and the challenges of critical urban theory. *City* 15(2): 225–240.

Bridge, Gary and Sophie Watson, eds. (2010) *The Blackwell City Reader*, second edition. Oxford: Blackwell.

Briganti, Chiara and Kathy Mezei, eds. (2012) *The Domestic Space Reader.* Toronto: University of Toronto Press.

Brown, Rebecca (2003) The cemeteries and the suburbs: Patna's challenges to the colonial city in South Asia. *Journal of Urban History* 29: 151–172.

Bull, Michael (2008) *Sound Moves: iPod Culture and Urban Experience*. London: Routledge.

Büscher, Monika, John Urry and Katian Witchger, eds. (2011) *Mobile Methods*. London and New York: Routledge.

Caldeira, Teresa (2000) *City of Walls: Crime, Segregation and Citizenship in São Paulo*. Berkeley, CA: University of California Press.

Caldeira, Teresa P. (2012) Imprinting and moving around: New visibilities and configurations of public space in São Paulo. *Public Culture* 24(2): 385–419.

Casas-Cortés, Maribel, Sebastian Cobarrubias and John Pickles (2014) The commons. In: Donald Nonini (ed.), *The Blackwell Companion to Urban Anthropology*, pp. 449–469. Oxford: Wiley-Blackwell.

Castells, Manuel (1983) *The City and the Grassroots: A Cross-cultural Theory of Urban Social Movements*. Berkeley, CA: University of California Press.

Castells, M. (1996). *The Rise of the Network Society, The Information Age: Economy, Society and Culture Vol. I*. Malden, MA: Blackwell Publishers.

Castells, M. (2013). *Communication Power*. Oxford: Oxford University Press.

Centrale Gezondheidsraad (1913) *Rapport omtrent de voorzieningen die op sanitair gebied te Willemstad waren te treffen ten einde deze haven te doen beantwoorden aan de hoogere eischen die het, met het oog op de opening van het Panamakanaal te verwachten grooter scheepvaartverkeer, zal stellen*. Willemstad: Centrale Gezondheidsraad.

Chappell, Ben (2012) *Lowrider Space: Aesthetics and Politics of Mexican American Custom Cars*. Austin, TX: University of Texas Press.

Chatterjee, Partha (2004) *The Politics of the Governed: Reflections on Popular Politics in Most of the World*. New York: Columbia University Press.

Checker, Melissa (2001) 'Like Nixon coming to China': Finding common ground in a multi-ethnic coalition for environmental justice. *Anthropological Quarterly* 74(3): 135–146.

Chiu, Chihsin (2009) Contestation and conformity: street and park skateboarding in New York City public space. *Space and Culture* 12(1): 25–42.

Clifford, James and George Marcus (1986) *Writing Culture: The Poetics and Politics of Ethnography*. Berkeley, CA: University of California Press.

Collier, Stephen J. (2011) *Post-Soviet Social: Neoliberalism, Social Modernity, Biopolitics*. Princeton: Princeton University Press.

Collins, Patricia H. (1993) Toward a new vision: Race, class, and gender as categories of analysis and connection. *Race, Sex & Class* 1(1): 25–45.

Comaroff, Jean and John L. Comaroff (2000) Millennial capitalism: First thoughts on a second coming. *Public Culture* 12(2): 291–343.

Condry, Ian (2006). *Hip-hop Japan: Rap and the Paths of Cultural Globalization*. Durham, NC: Duke University Press.

Cooper, Frederick (2005) *Colonialism in Question: Theory, Knowledge, History*. Berkeley, CA and Los Angeles, CA: University of California Press.

Crenshaw, Kimberley (1991) Mapping the margins: Intersectionality, identity politics, and violence against women of color. *Stanford Law Review* 43(6): 1241–1299.

Cresswell, Tim (2004) *Place: A Short Introduction*. Malden, MA: Blackwell.

Cresswell, Tim (2006) *On the Move: Mobility in the Modern Western World*. New York and Oxford: Routledge.

Cresswell, Tim (2010) Towards a politics of mobility. *Environment and Planning D* 28(1): 17–31.

Cunha, Manuela (2014) The ethnography of prisons and penal confinement. *Annual Review of Anthropology* 43: 217–233.

Cunningham, Hilary and Stephen Bede Scharper (2014) Futures. In: Donald Nonini (ed.), *The Blackwell Companion to Urban Anthropology*, pp. 486–497. Oxford: Wiley-Blackwell.

Cwerner, Saulo (2009) Helipads, heliports and urban air space: Governing the contested infrastructure of helicopter travel. In: Saulo Cwerner, Sven Kesselring and John Urry (eds), *Aeromobilities*, pp. 225–246. London: Routledge.

D'Andrea, Anthony (2014) 2013 Protests in Brazil: The kite and the byte in new forms of popular mobilization. *Anthropological Quarterly* 87(3): 935–942.

Daniels, Inge (2010). *The Japanese House*. London: Berg.

Daunton, Martin J. and Matthew Hilton, eds. (2001) *The Politics of Consumption: Material Culture and Citizenship in Europe and America*. Oxford: Berg.

Davila, Arlene (2004) *Barrio Dreams: Puerto Ricans, Latinos and the Neoliberal City*. Berkeley, CA: University of California Press.

de Boeck, Filip (2011) Inhabiting ocular ground: Kinshasa's future in the light of Congo's spectral urban politics. *Cultural Anthropology* 26(2): 263–286.

de Certeau, Michel (1984) *The Practice of Everyday Life*, translated by Steven Rendall. Berkeley, CA and Los Angeles, CA: University of California Press.

de Koning, Anouk (2009) *Global Dreams: Class, Gender, and Public Space in Cosmopolitan Cairo*. Cairo and New York: American University in Cairo Press.

de Koning, Anouk (2011a) Shadows of the plantation? A social history of Suriname's bauxite town Moengo. *New West Indian Guide* 85: 215–246.

de Koning, Anouk (2011b) Moengo on strike: The politics of labour in Suriname's bauxite industry. *European Review of Latin American and Caribbean Studies* 91: 31–47.

de Koning, Anouk (2015) Citizenship agendas for the abject: Amsterdam's youth and security assemblage in action. *Citizenship Studies* 19(2): 155–168.

de Koning, Anouk, Rivke Jaffe and Martijn Koster (2015) Introduction: Citizenship agendas in and beyond the nation-state. *Citizenship Studies* 19(2): 121–127.

De Soto, Hernando (2000) *The Mystery of Capital: Why Capitalism Triumphs in the West and Fails Everywhere Else*. London: Bantam.

Deeb, Lara and Mona Harb (2013) *Leisurely Islam: Negotiating Geography and Morality in Shi'ite South Beirut*. Princeton, NJ: Princeton University Press.

Derby, Lauren and Marion Werner (2013) The devil wears Dockers: Devil pacts, trade zones and rural-urban ties in the Dominican Republic. *New West Indian Guide* 87: 294–321.

Dickey, Sarah (2000) Permeable homes: Domestic service, household space and the vulnerability of class boundaries in urban India. *American Ethnologist* 27(2): 462–489.

Diphoorn, Tessa (2015) *Twilight Policing: Private Security in South Africa*. Berkeley, CA: University of California Press.

Drake, St. Clair and Horace R. Cayton (1945) *Black Metropolis: A Study of Negro Life in a Northern City*. New York: Harcourt, Brace and Company.

Dürr, Eveline (2003) Der abgesägte Fuß des spanischen Eroberers: Konflikte und kulturelle Identitäten im Südwesten der USA. *Zeitschrift für Ethnologie* 128(2): 173–194.

Dürr, Eveline and Rivke Jaffe (2012) Theorizing slum tourism: Performing, negotiating and transforming inequality. *European Review of Latin American and Caribbean Studies* 93: 113–123.

Dürr, Eveline and Rivke Jaffe (2014) Pollution. In: Donald Nonini (ed.), *The Blackwell Companion to Urban Anthropology*, pp. 414–427. Oxford: Wiley-Blackwell.

Duyvendak, Jan Willem (2011) *The Politics of Home: Belonging and Nostalgia in Europe and the United States*. Basingstoke: Palgrave Macmillan.

Eade, John and Michael Peter Smith (2011) *Transnational Ties: Cities, Migrations, and Identities*. New Brunswick, NJ: Transaction Publishers.

Epstein, Beth S. (2011) *Collective Terms: Race, Culture, and Community in a State-planned City in France*. New York and Oxford: Berghahn Books.

Eriksen, Thomas Hylland (2007) *Globalization: The Key Concepts*. Oxford and New York: Berg.

Evers, Clifton and Kirsten Seale, eds. (2014) *Informal Urban Street Markets: International Perspectives*. New York: Routledge.

Farias, Ignacio, and Thomas Bender, eds. (2012) *Urban Assemblages: How Actor-Network Theory Changes Urban Studies*. Abingdon and New York: Routledge.

Farmer, Paul (2004) An anthropology of structural violence. *Current Anthropology* 45(3): 305–325.

Fassin, Didier (2013) *Enforcing Order: An Ethnography of Urban Policing*. Cambridge: Polity.

Fawaz, Mona, Mona Harb and Ahmad Gharbieh (2012) Living Beirut's security zones: An investigation of the modalities and practice of urban security. *City & Society* 24(2): 173–195.

Feld, Steven and Keith H. Basso, eds. (1996) *Senses of Place*. Santa Fe, NM: School of American Research Press.

Feldman, Allen (1991) *Formations of Violence: The Narrative of the Body and Political Terror in Northern Ireland*. Chicago, IL: University of Chicago Press.

Ferguson, James (1999) *Expectations of Modernity: Myths and Meanings of Urban Life on the Zambian Copperbelt*. Berkeley, CA and Los Angeles, CA: University of California Press.

Ferguson, James (2005) Seeing like an oil company: Space, security, and global capital in neoliberal Africa. *American Anthropologist* 107(3): 377–382.

Fernandes, Leela (2006) *India's New Middle Class: Democratic Politics in an Era of Economic Reform*. Minneapolis, MN: University of Minnesota Press.

Fishman, Robert (1982) *Urban Utopias in the Twentieth Century: Ebenezer Howard, Frank Lloyd Wright, and Le Corbusier*. Cambridge, MA: MIT Press.

Florida, Richard (2002) *The Rise of the Creative Class, and How It's Transforming Work, Leisure, Community and Everyday Life*. New York: Basic Books.

Forman, Murray (2002) *The 'Hood Comes First: Race, Space and Place in Rap and Hiphop*. Middletown, CT: Wesleyan University Press.

Foster, George McClelland, and Robert V. Kemper, eds. (1974) *Anthropologists in Cities*. Boston, MA: Little, Brown.

Foster, George M. and Robert V. Kemper (2009) Anthropological fieldwork in cities. In: George Gmelch and Walter P. Zenner (eds), *Urban Life: Readings in Urban Anthropology*, fifth edition. Long Grove, IL: Waveland Press.

Foucault, Michel (1977) *Discipline and Punish: The Birth of the Prison*. New York: Vintage.

Gandhi, Ajay (2011) Crowds, congestion, conviviality: The enduring life of the old city. In: Isabelle Clark-Decès (ed.), *A Companion to the Anthropology of India*, pp. 202–222. Oxford: Wiley-Blackwell.

Garbin, David (2013) The visibility and invisibility of migrant faith in the city: Diaspora religion and the politics of emplacement of Afro-Christian churches. *Journal of Ethnic and Migration Studies* 39(5): 677–696.

Garriott, William, ed. (2013) *Policing and Contemporary Governance: The Anthropology of the Police in Practice*. New York: Palgrave Macmillan.

Ghannam, Farha (2002) *Remaking the Modern: Space, Relocation, and the Politics of Identity in a Global Cairo*. Berkeley, CA and Los Angeles, CA: University of California Press.

Gibson-Graham, J.K. (2014) Rethinking the economy with thick description and weak theory. *Current Anthropology* 55(S9), S147–S153.

Gilbert, Alan (2007) The return of the slum: Does language matter? *International Journal of Urban and Regional Research* 31(4): 697–713.

Gilroy, Paul (2001) Driving while Black, in D. Miller (ed.) *Car Cultures*. Oxford: Berg.

Gluckman, Max (1940) Analysis of a social situation in modern Zululand. *Bantu Studies* 14: 1–30, 147–174.

Gmelch, George and Walter P. Zenner, eds. (2009) *Urban Life: Readings in Urban Anthropology*, fourth edition. Long Grove, IL: Waveland Press.

Goffman, Erving (1963) *Behavior in Public Places: Notes on the Social Organization of Gatherings*. New York: The Free Press.

Goldberg, Daniel Theo (1993) 'Polluting the body politic': Racist discourse and urban location. In: Malcolm Cross and Michael Keith (eds), *Racism, the City and the State*, pp. 45–60. Oxford and New York: Routledge.

Goldstein, Daniel (2004) *The Spectacular City: Violence and Performance in Urban Bolivia*. Durham, NC: Duke University Press.

Goldstein, Daniel M. (2010) Toward a critical anthropology of security. *Current Anthropology* 51(4): 487–517.

Goldstein, Daniel M. (2014) Qualitative Research in Dangerous Places: Becoming an 'Ethnographer' of Violence and Personal Safety. DSD Working Papers on Research Security, No. 1. New York: SSRC.

Goonewardena, Kanishka (2005) The urban sensorium: Space, ideology and the aestheticization of politics. *Antipode* 37(1), 46–71.

Graham, Stephen (2011) *Cities under Siege: The New Military Urbanism*. London: Verso.

Graham, Steve and Simon Marvin (2001) *Splintering Urbanism: Networked Infrastructures, Technological Mobilities and the Urban Condition*. London and New York: Routledge.

Gregory, Steven (1998) *Black Corona: Race and the Politics of Place in an Urban Community*. Princeton, NJ: Princeton University Press.

Griskevicius, Vladas, Joshua M. Tybur and Bram Van den Bergh (2010) Going green to be seen: Status, reputation, and conspicuous conservation. *Journal of Personality and Social Psychology* 98(3): 392–404.

Guano, Emanuela (2002a) Ruining the president's spectacle: Theatricality and telepolitics in the Buenos Aires public sphere. *Journal of Visual Culture* 1(3): 303–323.

Guano, Emanuela (2002b) Spectacles of modernity: Transnational imagination and local hegemonies in neoliberal Buenos Aires. *Cultural Anthropology* 17(2): 181–209.

Gupta, Akhil and James Ferguson (1992) Beyond 'culture': Space, identity, and the politics of difference. *Cultural Anthropology* 7(1): 6–23.

Gupta, Akhil and James Ferguson, eds. (1997) *Anthropological Locations: Boundaries and Grounds of a Field Science*. Berkeley, CA: University of California Press.

Gusterson, Hugh (1997) Studying up revisited. *PoLAR: Political and Legal Anthropology Review* 20(1): 114–119.

Haldrup, M. (2011). Choreographies of leisure mobilities. In: Monika Büscher, John Urry and Katian Witchger (eds), *Mobile Methods*, pp. 54–71. London and New York: Routledge.

Hall, Stuart and Tony Jefferson, eds. (1975) Resistance through Rituals: Youth Subcultures in Post-war Britain. Working Papers in Cultural Studies, no. 7/8. Birmingham: CCCS.

Hancock, Mary and Smriti Srinivas (2008) Spaces of modernity: Religion and the urban in Asia and Africa. *International Journal of Urban and Regional Research* 32(3): 617–630.

Hannam, Kevin, Mimi Sheller and John Urry (2006) Editorial: Mobilities, immobilities and moorings. *Mobilities* 1(1), 1–22.

Hannerz, Ulf (1969) *Soulside: An Inquiry into Ghetto Culture*. New York: Columbia University Press.

Hannerz, Ulf (1980) *Exploring the City: Inquiries toward an Urban Anthropology*. New York: Columbia University Press.

Hansen, Karen T., Walter E. Little and B. Lynne Milgram, eds. (2013) *Street Economies in the Urban Global South*. Santa Fe, NM: SAR Press.

Hansen, Thomas Blom (2006) Performers of sovereignty: On the privatization of security in urban South Africa. *Critique of Anthropology* 26(3): 279–295.

Hansen, Thomas Blom and Oskar Verkaaik (2009) Introduction – urban charisma: On everyday mythologies in the city. *Critique of Anthropology* 29(1): 5–26.

Harrison, Faye (1988) Women in Jamaica's urban informal economy: Insights from a Kingston slum. *New West Indian Guide* 62 (3/4): 103–128.

Hart, Keith (2010) The informal economy. In: Keith Hart, J.-L. Laville and A.D. Cattani (eds), *The Human Economy*, 142–153. Cambridge: Polity Press.

Harvey, David (1989) From managerialism to entrepreneurialism: The transformation in urban governance in late capitalism. *Geografiska Annaler Series B* 71(1): 3–17.

Harvey, David (2003) The right to the city. *International Journal of Urban and Regional Research* 27(4): 939–941.

Harvey, David (2005). *A Brief History of Neoliberalism*. Oxford: Oxford University Press.

Harvey, David (2008) The right to the city. *New Left Review* 53: 23–40.

Hazen, Jennifer M. and Dennis Rodgers (2014) *Global Gangs: Street Violence across the World*. Minneapolis, MN: University of Minnesota Press.

Hebdige, Dick (1979) *Subculture: The Meaning of Style*. London: Routledge.

Heiman, Rachel, Carla Freeman and Mark Liechty, eds. (2012) *The Global Middle Classes: Theorizing Through Ethnography*. Santa Fe, NM: SAR Press.

Heyman, Josiah McC. (2014) Policing and security. In: Donald Nonini (ed.), *The Blackwell Companion to Urban Anthropology*, pp. 271–290. Oxford: Wiley-Blackwell.

Ho, Swee-Lin (2013) 'License to drink': White-collar female workers and Japan's urban night space. *Ethnography* 16(1) 25–50.

Holston, James (1989) *The Modernist City: An Anthropological Critique of Brasília*. Chicago, IL: University of Chicago Press.

Holston, James, ed. (1999) *Cities and Citizenship*. Durham, NC: Duke University Press.

Holston, James (2008) *Insurgent Citizenship. Disjunctions of Democracy and Modernity in Brazil*. Princeton, NJ: Princeton University Press.

Holston, James (2009) Insurgent citizenship in an era of global urban peripheries. *City & Society* 21(2): 245–267.

Holston, James and Arjun Appadurai (1999) Cities and citizenship. In: James Holston (ed.) *Cities and Citizenship* pp. 2–18. Durham, NC: Duke University Press.

hooks, bell (2003) The oppositional gaze: Black female spectators. *The Feminism and Visual Culture Reader* pp. 94–104. London and New York: Routledge.

Horst, Heather and Daniel Miller (2005) From kinship to link-up: Cell phones and social networking in Jamaica. *Current Anthropology* 46(5): 755–778.

Hymes, Dell (1972) *Reinventing Anthropology*. New York: Pantheon Books.

Imrie, Rob (1996) *Disability and the City: International Perspectives*. London: Paul Chapman.

Ingold, Tim and Jo Lee Vergunst, eds. (2008) *Ways of Walking: Ethnography and Practice on Foot*. Aldershot: Ashgate Publishing.

Isenhour, Cindy, Gary McDonogh and Melissa Checker, eds. (2014) *Sustainability in the Global City: Myth and Practice*. Cambridge: Cambridge University Press.

Ismail, Salwa (2014) The politics of the urban everyday in Cairo: Infrastructures of oppositional action. In: Susan Parnell and Sophie Oldfield (eds), *The Routledge Handbook on Cities of the Global South*, pp. 269–280. Abingdon and New York: Routledge.

Istomin, Kirill V. and Mark J. Dwyer (2009) Finding the way: a critical discussion of anthropological theories of human spatial orientation with reference to reindeer herders of northeastern Europe and Western Siberia. *Current Anthropology* 50(1): 29–49.

Jackson, Emma (2012) Fixed in mobility: Young homeless people and the city. *International Journal of Urban and Regional Research* 36(4): 725–741.

Jaffe, Rivke (2012a) Criminal dons and extralegal security privatization in downtown Kingston, Jamaica. *Singapore Journal of Tropical Geography* 33(2): 184–197.

Jaffe, Rivke (2012b) Talkin' 'bout the ghetto: Popular culture and urban imaginaries of immobility. *International Journal of Urban and Regional Research* 36(3): 674–688.

Jaffe, Rivke (2012c) The popular culture of illegality: Crime and the politics of aesthetics in urban Jamaica. *Anthropological Quarterly* 85(1): 79–102.

Jaffe, Rivke (2013) The hybrid state: Crime and citizenship in urban Jamaica. *American Ethnologist* 40(4): 734–748.

Jaffe, Rivke (2014) Hip-hop and urban studies. *International Journal of Urban and Regional Research* 38(2): 695–699.

Jaffe, Rivke (2015) Between ballots and bullets: Elections and citizenship in and beyond the nation-state. *Citizenship Studies* 19(2) 128–140.

Jaffe, Rivke (2016) *Concrete Jungles: Urban Pollution and the Politics of Difference in the Caribbean.* New York and Oxford: Oxford University Press.

Jaffe, Rivke and Eveline Dürr (2010) Introduction: Cultural and material forms of urban pollution. In: Eveline Dürr and Rivke Jaffe (eds), *Urban Pollution: Cultural Meanings, Social Practices*, pp. 1–29. Oxford and New York: Berghahn.

Jayne, Mark (2006) *Cities and Consumption.* Oxford and New York: Routledge.

Jirón, Paola (2011) On becoming 'la sombra/the shadow'. In: Monika Büscher, John Urry and Katian Witchger (eds), *Mobile Methods*, pp. 36–53. London and New York: Routledge.

Johnston, Josée (2008) The citizen-consumer hybrid: Ideological tensions and the case of whole foods market. *Theory and Society* 37(3): 229–270.

Juris, Jeffrey (2012) Reflections on #Occupy everywhere: Social media, public space, and emerging logics of aggregation. *American Ethnologist* 39(2): 259–279.

Kanna, Ahmed (2011) *Dubai: The City as Corporation.* Minneapolis, MN: University of Minnesota Press.

Kaviraj, S. (1997) Filth and the public sphere: Concepts and practices about space in Calcutta. *Public Culture* 10(1): 83–113.

Kearney, Michael (1995) The local and the global: The anthropology of globalization and transnationalism. *Annual Review of Anthropology* 24: 547–565.

Kelly, Ann H. and Javier Lezaun (2014) Urban mosquitoes, situational publics, and the pursuit of interspecies separation in Dar es Salaam. *American Ethnologist* 41(2): 368–383.

Kindstrand, Love (2011) The politicization of precarity: Anti-nuke protests in Japan since the great Tohoku earthquake. Fieldsights – hot spots, *Cultural Anthropology Online*, 26 July, 2011, http://www.culanth.org/fieldsights/300-the-politicization-of-precarity-anti-nuke-protests-in-japan-since-the-great-tohoku-earthquake.

King, Anthony D. (1990a) *Global Cities: Post-imperialism and the Internationalization of London.* London and New York: Routledge.

King, Anthony D. (1990b) *Urbanism, Colonialism, and the World-Economy: Cultural and Spatial Foundations of the World Urban System.* New York: Routledge.

King, Anthony D. (2004) *Spaces of Global Cultures: Architecture, Urbanism, Identity.* Abingdon and New York: Routledge.

Klaufus, Christien (2012) The symbolic dimension of mobility: Architecture and social status in Ecuadorian informal settlements. *International Journal of Urban and Regional Research* 36(4): 689–705.

Kong, Lily (2010) Global shifts, theoretical shifts: Changing geographies of religion. *Progress in Human Geography* 34(6): 755–776.

Koptiuch, Kristin (1991) Third-worlding at home. *Social Text* 28: 87–99.

Kusenbach, Margarethe (2003) Street phenomenology: The go-along as ethnographic research tool. *Ethnography* 4(3): 455–485.

Kusno, Abidin (2004) Whither nationalist urbanism? Public life in Governor Sutiyoso's Jakarta. *Urban Studies* 41(12): 2377–2394.

Kusno, Abidin (2010) *The Appearances of Memory. Mnemonic Practices of Architecture and Urban Form in Indonesia.* Durham, NC: Duke University Press.

Larkin, Brian (2013) The politics and poetics of infrastructure. *Annual Review of Anthropology* 42: 327–343.

Lazar, Sian (2004) Personalist politics, clientelism and citizenship: Local elections in El Alto, Bolivia. *Bulletin of Latin American Research* 23(2): 228–243.

Lazar, Sian (2008) *El Alto, Rebel City: Self and Citizenship in Andean Bolivia.* Durham, NC: Duke University Press.

Lazar, Sian (2014) Citizenship. In: Donald Nonini (ed.), *The Blackwell Companion to Urban Anthropology*, pp. 65–82. Oxford: Wiley-Blackwell.

Lefebvre, Henri (1991) *The Production of Space*. Oxford: Blackwell.

Lefebvre, Henri (1996) *Writings on Cities*. Oxford: Blackwell.

Levitt, Peggy, and Nina Glick Schiller (2004) Conceptualizing simultaneity: A transnational social field perspective on society. *International Migration Review* 38(3): 1002–1039.

Lewis, Oscar (1966) *La Vida: A Puerto Rican Family in the Culture of Poverty: San Juan and New York*. New York: Random House.

Leydet, Dominique (2014) Citizenship. In: Edward N. Zalta (ed.), *The Stanford Encyclopedia of Philosophy* (Spring 2014 Edition). Accessible online at http://plato.stanford.edu/archives/ spr2014/ entries/citizenship/.

Lindley, Anna (2010) *The Early Morning Phone Call: Somali Refugees' Remittances*. New York: Berghahn Books.

Löfgren, Orvar (1984) The sweetness of home: Class, culture and family life in Sweden. *Ethnologica Europea* 14: 44–64.

Lofland, Lyn H. (1989) Social life in the public realm: 'A review'. *Journal of Contemporary Ethnography* 17(4): 453–482.

Low, Setha M. (1996) The anthropology of cities: Imagining and theorizing the city. *Annual Review of Anthropology* 25: 383–409.

Low, Setha M., ed. (1999) *Theorizing the City: The New Urban Anthropology Reader*. New Brunswick, NJ: Rutgers University Press.

Low, Setha M. (2000) *On the Plaza: The Politics of Public Space and Culture*. Austin, TX: University of Texas Press.

Low, Setha M. (2003) *Behind the Gates: Life, Security and the Pursuit of Happiness in Fortress America*. New York: Routledge.

Low, Setha M. (2011) Claiming space for an engaged anthropology: Spatial inequality and social exclusion. *American Anthropologist* 113(3): 389–407.

Low, Setha M. (2014) Spatialities. In: Donald Nonini (ed.), *The Blackwell Companion to Urban Anthropology*, pp. 15–27. Oxford: Wiley-Blackwell.

Low, Setha M. and Denise Lawrence-Zúñiga, eds. (2003) *The Anthropology of Space and Place: Locating Culture*. Malden, MA: Blackwell.

Lutz, Catherine (2014) Cars and transport: The car-made city. In: Donald Nonini (ed.), *The Blackwell Companion to Urban Anthropology*, pp. 142–153. Oxford: Wiley-Blackwell.

Lynch, Kevin (1960) *The Image of the City*. Cambridge, MA: MIT Press.

MacGaffey, Janet and Remy Bazenguissa-Ganga (2000) *Congo-Paris: Transnational Traders on the Margins of the Law*. Bloomington, IN: Indiana University Press, and Oxford: James Currey, in association with the International African Institute.

Maeckelbergh, Marianne (2012) Mobilizing to stay put: Housing struggles in New York City. *International Journal of Urban and Regional Research* 36(4): 655–673.

Marshall, T. H. (1950) *Citizenship and Social Class and Other Essays*. Cambridge: Cambridge University Press.

Massey, Doreen (2004) Geographies of responsibility. *Geografiska Annaler: Series B, Human Geography* 86(1): 5–18.

Mathews, Gordon (2007) Chungking Mansion: A center of low-end globalization. *Ethnology* 46(2) 169–183.

Mathews, Gordon (2011) *Ghetto at the Center of the World: Chungking Mansions, Hong Kong*. Chicago, IL: Chicago University Press.

Maxwell, Andrew H. (1998) Motorcyclists and community in post-industrial urban America. *Urban Anthropology and Studies of Cultural Systems and World Economic Development* 27(3/4): 263–299.

McCallum, Cecilia (2005) Racialized bodies, naturalized classes: Moving through the city of Salvador da Bahia. *American Ethnologist* 32(1): 100–117.

McMichael, Philip (1998) Development and structural adjustment. In: James G. Carrier and Daniel Miller (eds) *Virtualism: A New Political Economy* pp. 95–116. Oxford: Berg.

McRobbie, Angela (1980) Settling accounts with subcultures: A feminist critique. *Screen Education* 34(1): 37–49.

Merry, Sally Engle (2001) Spatial governmentality and the new urban social order: Controlling gender violence through law. *American Anthropologist* 103(1): 16–29.

Milgram, B. Lynne (2014) Remapping the edge: Informality and legality in the Harrison Road Night Market, Baguio City, Philippines. *City and Society* 26(2): 153–174.

Miller, D. (ed) (2001) *Car Cultures*. Oxford: Berg.

Mitchell, Don (2003) *The Right to the City: Social Justice and the Fight for Public Space*. New York: Guilford Press.

Mitchell, J. Clyde (1956) *The Kalela Dance*. Manchester: Manchester University Press.

Mitlin, Diana and Sheela Patel (2014) The urban poor and strategies for a pro-poor politics: Reflections on slum/shack dwellers international. In: Susan Parnell and Sophie Oldfield (eds), *The Routledge Handbook on Cities of the Global South*, pp. 296–308. Abingdon and New York: Routledge.

Modan, Gabriella Gahlia (2007). *Turf Wars: Discourse, Diversity, and the Politics of Place*. Malden, MA: Blackwell.

Modest, Wayne and Anouk de Koning, eds (forthcoming) Special issue: Anxious politics and the European city. *Patterns of Prejudice*.

Morgen, Sandra and Jeff Maskovsky (2003) The anthropology of welfare 'reform': New perspectives on US urban poverty in the post-welfare era. *Annual Review of Anthropology* 32: 315–338.

Moser, Caroline and Cathy McIlwaine (2004) *Encounters with Violence in Latin America: Urban Poor Perspectives from Colombia and Guatemala*. London: Routledge.

Moyer, Eileen (2004) Popular cartographies: Youthful imaginings of the global in the streets of Dar es Salaam, Tanzania. *City & Society* 16(2): 117–143.

Moyer, Eileen (2005). Street-corner justice in the name of Jah: Imperatives for peace among Dar es Salaam street youth. *Africa Today* 51(3): 31–58.

Muehlebach, Andrea (2012) *The Moral Neoliberal: Welfare and Citizenship in Italy*. Chicago, IL: University of Chicago Press.

Mullings, Leith (1987) *Cities of the United States: Studies in Urban Anthropology*. New York: Columbia University Press.

Mususa, Patience (2012a) Mining, welfare and urbanisation: The wavering urban character of Zambia's Copperbelt. *Journal of Contemporary African Studies* 30(4): 571–587.

Mususa, Patience (2012b) Topping up: Life amidst hardship and death on the Copperbelt. *African Studies* 71(2): 304–322.

Nader, Laura (1972) Up the anthropologist – Perspectives gained from studying up. In: Dell Hymes (ed.), *Reinventing Anthropology*, pp. 284–311. New York: Pantheon Books.

Nas, Peter J.M. and Reint Sluis (2002) In search of meaning: Urban orientation principles in Indonesia. In: Peter J.M. Nas (ed.), *The Indonesian Town Revisited*, pp. 130–146. Münster: Lit.

Navaro-Yashin, Yael (2012) *The Make-believe Space: Affective Geography in a Postwar Polity*. Durham, NC: Duke University Press.

Newell, Sasha (2012a) *The Modernity Bluff: Crime, Consumption, and Citizenship in Côte D'Ivoire*. Chicago, IL: University of Chicago Press.

Newell, Sasha (2012b) *Le Goût des Autres*: Ivoirian fashion and alterity. *Etnofoor* 24(2): 41–57.

Noble, Greg (2005) The discomfort of strangers: Racism, incivility and ontological security in a relaxed and comfortable nation. *Journal of Intercultural Studies* 26(1): 107–120.

Nonini, Donald M., ed. (2014) *The Blackwell Companion to Urban Anthropology*. Oxford: Wiley-Blackwell.

Nordstrom, Carolyn (2007) *Global Outlaws: Crime, Money and Power in the Contemporary World*. Berkeley, CA: University of California Press.

Nordstrom, Carolyn and Antonius C.G.M. Robben, eds. (1995) *Fieldwork under Fire: Contemporary Studies of Violence and Survival*. Berkeley, CA: University of California Press.

Nuijten, Monique and Martijn Koster, eds. (forthcoming) Special issue: Close encounters: Ethnographies of the coproduction of space by the urban poor. *Singapore Journal of Tropical Geography*.

Nuijten, Monique, Martijn Koster and Pieter de Vries (2012) Regimes of spatial ordering in Brazil: Neoliberalism, leftist populism and modernist aesthetics in slum upgrading in Recife. *Singapore Journal of Tropical Geography* 33(2): 157–170.

O'Neill, Bruce (2014) Cast aside: Boredom, downward mobility, and homelessness in post-communist Bucharest. *Cultural Anthropology* 29(1): 8–31.

O'Neill, Kevin Lewis (2010) *City of God: Christian Citizenship in Postwar Guatemala*, Berkeley, CA: University of California Press.

Öncü, Ayse and Petra Weyland (1997) *Space, Culture and Power*. London: Zed Books.

Oosterbaan, Martijn (2009) Sonic supremacy. Sound, space and charisma in a favela in Rio de Janeiro. *Critique of Anthropology* 29(1): 81–104.

Oosterbaan, Martijn, ed. (2014) Special issue: Public religion and urban space in Europe. *Social & Cultural Geography* 15(6): 591–682.

Ortner, Sherry B. (2010) Access: Reflections on studying up in Hollywood. *Ethnography* 11: 211–233.

Pardo, Italo and Giuliana B. Prato, eds. (2012) *Anthropology in the City: Methodology and Theory*. Farnham and Burlington, VT: Ashgate.

Pardue, Derek (2008) *Ideologies of Marginality in Brazilian Hip Hop*. New York: Palgrave Macmillan.

Parker, Martin, George Cheney, Valérie Fournier and Chris Land, eds. (2014) *The Routledge Companion to Alternative Organization*. Abingdon and New York: Routledge.

Parreñas, Rhacel Salazar (2001) *Servants of Globalization: Women, Migration and Domestic Work*. Stanford, CA: Stanford University Press.

Pellow, Deborah and Denise Lawrence-Zúñiga (2014) Built structure and planning. In: Donald M. Nonini (ed.), *A Companion to Urban Anthropology*, pp. 85–102. Malden, MA: Wiley-Blackwell.

Perlman, Janice (1976) *The Myth of Marginality: Urban Poverty and Politics in Rio de Janeiro*. Berkeley, CA and Los Angeles, CA: University of California Press.

Perlman, Janice (2010) *Favela: Four Decades of Living on the Edge in Rio de Janeiro*. Oxford: Oxford University Press.

Perry, Richard W. (2000) Governmentalities in city-scapes: Introduction to the symposium. *PoLAR: Political and Legal Anthropology Review* 23(1): 65–72.

Peterson, Marina (2012) *Sound, Space, and the City: Civic Performance in Downtown Los Angeles*. Philadelphia, PA: University of Pennsylvania Press.

Phadke, Shilpa (2007) Dangerous liaisons: Women and men: Risk and reputation in Mumbai. *Economic and Political Weekly* 42(17): 1510–1518.

Pink, Sarah (2008) An urban tour: The sensory sociality of ethnographic place-making. *Ethnography* 9(2): 175–196.

Porter, Amy L. (2008) Fleeting dreams and flowing goods: Citizenship and consumption in Havana, Cuba. *Political and Legal Anthropology Review* 31(1): 134–149.

Prashad, Vijay (1994) Native dirt/imperial ordure: The cholera of 1832 and the morbid resolutions of modernity. *Journal of Historical Sociology* 7(3): 243–260.

Pratten, David and Atreyee Sen (2007) *Global Vigilantes: Perspectives on Justice and Violence*. London: Hurst.

Priya Uteng, T. and Tim Cresswell, eds. (2008) *Gendered Mobilities*. Aldershot: Ashgate.

Rabinow, Paul (1989) *French Modern: Norms and Forms of the Social Environment*. Chicago, IL: University of Chicago Press.

Rabinow, Paul (2003) Ordonnance, discipline, regulation: Some reflections on urbanism. In: Setha Low and Denise Lawrence-Zúñiga (eds), *The Anthropology of Space and Place: Locating Culture*, pp. 353–362. Malden, MA: Blackwell.

Rademacher, Anne M. (forthcoming) Urban political ecology. *Annual Review of Anthropology* 44.

Ramos-Zayas, Ana Y. (2012) *Street Therapists: Race, Affect, and Neoliberal Personhood in Latino Newark.* Chicago, IL: University of Chicago Press.

Rao, Ursula (2013) Tolerated encroachment: Resettlement policies and the negotiation of the licit/illicit divide in an Indian metropolis. *Cultural Anthropology* 28(4): 760–779.

Rattray, Nicholas A. (2013) Contesting urban space and disability in highland Ecuador. *City and Society* 25(1): 25–46.

Redfield, Robert (1941) *The Folk Culture of Yucatan.* Chicago, IL: University of Chicago Press.

Riis, Jacob A. (1890) *How the Other Half Lives: Studies among the Tenements of New York.* New York: Charles Scribner's Sons.

Robinson, Jennifer (2002) Global and world cities: A view from off the map. *International Journal of Urban and Regional Research* 26(3): 531–554.

Rodgers, Dennis (2004) 'Disembedding' the city: Crime, insecurity and spatial organization in Managua, Nicaragua. *Environment and Urbanization* 16(2): 113–123.

Rodgers, Dennis and Bruce O'Neill (2012) Infrastructural violence: Introduction to the special issue. *Ethnography* 13(4): 401–412.

Rofel, Lisa (1997) Rethinking modernity: Space and factory discipline in China. In: Akhil Gupta and James Ferguson (eds), *Culture, Power, Place: Explorations in Critical Anthropology,* pp. 155–178. Durham, NC: Duke University Press.

Rogers, Susan Carol (2001) Anthropology in France. *Annual Review of Anthropology* 30: 481–504.

Rose, Gillian (1993) *Feminism and Geography: The Limits of Geographical Knowledge.* Cambridge: Polity Press.

Roseberry, William (1996) The rise of yuppie coffees and the reimagination of class in the United States. *American Anthropologist* 98(4): 762–775.

Rotenburg, Robert (2014) Nature. In: Donald Nonini (ed.), *The Blackwell Companion to Urban Anthropology,* pp. 383–393. Oxford: Wiley-Blackwell.

Rotenberg, Robert L. and Gary V. McDonogh (1993) *The Cultural Meaning of Urban Place.* Westport, CT: Greenwood.

Ryzova, Lucie (2013) The battle of Cairo's Muhammad Mahmoud Street. *Cultural Anthropology Online*, 12 May 2013, accessed at http://www.culanth.org/fieldsights/232-the-battle-of-cairo-s-muhammad-mahmoud-street

Samuels, Annemarie (2010) Remaking neighbourhoods in Banda Aceh: Post-tsunami reconstruction of everyday life. In: Matthew Clarke, Ismet Fanany and Sue Kenny (eds), *Post-Disaster Reconstruction: Lessons from Aceh,* pp. 210–226. London: Earthscan.

Sanjek, Roger (1990) Urban anthropology in the 1980s: A world view. *Annual Review of Anthropology* 19: 151–186.

Sassen, Saskia (1996) Whose city is it? Globalization and the formation of new claims. *Public Culture* 8(2): 205–223.

Sassen, Saskia (2000) Spatialities and temporalities of the global: Elements for a theorization. *Public Culture* 12(1): 215–232., NJ: Princeton University Press.

Sassen, Saskia (2001) *Global City: New York, London, Tokyo.* 2nd revised ed. Princeton, NJ: Princeton University Press.

Sassen, Saskia (2005) The global city: Introducing a concept. *Brown Journal of World Affairs* 11(2): 27.

Scheper-Hughes, Nancy and Philippe Bourgois (2004) Introduction: Making sense of violence. In: Nancy Scheper-Hughes and Philippe Bourgois (eds), *Violence in War and Peace,* pp. 1–31. Malden, MA: Blackwell.

Schwenkel, Christina (2013) Post/socialist affect: Ruination and reconstruction of the nation in urban Vietnam. *Cultural Anthropology* 28(2): 252–277.

Scott, James (1998) *Seeing Like a State: How Certain Schemes to Improve the Human Condition Have Failed.* New Haven, CT: Yale University Press.

Secor, Ann J. (2002) The veil and urban space in Istanbul: Women's dress, mobility and Islamic knowledge. *Gender, Place and Culture* 9(1): 5–22.

Sennett, Richard (2010) The Public Realm. In: Gary Bridge and Sophie Watson (eds), *The Blackwell City Reader*, second edition, pp. 261–272. Oxford: Blackwell.

Sheller, Mimi and John Urry (2006) The new mobilities paradigm. *Environment and Planning A* 38: 207–226.

Shirlow, Peter and Brendan Murtagh (2006) *Belfast: Segregation, Violence and the City*. London: Pluto Press.

Sieber, Tim, Graça Índias Cordeiro and Lígia Ferro (2012) The neighborhood strikes back: Community murals by youth in Boston's communities of color. *City & Society* 24(3): 263–280.

Sletto, Bjørn Ingmunn (2009) 'We drew what we imagined.' *Current Anthropology* 50(4): 443–476.

Sluka, Jeffrey A. (2012 [1995]) Reflections on managing danger in fieldwork: Dangerous anthropology in Belfast. In: Antonius C.G.M. Robben and Jeffrey A. Sluka (eds), *Ethnographic Fieldwork: A Reader*, second edition, pp. 283–295. Malden, MA: Wiley-Blackwell.

Smart, Alan and Filippo M. Zerilli (2014) Extralegality. In: Donald Nonini (ed.), *The Blackwell Companion to Urban Anthropology*, pp. 222–238. Oxford: Wiley-Blackwell.

Smart, Alan and Josephine Smart (2003) Urbanization and the global perspective. *Annual Review of Anthropology* 32: 263–285.

Smith, Neil (2002) New globalism, new urbanism: Gentrification as global urban strategy. *Antipode* 34(3): 427–450.

Sopranzetti, Claudio (2014) Owners of the map: Mobility and mobilization among motorcycle taxi drivers in Bangkok. *City & Society* 26(1): 120–143.

Spirou, Costas (2011) *Urban Tourism and Urban Change: Cities in a Global Economy*. New York and Oxford: Routledge.

Stoller, Paul (1996) Spaces, places, and fields: The politics of West African trading in New York City's informal economy. *American Anthropologist* 98(4): 776–788.

Susser, Ida (1982) *Norman Street*. New York: Oxford University Press.

Susser, Ida (1996) The construction of poverty and homelessness in US cities. *Annual Review of Anthropology* 25: 411–435.

Susser, Ida and Jane Schneider, eds. (2003) *Wounded Cities: Destruction and Reconstruction in a Globalized World*. New York: Berg.

Swanson, Kate (2007) Revanchist urbanism heads south: The regulation of indigenous beggars and street vendors in Ecuador. *Antipode* 39(4): 708–728.

Swyngedouw, Erik (1996) The city as a hybrid: On nature, society and cyborg urbanization. *Capitalism Nature Socialism* 7(2): 65–80.

Thomas, William I. and Florian Znaniecki (1918–1920) *The Polish Peasant in Europe and America: Monograph of an Immigrant Group*, five volumes. Chicago, IL: University of Chicago Press.

Truitt, Allison (2008) On the back of a motorbike: Middle-class mobility in Ho Chi Minh City, Vietnam. *American Ethnologist* 35(1): 3–19.

Tuan, Yi-Fu (1974) *Topophila: A Study of Environmental Perception, Attitudes and Values*. Englewood Cliffs, NJ: Prentice Hall.

Ulysse, Gina A. (2007). *Downtown Ladies: Informal Commercial Importers, a Haitian Anthropologist and Self-Making in Jamaica*. Chicago, IL: University of Chicago Press.

van den Berg, Marguerite and Willem Schinkel (2009) Women from the catacombs of the city: Gender notions in Dutch culturist discourse. *Innovation* 22(4): 393–410.

van Schendel, Willem and Itty Abraham, eds. (2005). *Illicit Flows and Criminal Things: States, Borders, and the Other Side of Globalization*. Bloomington, IN and Indianapolis, IN: Indiana University Press.

Vargas, João H.C. (2006) When a favela dared to become a gated condominium: The politics of race and urban space in Rio de Janeiro. *Latin American Perspectives* 33(4): 49–81.

Verkaaik, Oskar, ed. (2013) *Religious Architecture: Anthropological Perspectives*. Amsterdam: Amsterdam University Press.

Vivanco, Luis A. (2013) *Reconsidering the Bicycle: An Anthropological Perspective on a New (Old) Thing*. New York and Oxford: Routledge.

von Lieres, Bettina and Laurence Piper, eds. (2014) *Mediated Citizenship: The Informal Politics of Speaking for Citizens in the Global South*. Basingstoke: Palgrave Macmillan.

Wacquant, Loïc (2002) From slavery to mass incarceration: Rethinking the 'race question' in the US. *New Left Review* 13(1): 41–60.

Weber, M. (1966). *The City*. Translated and edited by Don Martindale and Gertrud Neuwirth. New York: Free Press.

Wedel, Janine R., Cris Shore, Gregory Feldman and Stacy Lathrop (2005) Toward an anthropology of public policy. *Annals of the American Academy of Political and Social Science* 600: 30–51.

Weiss, Brad (2009) *Street Dreams and Hip Hop Barbershops: Global Fantasy in Urban Tanzania*. Bloomington, IN: Indiana University Press.

WHO (World Health Organization) (2011) *World Report on Disability*. Geneva: World Health Organization.

Whyte, William Foote (1943) *Street Corner Society: The Social Structure of an Italian Slum*. Chicago, IL: University of Chicago Press.

Whyte, William H. (2001 [1980]) *The Social Life of Small Urban Spaces*. New York: Project for Public Spaces.

Wilson, Elizabeth (2001) *The Contradictions of Culture: Cities, Culture, Women*. London: Sage.

Wirth, Louis (1928) *The Ghetto*. Chicago, IL: University of Chicago Press.

Wirth, Louis (1938) Urbanism as a way of life. *American Journal of Sociology* 44(1): 1–24.

Yazıcı, Berna (2013) Towards an anthropology of traffic: A ride through class hierarchies on Istanbul's roadways. *Ethnos* 78(4): 515–542.

Yeoh, Brenda S. (1996) *Contesting Space: Power Relations and the Urban Built Environment in Colonial Singapore*. Kuala Lumpur: Oxford University Press.

Young, Iris Marion (1990) *City Life and Difference*. Princeton, NJ: Princeton University Press.

Zandbergen, Dorien (2015) 'Best practice' story telling on smart cities, and why we need better genres. Blog, accessed at http://urbanstudies.uva.nl/blog/urban-studies-blog-series/urban-studies-blog-series/content/folder/best-practice-story-telling-on-smart-cities---and-why-we-need-better-genres.html.

Zeiderman, Austin (forthcoming) *Endangered City: The Politics of Security and Risk in Bogotá*. Durham, NC: Duke University Press.

Zhang, Li (2002) Spatiality and urban citizenship in late socialist China. *Public Culture* 14(2): 311–334.

Zukin, Sharon (1995) *The Cultures of Cities*. Oxford: Blackwell.

Zukin, Sharon (2011) *Naked City: The Death and Life of Authentic Urban Places*. Oxford: Oxford University Press.

Index